T.

O.S

24.

24.

4.

AUTHOR

TITLE Be

ACCESSION
O.5.

WITHDRAWN FROM
THE LIBRARY

UNIVERSITY OF
WINCHESTER

KA 0052502 2

THE BEGINNINGS OF

INDUSTRIAL BRITAIN

by

S. D. Chapman, B.Sc.(Econ.), Ph.D., M.A.

Pasold Lecturer in Textile History, University of Nottingham

&

J. D. Chambers, B.A., Ph.D.

Emeritus Professor of Economic History, University of Nottingham

with original photographs by

T. R. Sharpe, M.A.

UNIVERSITY TUTORIAL PRESS LTD

9-10 Great Sutton Street

LONDON, E.C.1

All rights reserved. No portion of the book
may be reproduced by any process without
written permission from the publishers.
© *S. D. Chapman, J. D. Chambers, and T. R. Sharpe*, 1970.

Published 1970

KING ALFRED'S COLLEGE
WINCHESTER

942.07
CHA

O.S
72237

SBN: 7231 0169 8

PRINTED IN GREAT BRITAIN BY UNIVERSITY TUTORIAL PRESS LTD, FOXTON, NEAR CAMBRIDGE

Contents

Acknowledgements

Our principal debt is to the large company of economic historians whose research and writing has developed the subject so impressively within the last twenty years and necessitated a frequent redrawing of the contours of the subject. It is impossible, in an introductory work of this kind, to acknowledge all these debts, and we have had to restrict ourselves to a short reading list of more advanced texts where the reader will find good bibliographies of the books, articles, and theses that at present form the foundations of our subject.

The preparation of photographs and line drawings for this work has taken as much time as the writing of the text, and friends in different parts of the country have been most generous in sending us details of subject material in their own localities. We are particularly grateful to Miss Julia Mann, Mr K. G. Ponting, and Dr Jennifer Tann for details of sites in the West of England, to Mr A. R. Mountford for help with sites and illustrations on the Potteries, to Dr Eric Sigsworth and Mr D. W. Crossley for suggestions on the West Riding and Sheffield respectively, and to Mr C. A. Jewell, Keeper of the Museum of English Rural Life at Reading University, for material from the Museum's photographic library. Several business concerns, Josiah Wedgwood and Sons Ltd, Allied Ironfounders Ltd (Coalbrookdale), Rabone & Petersen, Marling & Evans, Westminster Bank Ltd, and the Port of London Authority have provided materials or facilities; the curators of the Welsh Folk Museum, the Birmingham Science Museum, and West Yorkshire Folk Museum (Shibden Hall) have kindly allowed us to photograph some of their exhibits; the librarians of the Royal Society and of public libraries of Birmingham, Dudley, Derby, and Nottingham have been generous in sending us material, and among numerous private individuals who have lent their support we would particularly like to acknowledge the help of Mr F. A. M. Fitzroy-Newdegate for permission to print material from the archives at Newdegate Hall, Alderman Wesley Perrins for opportunities to photograph his collection of material on Black Country nail trade, and Frank Atkinson of the Bowes Museum.

Finally we should like to record our thanks to Charles Moseley of University Tutorial Press Ltd for invaluable help and guidance during the period that this work has been in preparation, and to Tom Sharpe who travelled the country taking photographs to illustrate our text.

S. D. C.

J. D. C.

Introduction

There have been many studies of the rise of industrialism since Arnold Toynbee wrote his famous book, *Industrial Revolution*, in 1884, and the various authors have approached their task from many different points of view. These have been made the subject of a valuable discussion in two recent publications[1] which are readily accessible to students, and no useful purpose would be served by re-opening it here. Perhaps the most enduring impression that it leaves is the extent to which the picture available to the students of the Industrial Revolution to-day has grown in complexity since Arnold Toynbee wrote; and this tendency continues as fresh sources of evidence are explored and new ideas are brought to bear upon it. It is part of our task, so far as the limitations of this book permit, to present the outlines of this picture in the light of the most recent contributions to it, and to introduce students to the methods, practical as well as theoretical, which have been found most useful in interpreting it.

On the practical side, we propose to make use of the record left by the rise of industrialism on the landscape itself. The record may take the form of early examples of machinery, workshops, and factories, of contemporary working-class houses (many of which are in use to-day), of canals, early railways, of chapels, schools, and churches built by employers for their work-people. All these are examples drawn from the relatively new subject of Industrial Archaeology about which several books have been published provided with lavish illustrations, though none has a text to match the visual impact. There is, moreover, a wealth of material still lying in wait for the enterprising photographer, as Mr Sharpe shows in his photographs in this book, nearly all of which appear for the first time; we hope that our readers will be stimulated to make their own collections by independent work in their own localities. There is no better way of visualising the physical and human problems faced by the early factory masters and workers in creating the new industrial communities than by actual investigation on the spot with both tape measure and camera. Such practical work helps to recapture the spirit of the time; but it also serves as a reinforcement, and sometimes as a corrective, of long accepted views based on contemporary accounts in newspapers, pamphlets, or speeches which were as much liable to bias as they are now, while the Reports of Parliamentary bodies in the Blue Books on which historians have relied so heavily were probably more influenced by the virulence of party strife than they would be to-day.

The methods of Industrial Archaeology, however, are an aid to, not a substitute for, a close study of the events themselves. They are historical events, but with an economic content and we must think in economic terms; and just as in political history use is made of terms and concepts drawn from political and constitutional theory, so in economic history it is necessary to make use of concepts drawn from economics where these help to explain the facts. In particular we shall have to understand the concept of the *entrepreneur* and of fixed and circulating capital, and we shall have to think in terms of supply and demand and their effect on wages and prices, of expansion and contraction of the market, of perfect competition and monopolistic tendencies, and of commercial crises and the trade cycle. A background knowledge of the theory of national income and of banking and credit creation is valuable if not indispensable, even for beginners. We shall have to make use of statistics of trends in production, population, prices, and income, and realise the importance of being critical of their origin and reliability. These ideas are not difficult even for those new to

---

[1] M. W. Flinn, *The Origins of the Industrial Revolution* (1966), and R. M. Hartwell, *The Industrial Revolution* (Historical Association Pamphlet, 1965).

the subject, and as far as possible we have explained economic terms as they arise; but it is the essential importance of economic ideas and the necessity to apply them that must be stressed at the outset.

Though Britain is a small country, the physical, industrial, social, intellectual, and cultural differences between the regions are sometimes found to be more striking than the similarities, and the economic historian, seeking to generalise in terms of national trends and uniform tendencies, can readily expose himself to the criticism of his colleagues and students. The authors, who themselves served their research apprenticeship in the study of the development of a particular region, are very conscious of the differing pace of change in various parts of the country, and in different industries and firms in one locality. They have tried to do justice to this aspect of their subject by linking their generalisations with case studies of individual firms, industries, and regions. It is of course the usual practice to illustrate a principle with suitable examples, but we hope that our readers will recognise our case histories as being more full than those usually found in outline histories, and identify this approach as a distinguishing feature of this introductory text.

In brief, then, the justification for the present work is the need for an introduction that will keep students abreast of the ever-changing configuration of our subject by including some of the fruits of much recent research and, in particular, case studies, by insisting on the relevance of elementary economics, and by directing attention to field work as a necessary aid to and reinforcement of understanding. The authors will be well satisfied if their readers come to regard this book as no more than a starting-point for the pursuit of their interest.

I

Industry Large and Small Before the Industrial Revolution

Plate I.1.   A stone anvil used in the nailing trade.   (*S. D. Chapman.*)

In the seventeenth century, and indeed for most of the period covered by this book, the traditional village craftsman was still the most important industrial producer in Britain. Every locality had its smith, carpenter, baker, tailor, and bricklayer, who was both worker and capitalist. For such men the limited local demand offered no real opportunity for expansion of their business, which was often handed on, more or less intact, from father to son for generations. In the towns these crafts were still often organised in guilds, though the traditional authority of the bodies was often ignored or by-passed by the seventeenth century. Some craft industries continued unchanged through the eighteenth and most of the nineteenth centuries, not only in rural Britain but also, in a few instances, in the big manufacturing towns like London, Birmingham, and Manchester.

Beside these traditional and ubiquitous local crafts the sixteenth and seventeenth centuries saw the emergence of specialised industries, concentrated in particular districts or regions. It is possible to distinguish three types of specialised industries. The *mineral industries*—those concerned with the mining or extraction of coal, iron, lead, tin, and salt—were necessarily concentrated because the accessible and marketable natural resources were highly localised. What economists call *the consumption industries*—the preparation of commodities of popular consumption such as beer, tobacco, sugar, soap, paper, glass, and pottery—had to be close to large centres of population in an age when transport was slow and expensive. In the seventeenth century London, ten times the size of its nearest rival, attracted a high proportion of those industries. The third type of specialised industry is not so easy to account for. The manufacture of textiles and metallurgical goods were carried on as *rural domestic industries* in most English counties, but a few districts had a much higher concentration than most. The concentration of the English woollen industry in the West Country, East Anglia, and the West Riding of Yorkshire can partly be explained by reference to factors like the availability of water power, the settlement of refugees from the Continent in Devon and Essex in the sixteenth century and the accessibility to ports and urban markets like London and Bristol. But clearly this is not the whole story since other parts of the country could show similar conditions. In the absence of detailed evidence we must surmise that the explanation for industrial concentration of this kind must be in terms of the internal economies of the district—that is, the development of merchant specialism, labour skills, and ancillary services that can tie an industry to a district after its original reason for being there has disappeared. The internal economies of a manufacturing district can be contrasted with its external economies, *i.e.* its natural resources (water power, coal, supply of raw materials), labour supply, and accessibility to markets. Similarly other branches of the textile industry—cotton, silk, linen, hosiery, and lace—also became highly concentrated in the seventeenth and eighteenth centuries. The metallurgical industries also became highly localised, particularly in Birmingham and the Black Country, Sheffield, and South Lancashire, and though it is not difficult to identify external economies that each possessed, the emergent specialisms of these districts must be connected with the cumulative skills of generations of anonymous specialists, rather than the physical resources of the neighbourhood.

In order to make a more detailed study of industrial specialisation before the industrial revolution we must study each of the three types in turn.

The Mineral Industries

The rise of the coal industry in Britain took place sooner than in any other European country, with the possible exception of Belgium. The period of most rapid growth is said to have been between about 1540 and the start of the English Civil War (1642). An American scholar, Professor J. U. Nef, estimated that in 1551-60 production was 210,000 tons, while in 1681-90 it was 2,982,000 tons.

This was owing to a number of coincident factors. England possessed an abundance of accessible coal, near rivers, which were the main transport arteries before the building of the canals. The rich coal seams of County Durham were not only situated close to the River Tyne, but also had easy access to the North Sea, and hence to the London market. The pits at Broseley and Coalbrookdale, which formed the basis of an early centre of industry, were served by the Severn, the country's longest navigable river. Mining at Worsley and St Helens, on the Lancashire coalfield, was encouraged by the proximity of the River Irwell and the River Mersey. Another early centre of coal mining, at Wollaton and Strelley, near Nottingham, had the advantage of being near the Trent.

However, the immediate stimulus to the growth of the coal industry was the exhaustion of the country's accessible timber supplies. In the later sixteenth century the heavy and extravagant consumption of timber by a few industries began to push up its price, and in 1559 a writer complained that wood had risen from a penny to two shillings a load "by reason of the iron mills". At this period it is said to have taken 5,000 cubic feet of wood to obtain sufficient charcoal to smelt one ton of ore, so the complaint seems quite plausible. However, it must also be remembered that ship-building absorbed large quantities of hardwoods—in the seventeenth century it took "40 great oaks" to build a man-o-war—and the brewers and glass makers bought tens of thousands of wagon loads of timber each year by the end of the sixteenth century. With the inflation of timber prices coal was used as a substitute wherever it could be obtained cheaply.

The most important coalfield up to the last quarter of the eighteenth century was, of course, Tyneside. Under successive Bishops of Durham the exploitation of this field was unprofitable because of the conditions imposed—short-term leases, restrictions on output, and high royalties. The transference of much of this land to the Crown at the dissolution of the monasteries (in 1533 and 1536) brought cheap, long leases, with no significant restrictions. As London grew rapidly, Tyneside benefited by increasing the supply of "sea coal" to the metropolis.

The basic factor in the organisation of the coal industry was that the legal owner of a coal seam was the owner of the land above. The great landowners, the aristocracy and gentry, played, therefore, a major role in the development of the industry.

The availability of a source of fuel alternative to wood enabled the Tudor industries of England to maintain the momentum of their growth. This was particularly so with urban industries, especially in London, where the scarcity of timber fuel was first felt. The constant supply of "sea coal" from Tyneside by a growing fleet of sailing ships allowed the consumption industries of London to continue to increase the scale of their operations, and indeed it has been pointed out that Tyneside coal was the prerequisite of the continued growth of London itself, for without coal to warm their homes the householders of the metropolis must have been taxed out of town by the increasing price of timber.

The cheapness of coal on the coalfields and in areas adjacent to the navigable rivers that ran through them was an effective stimulant to some other industries. In the course of the seventeenth century coal was substituted for wood in every industry except iron smelting, where the technique of using coke was not discovered until the early eighteenth

Plate I.2. The Staffordshire "Ten-yard" seam. A nineteenth-century print of Bradley mine, near Bilston. (*Birmingham Reference Library.*)

century and not generally known until its second half. The most important beneficiaries were the metallurgical industries. The Black Country owed its early development to the famous "ten yard" seam of the South Staffordshire coalfield, over which there already stood hundreds of forges at the Restoration. The smelting of copper, lead, and tin was done with coal and the glass industry found it possible to use coal for all its heating. The principal provincial centres of the glass industry (Stourbridge, Newcastle, and Bristol) owed their situation chiefly to their proximity to coal seams. The need to transport coal also created the beginnings of the modern transport system. The ever-growing London market for coal created a fleet of colliers regularly sailing up and down the east coast between Newcastle and the Thames. In 1550 it is said that there were only two British ships engaged in this trade, but by about 1700 there were something like 1,600, only one-fifth of which were owned by foreigners. Until the canal age began in the second half of the eighteenth century, the rivers and the sea were the transport arteries of the country. The first substantial improvement in the primitive transport system took place when some of the rivers passing through the coalfields were made more navigable by dredging, widening, straightening their courses, and building locks

where necessary. Thus in 1719 the little River Douglas was made into a "navigation" to create an outlet for the superior "cannel" coal of Wigan, and the following year the Rivers Mersey and Weaver were canalised to link the coal measures of St Helens with the salt deposits of north Cheshire (see Chap. VI). Another significant development connected with coal mining was the building of wagon-ways to carry the coal from the pit-head to the barges waiting by the jetties on the rivers. These railroads were originally wooden guides along which horses pulled trains of coal trucks. In the early eighteenth century wrought iron rails began to replace wooden guides, but it was another century before the pioneers of the modern railways began to use steam locomotives successfully on the colliery railroads. However, this is to anticipate a later phase of economic development; for the time being it is sufficient to say that those scholars who have attempted to identify the original colliery wagon-way—in Nottingham, St Helens, and Newcastle—all place the date soon after 1600.

The development of the coal industry was also the key to another crucial development in this seed-time of modern industry. The drainage of coal and lead mines was a perennial problem and in the seventeenth century some very expensive soughs (drainage tunnels) were excavated in attempts

Plate I.3.   Early iron rails at Coalbrookdale.

close to the natural resources. The blast furnace produced "pigs" of a thousand lbs. or more which were refined into wrought iron at a forge, or refinery forge as we might call it. At the chafery forge the wrought iron was shaped into a form suitable for the smiths or the rolling and slitting mills, which rolled the metal into sheets and cut it into rods before sending it to merchants for distribution to nailers, lockmakers, and similar metal workers. The chafery forges could use coal as their source of heat, and so too could the slitting and rolling mills and the smiths. Thus these later processes tended to be attracted towards the coalfields and towards their main customers in the towns. The iron industry was thus highly dispersed, the first process being tied to the forests while the finishing processes were drawn towards the markets.

British iron ores contained a high proportion of impurities and were expensive to smelt compared with the higher grade Swedish ores. Freight rates from the Baltic were low compared with the cost of overland transport so that, despite a Swedish export duty and a British import one, considerable quantities of Swedish bar iron were imported. This situation favoured the growth of an iron industry on the north-east coast and districts (like Sheffield, for instance), that had river connections with the ports.

Until quite recently it was generally supposed that the charcoal iron industry was in a state of stagnation, if not decline, in the eighteenth century, owing to the increasing shortage of timber. Research on the different regions suggests that this may be wrong. The old centre of the industry in the Weald was probably declining, but the West Midlands, South Yorkshire, Furness, and South Wales could show vigorous activity. Moreover, the timber needs of the charcoal iron industry were quite different from

Plate I.4.   A coal-mining horse gin. (*Courtesy of the West Yorkshire Folk Museum, Shibden Hall, Halifax.*)

to drain off the water. One completed by Sir Roger Bradshaigh near Wigan in 1670 is said to have taken sixteen years to build. However, soughs were only possible in hilly country and elsewhere horse-driven pumps had to be used. In 1631 we first hear of an attempt "to raise water from coal-pits by fire" and subsequent experiments led, at the end of the century, to the introduction of Savery's atmospheric pump, the ancestor of the steam engine.

The Newcastle coal trade was certainly one important reason for the ship-building industry of the north-east coast that came into existence in the decades around 1700. The large and expensive East Indiamen continued to be built on the Thames, but an increasing number of cheaper ships (originally only to serve the coal trade) were built at Whitby, Newcastle, on the Tyne estuary, and at Scarborough, Stockton, and Sunderland.

Like the coal industry in its early stages the iron industry was developed by men of substantial capital. There were three or four basic processes in the iron industry up till the last quarter of the eighteenth century when the traditional charcoal iron industry gave way to an industry using coke as its fuel. The ore was smelted in a blast furnace which, because of the high cost of transport, was necessarily situated

Plate I.5. Newcomen's "Atmospheric" engine, based on a 1717 engraving. (*Courtesy David and Charles Ltd, Thomas Newcomen.*)

those of other major consumers, such as builders and shipyards. Charcoal for iron making was obtained from young trees, which could be conveniently obtained from recently-planted woodlands, leaving the more sturdy trees for further growth and other uses. It is known that sylviculture was practised by many landowners from the period of the Restoration onwards, and consequently too much should not be made of the undoubted shortage of mature timber.

The great expansion of iron production that began in the reign of Elizabeth was at first directed by the landowners, the nobility, and gentry. The greatest

ironmasters were peers of ancient lineage like George Talbot, ninth Earl of Shrewsbury, who had ironworks near Sheffield, and the Duke of Norfolk, whose foundries were in the Sussex Weald, the traditional English centre of the industry. The Earls of Rutland ran a foundry at Rievaulx (Yorkshire); the Earls of Devonshire had several foundries in Derbyshire. A scholar has calculated that of the Elizabethan aristocratic families no less than 22 per cent. owned ironworks at the end of the sixteenth century.

This early lead was, however, soon usurped by thrusting men of more humble birth. The interest in industry of the great nobles was typically ephemeral; after the initial excitement of starting the business they tended to delegate the running of their enterprises to agents or contractors. The Foleys of Stourbridge, Worcestershire, were the first middle-class family to head the table of iron producers. Richard Foley (*c.* 1580-1657), the son of a Dudley nailer, began his career selling nails but shortly became master of a forge. His fortune probably dates from his introduction of the rolling and slitting mill from the Continent, the first of which he built near Stourbridge about 1627. He also owned a furnace at West Bromwich. His son, Thomas Foley, built up the business and in 1669 owned four furnaces, thirteen forges, four slitting mills, and a warehouse, together valued at £68,830. The grandsons were associated in partnerships controlling ironworks in the Stourbridge district, north Staffordshire, Cheshire, Derbyshire, Nottinghamshire, and the Forest of Dean. At the beginning of the eighteenth century they had financial links with over forty ironworks, all supplying rods and wire to the rapidly growing metallurgical industries of Birmingham and the Black Country.

The largest single industrial organisation built up before the Industrial Revolution was again in the iron industry and trade and again had its origins in Stourbridge. Sir Ambrose Crowley, the son of an iron merchant, was sent to London to serve his apprenticeship in a City warehouse. The foundations of Crowley's success were his contracts for supplying the Royal Navy, for the army and navy departments offered the largest orders to be had at this period. In 1682 Crowley branched out into manufacturing by opening a nail factory at Sunderland (Co. Durham) whose location was convenient for importing Swedish bar iron and sending nails to London by the convenient and regular collier. Within a decade he embarked on a much more ambitious concern with his industrial estate at Winlaton, near Newcastle-on-Tyne. By 1707 this comprised three factories, two slitting mills, two forges, four steel furnaces, innumerable smiths' workshops, and a range of warehouses. The output now included not only nails but a wide variety of manufactured metal goods whose origins were more usually connected with Birmingham. Crowley's mercantile interests remained centred on the City, where he had five warehouses as well as a wharf at Greenwich, adjoining his fine Jacobean house. He also maintained a chain of warehouses in the provinces—at Ware,

Wolverhampton, Walsall, and Stourbridge—with a nail manufacturing business at the last. The capital assets of the whole business were worth well over £100,000 at Crowley's death in 1713, and in the firm's heyday in the second quarter of the eighteenth century his son John probably employed more than a thousand workers. It is particularly to be noticed that Crowley established a factory system of production (*i.e.*, a concentration of workers in a building employing mechanised power) almost a century before the system came into general use in the textile industries, with all stages of the industry integrated under one owner's direction.

The Foleys and Crowleys are outstanding, but their careers were not different in type to those of dozens of other iron masters. Before the opening of the eighteenth century the iron industry was already a capitalistic structure, conducted on lines not essentially different to the direction of modern industry.

Consumption Industries

The growth of consumption industries in Britain in the Tudor and Stuart periods was largely a consequence of the growth of a large urban market, particularly London, whose population (including the suburbs and adjacent boroughs south of the river) rose from an estimated 130,000 in 1631 to 528,000 in 1695. London was easily the largest port of the country and the home of a large and growing number of wealthy merchants, some of whom were drawn from the provinces and foreign countries. Being the capital, residence there was necessary for the aristocracy, ambassadors, members of parliament (all with their retinues), the judiciary, and a growing number of lawyers. During the seventeenth century London became a centre for education (the Inns of Court became a "university of London" for the gentry, and private academies were multiplying). Merchants, scriveners, and goldsmiths developed the technique of deposit banking during the course of the century, and London began to emerge as the national money market. This concentration of population and wealth made London the centre for fashion, ostentation, and luxurious living, the nobility and gentry drawing income from the provinces to support their conspicuous consumption.

As the principal port of the country, London was able to import raw materials not only from other parts of Britain, but also from overseas. These were worked up in the capital and became the basis for industries like sugar refining, tobacco curing, and the silk manufacture. The needs of a large population fostered industries like tailoring, brick-making, furniture-making, and beer brewing in London. More significant, in the light of subsequent economic developments, were the industries called forth by the discriminating market: the demand for fine textiles, china and porcelain, soap, paper, and glass-ware, now articles of common use but at this time only purchasable by those of considerable substance. After the Restoration, sugar, paper, and beer began to be manufactured on a commercial scale in other centres of population, such as Bristol, Edinburgh, and Glasgow.

The growth of the consumption industries was encouraged by some other developments in the seventeenth century. The increasing trade of the country brought in manufactured goods from Europe and the Orient of a quality that could not be matched by British craftsmen. Nevertheless, the high price commanded by these imported textiles, pottery, furniture, and fine metal goods, stimulated attempts to imitate them in this country. Attempts to attain the standards of foreign crafts-men were very considerably helped by the migration of religious refugees to this country, particularly Huguenots after the revocation of the Edict of Nantes in 1685. The Huguenots included financiers and entrepreneurs of great ability, as well as crafts-men. Their influence was perhaps most marked in the paper industry, where they considerably improved the quality of white paper and so helped capture the home market from foreign suppliers. They brought new techniques to the manufacture of precision instruments, watches, cutlery, silk, and glass. The English government's attitude to industry and commerce was broadly paternalistic in the seven-teenth century, and they were ready to provide the benefit of protection to British industries, parti-cularly where these promised to displace some substantial import from abroad.

The scale on which the consumption industries were conducted of course varied, but broadly speaking they appear to have fallen between the large-scale capitalist enterprise of the coal and metal smelting industries on the one hand and the small domestic manufacturing units on the other. In the paper indus-try, for instance, there were some 150 to 200 mills in England by about 1720, concentrated in London and the Home Counties (particularly Kent and Buckinghamshire), with a handful of mills in Scotland and Ireland. The mills were worth in the region of £500 to £1,800 each, and most mills did not employ more than a score of workers. The glass industry also consisted of small units by to-day's standards. A member of one of the French emigré families that founded the Stourbridge industry in the very early years of James I's reign originally worked with only two assistants to make up the team of three that is still the basic producing unit in cut-glass works. At the Restoration his son rebuilt the glasshouse in stone at a cost of only £200. A hundred years later ten glasshouses in the Stourbridge district employed about 520 people—an average of about 50 in each.

The Domestic Industries

The domestic system of organisation, as we have already remarked, was characteristic of the regional textile industries and of the small metallurgical trades, of the kind just referred to in the last section. Every county in England and Wales manufactured some cloth, but there were three areas of concen-tration in the eighteenth century: the West Country, centred on Exeter (Devon), Trowbridge (Wiltshire), and Stroud (Gloucestershire); East Anglia, centred on Norwich; and the West Riding of Yorkshire, with centres at Leeds, Wakefield, and Halifax. The increasing reliance of the woollen industry on water power, the attraction of cheap rural labour, and the decay of the guild system had resulted in the migration of the industry from the old corpo-rate towns to the country districts. The towns

Plate I.6. Mr Hacking, a handloom weaver, at Colne in 1890. Both the loom and his clothing are similar to those com-monly seen at the beginning of the 19th century. (*Chapman.*)

themselves were the commercial, but not always the industrial heart of their district. By the early seventeenth century the cotton and linen industry found its principal home in Lancashire, the Clyde valley, and the Laggan Valley. Manchester, Glasgow, and Belfast were their respective commercial centres. The hosiery (or knitwear) industry was the speciality of the East Midlands, particularly the district around Nottingham, Leicester, and Derby, though it was not until after the middle of the eighteenth century that the provincial hosiery industry surpassed that of London, the traditional home of trades based on fashion. The silk industry was brought to the country by refugees from the Continent, and they and their descendants prospered in a number of places in different parts of the country, principally in Spitalfields and East London generally, and in Coventry, Norwich, and Macclesfield.

The specialisation of Birmingham and the Black Country in ironmongery covered a variety of products, with considerable local specialities within the region. In the seventeenth century the most distinctive products were buttons and buckles in many varieties (Birmingham), nails (Dudley and Stourbridge), and locks (Wolverhampton), but in the course of the next century the forge, lathe, and stamp found a whole variety of new products, of which pins, jewellery, coins, and coffin furniture are only instances. Some other districts specialised in other metal goods: Sheffield was then (as now) famed for its cutlery, Coventry and Clerkenwell (London) had watch-making industries, and several towns of south Lancashire specialised in craftsmen's tools.

Certain features of the domestic system of organisation were common to all these industries. The capitalist, organiser, and entrepreneur (*i.e.*, person who made the vital decisions about the quantities and qualities of goods that were to be produced) was the merchant. He invariably owned a warehouse at the centre of the industry (at Norwich, Leeds, Birmingham, or wherever else) and was variously known as merchant clothier, merchant ironmonger, merchant hosier, linen draper (in Lancashire), or some other appropriate title. He owned little fixed capital (*i.e.*, buildings and machinery), certainly at the beginning of the eighteenth century. Most of his capital was circulating, *i.e.*, tied up in stocks of raw materials, work in progress, stocks of the finished product, goods in transit, and credit to his customers.

The manufacturer was an artisan who owned considerably less capital than the merchant, but up to the end of the eighteenth century was often independent. He worked on his own premises and employed his own family as well as, quite often, a journeyman and an apprentice or two. Women were expected to contribute to the family income, if possible, by aiding their husbands; it was said in 1743 that "none but a fool will take a wife whose bread must be earned solely by his labour and who will contribute nothing towards it herself". Children were made to help with the simple chores of the domestic trade as soon as they were able to do so. The domestic work was carried on in the small crowded living room of the worker's cottage, or in towns, in a garret or cellar or other room that served as the living, sleeping, and working accommodation for the family. The most important exception to this was the Black Country, where the forges were necessarily built outside the cottages.

Domestic work was characteristically irregular. The poor condition of the roads, and dependence on the vagaries of wind and water for mechanical power, meant that there were often delays in obtaining materials, particularly in winter. (The domestic worker has sometimes been supposed to have enjoyed a pleasant alternation between indoor industrial work in the winter months and outdoor agricultural work in the summer. In fact he might often find that there was more manufacturing as well as farm work in the summer and autumn.) Quite apart from this, the workers themselves seem to have preferred long periods of leisure compensated by periods of excessive labour. After the work was taken or sent in to the warehouse on Friday or Saturday, Sunday was enjoyed as a games day (except where Puritans or, later on, Methodists were powerful) and "St Monday" and often "St Tuesday" were also spent as leisure days before a new and furious effort began to complete sufficient work for another week's subsistence. It is not difficult to account for these irregular habits. Labour, whether at the loom, stocking frame, or forge, was monotonous and exhausting. Hours were long, typically from dawn to dusk. The environment of work was often unhealthy, and deformities, pulmonary diseases, and eye strain were very common. Such conditions created periodically a sickening aversion to work, resulting in various forms of escapism—drinking, gambling, cruel or savage sports, rowdyism, and, indeed, anything for cheap excitement.

The Industrial Revolution

Nor was there anything idyllic about industrial relations under the domestic system. Often the connection with the merchant employer was remote. The worker only met the merchant's agent, a middleman who collected the work of a village or locality and carried it up to town. Most local studies point to the existence of strained relations between workers and employer; the result was often demonstrations, riots, and spontaneous strikes. At its worst the chasm which separated the merchant from his remote workers could create an irreconcilable division of interest; this was the situation which produced the original Luddite movement in the Midlands, with sustained industrial warfare against offending hosiers. In more normal circumstances, the workers constantly complained of under-payment and payment in truck (or kind), and the employers of embezzlement of materials, inferior workmanship, and rebellious attitudes.

This general framework has, of course, many regional and local variations. It is not possible in a short book of this kind to explore them all. The most that can be done is to study three or four examples at close range in order to illustrate some similarities and contrasts found within the system.

The West of England Clothing Industry

The domestic organisation of the industry was established in Gloucestershire, Wiltshire, Somerset, and Devon in the Tudor period. Dean Tucker, of Gloucester, provided what has been taken to be the classic description of the West of England clothier, in 1757. The woollen industry of the West, he wrote, was conducted by "one person with a great stock and large credit, who buys the wool, pays for the spinning, weaving, milling, dyeing, shearing, dressing, etc. That is, he is master of the whole manufacture from first to last and perhaps employs a thousand persons under him". This account of his wealth is supported, seemingly, by the monuments in the churches of the old clothing districts, the charitable bequests to the poor of the clothing towns, the fine houses built in town and countryside by the "gentlemen clothiers", and the still attractive houses adjoining the many surviving mills. In point of fact, however, the wealthy élite have acquired prominence at the expense of their more numerous (though less well-to-do) rivals. Until the end of the eighteenth century a substantial number of clothiers combined manufacturing with farming, or travelled with and sold their goods as

Plate I.7. An early wool merchant's house in Bradford-on-Avon. (*National Buildings Record; Batsford Ltd.*)

retailers; only a handful of clothiers could have employed anything like a thousand workpeople. The smaller clothiers sent their wool and finished cloths to specialists, who undertook the preparatory and finishing processes for a commission. It is probable that the number of farmer-clothiers declined gradually over the period during which the domestic system was widespread, the small clothier disappearing during the French Wars.

The general organisation of the West of England trade is illustrated in the diagram (p. 12). The clothiers bought their wool from local markets and a group of itinerant middlemen known as "wool broggers". (These travelled the villages of the west and south of England buying up the small clips of wool.) Farmer-clothiers would also contribute some of their own fleeces, of course. Carding and spinning occupied something like half the total labour force of the industry, and was mostly done by women and girls. By the eighteenth century there was a shortage of spinners because of the large numbers needed. It was by no means unusual for a clothier to send his wool 20 miles or more to be spun; for instance, Stroud clothiers employed many poor families in Cheltenham. The weavers were nominally independent of the clothiers, but from the first half of the sixteenth century the clothiers began buying up looms, and so acquired increasing control of the workmen that were employed in their own homes. The sale of the cloths in London was handled exclusively, from the early seventeenth century, by the factors at Blackwell Hall, the London cloth market. Other cloths were sold at the great international fairs, notably at Stourbridge (Cambs), Bristol, and Exeter. Local markets and direct sale to shopkeepers played only a minor role in the distribution of the products of this industry.

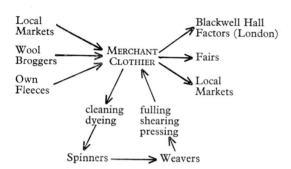

THE LANCASHIRE COTTON INDUSTRY

The domestic organisation of the Lancashire linen and cotton industry is first noticed towards the end of the sixteenth century; the pattern is similar to that which we have described for the West of England, except that the raw material (cotton) had to be imported from abroad. The central figure was the linen draper, who became known as the merchant (or merchant clothier) as the eighteenth century advanced. He bought raw cotton in London, Liverpool, Bristol, Lancaster, or Glasgow, and occasionally abroad. He might have a partner or agent in London or Liverpool or one of the other ports, or he might buy from the agents of London merchants in Manchester. The linen drapers advanced the cotton and yarn to an intermediate class of country manufacturers known as fustian makers or chapmen. It was these men who employed the spinners and weavers of the various country districts—Bury, Bolton, Chorley, Blackburn, Wigan, Warrington, and other Lancashire towns which were then but villages. The fustian weavers often combined their work in the loom with some agricultural occupation. They invariably owned their own machines. Spinning, in Lancashire as elsewhere, was the time-honoured occupation of the "labouring poor". Like the merchant clothiers of the West of England, the linen drapers sold through various channels. Some of their cloths went to their London agents or partners, or their connections at Liverpool, Lancaster, and other ports. Other cloths were sent directly to the great fairs which survived from the Middle Ages as great

Plate I.8.   Spinning.   (*Taken at St Fagan's, Cardiff.*)

Plate I.9.   Weaving.   (*Taken at St Fagan's, Cardiff.*)

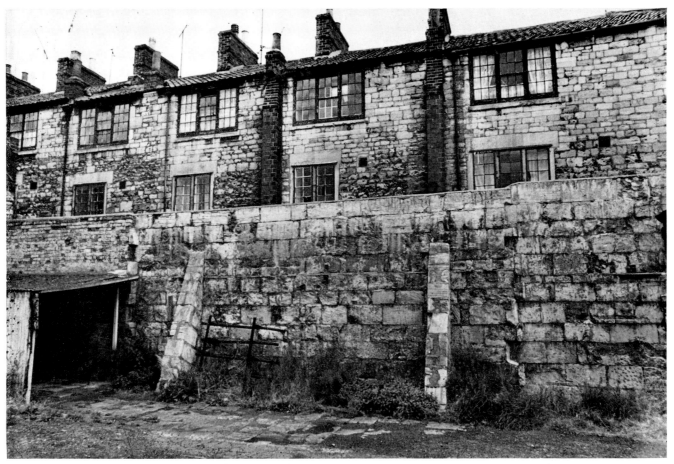

Plate I.10. Clothiers' houses at Trowbridge, Wilts.

international marts. Others again went to shop-keepers, local markets, and to the numerous hawkers and pedlars who, when shopkeeping was still in its infancy even in the towns, had their rounds through the villages and hamlets of a still predominantly rural England.

THE HOSIERY INDUSTRY

The stocking frame was the invention of minor mechanical genius, Rev. William Lee, of Calverton, near Nottingham. Lee took his invention to London in an unsuccessful attempt to obtain a patent from Queen Elizabeth, and though some of his workmen returned to their home county, the early framework knitting industry was based on the metropolis. Knitted fabrics differ from woven ones in that only one thread is used, the material being created by throwing up a series of loops which are secured by a second interlocking row of loops. The domestic system in the hosiery industry was greatly encouraged after 1728, when the Nottingham justices refused to recognise the restricting ordinances of the London Company of Framework Knitters, and the industry began to migrate from London to the greater freedom of the provinces. The organisation that emerged was basically similar to that of Lancashire. (It is summarised in diagrammatic form on p. 14.)

There was some tendency for Leicester merchant hosiers to specialise in worsted hosiery, Nottingham hosiers to specialise in cotton, and Derby hosiers (a much smaller group) to confine themselves to silk, but this division of function was never complete; in particular, there was a good deal of silk hosiery manufactured in Nottingham. The bag hosiers were middlemen who, by the 1780s, are to be found in manufacturing villages some way from the hosier's warehouse distributing yarn and collecting and forwarding the completed work.

13

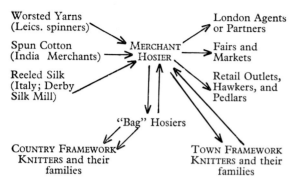

The work of combing and spinning worsted was carried on in Leicester and its neighbourhood. Combing, which required strength and skill, was considered a man's occupation; spinning occupied "married and unmarried women, widows, aged and infirm persons, and children". In 1663 these were estimated at 2,000 people, in 1788, on the eve of the transition to mechanised spinning, at 18,500. Framework knitters worked with their families, a cottage often containing two or three frames. Children learned to work in the frame as soon as they could reach the pedals at 10-12 years of age. Women carried on the supplementary work of winding thread and sizing and seaming the hose. The only industrial processes for which the merchant hosier made himself responsible were dyeing and bleaching apart from keeping a few frames at his warehouse for special orders. The number of stocking frames employed in the provinces is said to have increased from about 150 in 1664 to 25,000 in 1812.

Plate I.11. Nailmaker's equipment.

THE NAIL TRADE OF THE WEST MIDLANDS

The nail industry was probably the largest of all the industries using iron, and certainly one of the

earliest to be established, so that it provides a useful illustration of the domestic system in the metal trades and a starting point for later consideration of industrial development in that industry. From the earliest period for which we have records there was a wide sprinkling of nailers over the West Midland counties. In the early seventeenth century the Black Country trade was further stimulated by the establishment of rolling and slitting mills along the Stour and the Tame. The iron mills provided the rods of

Plate I.12. Nailmaker and holdfast maker, Halesowen.

iron which were the raw material of the nailers. Before the Civil Wars there were said to be 20,000 smiths and nailers within a ten mile radius of Dudley Castle.

The domestic system was in existence in the nailing industry from the sixteenth century, if not before. The organisation of the industry bears a basic resemblance to other industries conducted on the same system. (See diagram on p. 16.)

The nail masters had their warehouses in Birmingham, Dudley, Stourbridge, Bromsgrove, and other centres of the industry. They were served by a vast army of nail-makers through a corps of middlemen known as nail factors or (in the nineteenth century) "foggers". The nailer and his family worked

Plate I.13. Nailmakers' cottages and workshops at Mushroom Green, near Dudley.

Plate I.14. Some products of the Black Country Nailing Industry.

Plate I.15. Using a "springy pole" lathe. (See p. 90.) Chainmaker at Halesowen.

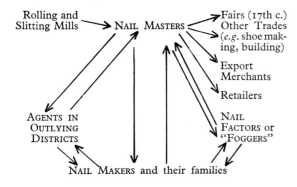

in a small shed or workshop adjoining his cottage. Other nailers rented a stall in a shop owned by another nailer. Numerous of these family workshops have survived in the Black Country until recently; an example is shown on p. 15. The family was responsible for all the processes by which the iron rod was converted into nails; there was no specialisation, except that the younger members of the family would begin on simple tasks like dipping the red hot tips of the nails in cold water to harden them. A large number of women worked in the trade, some of them resorting to it when domestic spinning declined. They specialised in "thousand work", or the smaller hob nails. A traveller on the road from Walsall to Birmingham observed them at work in 1741, "stripped of their upper garments, and not overcharged with their lower, wielding the hammer with all the graces of their sex. The beauties of their faces were rather eclipsed by the smut of the anvil . . . ."

The nailers were noted for their poverty from at least the early part of the eighteenth century. Their conditions of work were confined and unhealthy. Children began to help their parents from five years of age and worked regularly with their families at seven, blowing the bellows or dipping nails. The nailers' poor mud-walled thatch-roofed huts survived in the heart of the nailing country (at Lye, near Stourbridge) into this century, evidence of their continued poverty.

Craft Invention

So far the traditional structure of industry has been described as though the techniques of production were static. This is substantially true until the early or middle decades of the eighteenth century. There were of course important industrial innovations before this time, such as the stocking frame and the rolling mill which have already been mentioned; but industrial techniques were simple and traditional, craft "mysteries" that were handed on unchanged from one generation to the next. The significant change that came about in the early eighteenth century was that craftsmen in some of the centres of industry, such as Birmingham, Manchester, Nottingham, Sheffield, Blackburn, and Wolverhampton, began to contrive new products or to increase the output of their workshops. By the second half of the century this had become a popular practice. This development is readily illustrated from the experience of Birmingham. The traditional tools of the Birmingham district were the forge and hammer, largely occupied in making nails; some would produce other traditional products like the metal parts of harness, and knives, swords, and chains. Locks were added in the early seventeenth century. The availability of sheet metal in large quantities from the new rolling mills provided an opportunity to make other metal goods. The first, and for long the most popular, sheet-metal products were buttons and buckles. The manufacture of the metal buttons demanded by eighteenth-century fashion was at first a tedious and expensive process, for every ornament that appeared on the face had to be added or engraved by hand. The press, stamp, and lathe were improved to expedite the process of cutting out the shapes, and every visitor to the town bore testimony to the constant attempts that were made to improve the craftsmanship. One noticed that there were "an infinity of small improvements which each workman has and sedulously keeps secret from all the rest"; another remarked that "Such has been the rapidity of invention, and the elegance of design, that the public has been incessantly presented with new and exquisite patterns". Out of this ferment of ideas there emerged a whole range of new products, originally depending on the skill of the button maker. The stamp, press, and lathe were adapted to produce new articles such as cabinet ornaments, coffin furniture, Sheffield plate, coins, and medals, engraving plates for printing, jewellery, pins, and pistols. Not only all kinds of metals, but also glass, porcelain, papier-maché, leather, and mother of pearl were used for button-making. In course of time these materials were used for other products, particularly those requiring skill or artistic ability such as Japan ware (*c.* 1740) and, by about 1800, optical instruments. In the second half of the eighteenth century Birmingham became the natural home for inventive artisans. "Here the man of invention who has already formed a model of any machine . . . . may readily have the proof of the goodness or imperfection of his design without being subject to the trouble, delay, and expense which experiments made at a distance from hence necessarily occasioned. . .", an observer noted in 1777. There was a community of inventive minds, daily stimulating each other by the competition of superior products or workmanship. At the industrial and commercial centre of the manufacturing district merchants and others with capital were ready to patronise new techniques for which they foresaw a market.

The growth of craft invention in industrial towns had important consequences for the distribution of wealth and poverty. Not surprisingly, the towns attracted the most ambitious and able young men from the manufacturing villages for miles around seeking higher wages and outlet for their skill. As new trades came into existence the original and basic manufacture of the district was forced, in the process of competition for land, power resources, capital, and skilled labour, from the town into its rural environs. Thus the towns became the home of mechanics working on the newest and most remuner-

ative products, while the surrounding countryside took the less skilled and often poorly paid work. Birmingham artisans, for instance, were envied for their skill and prosperity, while the nailers, who were increasingly found on the periphery of the manufacturing region, were noted for their poverty. A similar contrast is found in the hosiery districts. The men working on fashion hosiery and lace net in Nottingham and Leicester earned from three to five times as much as the framework knitters of the country manufacturing districts, whose weekly earnings of 10s.-12s. was hardly reckoned enough for a subsistence. About two-thirds of the men in the trade made their livings from the basic process at the end of the eighteenth century. A parallel situation existed in Lancashire and the Cheshire and Derbyshire borders. Weavers making "fustians", the thick twilled cotton cloth which was the traditional product of the region, earned little more than a subsistence, while those who were able to tackle muslins, calicoes, and cambrics, the new and finer cloths of the last three decades of the eighteenth century, could earn five times that amount. The significance of these variations in earnings will become apparent when, in Chapter VII, we look at the social consequences of industrial change.

THE STOCKING FRAME

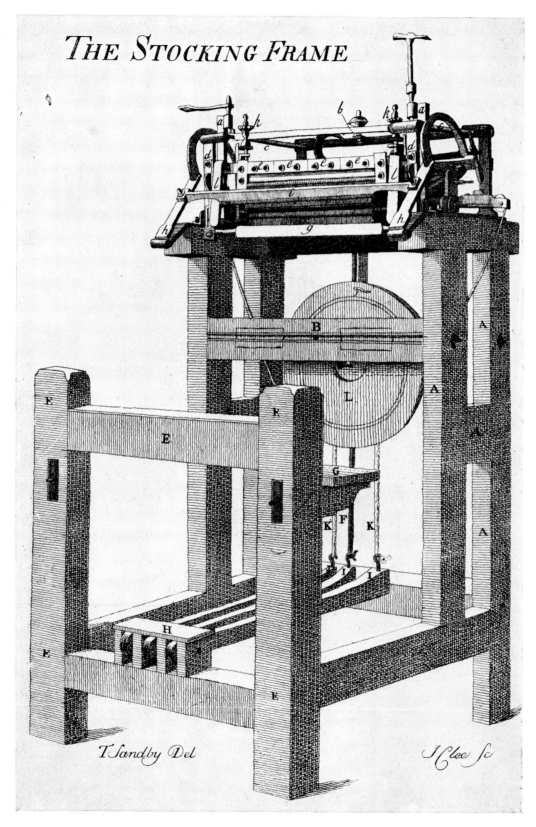

Plate II.1. An engraving in Charles Deering, *Nottinghamia Vetus et Nova* (1751). This machine is thought to be the most delicate mechanism used in British industry before the advent of the factory system.

II

The Origins of the Industrial Revolution

What Is an Industrial Revolution?

The concept of an industrial revolution is not difficult to understand: it is the period during which the economy of a backward or undeveloped country is transformed into a modern industrial economy. This change took place in Britain in the eighteenth and early nineteenth centuries, and subsequently in a number of other countries—France, the U.S.A., Germany, Japan, Russia, Sweden, and Canada, roughly in that order. The British industrial revolution took place before the time when most governments felt the need to collect statistics about national industry and trade, so that the only figures of growth available are very approximate estimates based on incomplete data. The first scholars to study British economic growth in the eighteenth century relied mainly on qualitative evidence and thought they discerned the major period of change in the last thirty years or so of the century, when some spectacular changes in the structure of the cotton and iron industries, and of transport services, took place. But the process of change was more complicated than the pioneers suspected, and attempts to trace its origins took researchers to the late sixteenth and the seventeenth centuries. T. S. Ashton entitled his best known book *The Industrial Revolution, 1760-1830*, but more recent research would take a date around 1740 as a starting point, and might wish to extend the period to 1850. Thus, although nobody disputes the existence of an industrial revolution in Britain, there is not yet sufficient statistical evidence or scholarly agreement to decide finally when it was taking place.

The definition of the industrial revolution leads to the more fundamental question of how this sudden and extraordinary growth in the economy was brought about. Who made the critical investment decisions and why were they made at the particular time? In a private enterprise economy like that of Britain decisions are made by a multitude of individuals and firms, the great majority of whose careers have escaped historical record. The meaningful question to ask is therefore: "What conditions suddenly favoured intensive industrial investment in the period after about 1780?" Because of the complexity of human relationships and the paucity of precise historical evidence, there is no easy answer to this question; but it is possible to identify the main factors with a fair degree of certainty.

We may begin by noting that in order to increase the flow of commodities or of services in a private

Plate II.2. Statue of Joseph Priestley, Matthew Boulton, and James Watt, at Birmingham.

enterprise economy six conditions must maintain:

(1) The support or acquiescence of the government.

(2) Business enterprise must be available—that is, men with the ability, training, energy, vision, and determination necessary to build up an industrial or

19

commercial organisation. (The term "business man" is not a very satisfactory one so the word *entrepreneur* is used to indicate the person—or partnership or corporation—that takes the important decisions about what shall be produced, the technical processes that will be employed, and when the product shall be put on the market.)

Entrepreneurs need:

(3) A market for the product or service they plan to provide.

(4) Capital, to acquire land, buildings, plant, etc., and raw materials.

(5) A labour force which can be trained to new methods of production.

(6) A knowledge of technology which is at least the equal of their competitors.

We may examine each of these requirements in turn in the context of eighteenth-century Britain.

Government and Society

In the eighteenth century British society consisted of a number of classes, but in practice it was not always easy to identify which class a man or his family belonged to as there were no clear class demarcations and (then as now) a close examination of the membership of any class revealed very significant differences between the most wealthy and the least well-off of those claiming to belong to it.

The reasons for this fluid social structure are worth analysing. One of the reasons was the decay of the medieval regulations which had restricted entry to the skilled industrial, trading, and merchant groups, while old trades (particularly the woollen industry) had migrated into the countryside beyond the jurisdiction of the chartered towns, and new trades had sprung up free of guild and corporate controls. This opened up the avenues through which men of humble

Plate II.3. Apprentice's Indentures. (*Derby Public Library.*)

origins might ascend from the status of journeyman (or wage-earner) to independent manufacturer and merchant. By the eighteenth century the aristocracy and gentry were crowded with the sons and grandsons of men who had made their fortunes in trade (at home or in the colonies), or in the professions or government service, and had invested their savings in landed estate. On the other hand, many noblemen had industrial and commercial interests, particularly in the exploitation of the mineral resources of their estates, and of course the management or supervision of a large estate was itself "big business". Moreover, the younger sons of the landowning classes were constantly being dispersed into industry and trade by the practice of primogeniture; the eldest son inherited the whole of the estate, while the younger ones had to make their own way in the world. Some younger sons were of course found places in the army and navy, the Church, the civil service, and the law, but a substantial number, particularly the sons of lesser landowners, were apprenticed to prosperous merchant houses. In Leicester, to take just one provincial town as an example, one-third of the 146 youths apprenticed to merchant hosiers between 1750 and 1800 were sons of landed proprietors of one type or another. The fathers of these young men were able to pay the higher apprenticeship premiums and so secure connections with the better-established merchant houses. In London the sons of country gentlemen were said to provide the largest single source of recruits to the merchant houses at the middle of the eighteenth century.

There was thus a constant movement of men from one social class to another, both up and down the social scale, and the prospect of winning both fortune and higher social status by application to business was a sufficient incentive for hundreds of Dick Whittingtons. At the apex of the social pyramid the ambition to pass on the family estate intact and secure the future of other sons and the daughters by expensive apprenticeship premiums (£1,000 was not unknown in London at the middle of the eighteenth century) or dowries helped to ensure that no business talent need be dissipated in the kind of enforced idleness for which the court of Louis XIV became notorious.

The British government cannot be said to have had an industrial policy in the eighteenth century. The Tudors and early Stuarts had passed a number of statutes collectively referred to in older textbooks as the Mercantilist System, but in fact they were less a system than a series of expedients devised to meet the problem of unemployment and "short time" in a backward economy. The most important Act was the Statute of Artificers (1563) which insisted that the qualification for a craftsman should be a seven-year apprenticeship and enjoined Justices of the Peace to fix wage rates in consultation with the responsible parties. However, by the eighteenth century the Justices were increasingly reluctant to enforce statutes "in restraint of trade" and by degrees the Statute of Artificers and the other apparatus of central and local government economic regulation fell into decay. Organised labour frequently petitioned parliament and the town and county Justices to enforce the law and to introduce new paternalistic laws or regulations, but they met with only occasional success. Because of this negative attitude, entrepreneurs suffered few significant restraints. They enjoyed the freedom to develop their manufacturing and commercial interests as they saw fit.

The lack of government policy was not lethargy so much as a philosophy commonly referred to as *laisser-faire, laisser-passer*, a view that the role of the state in economic life should be minimal. This can best be understood in the light of a simple idea that was very popular throughout the eighteenth century. When Sir Isaac Newton demonstrated that the movements of the planets and stars were in accordance with simple and regular laws, one important result was that the theory that there must be simple, natural laws that governed relationships between man and man seemed to have received support. Quite a bit of the philosophical thought of the eighteenth and nineteenth centuries was preoccupied with the search for readily intelligible but profound laws whose recognition would enable a country to attain the millenium. The passion for enacting constitutions, practical or otherwise, which would enshrine simple fundamental laws providing the framework for the government of a country is characteristic. The United States constitution is the earliest surviving example. In Britain, the most influential attempt to establish a science of society was Dr Adam Smith's book, *The Wealth of Nations* (1776).

The basic propositions of *The Wealth of Nations* were concerned with the two basic groups of people in any economy, consumers and producers. It is desirable, argued Smith, that the adult consumer should enjoy the maximum free choice to buy what he likes as he must be held to be the judge of his own interests. It is equally desirable for producers to be free to meet those needs. Self-interest will ensure that entrepreneurs produce what consumers want because if they do not they will lose money sooner or later. Those who respond most efficiently to consumers' needs will (other things being equal) profit most. The economy is thus basically self-regulating and paternalistic government is unnecessary.

Adam Smith pressed his argument further by defining the functions of the government in the economy. The first function was that of military defence, the second that of ensuring internal order, and the third—more difficult to summarise—was given as "the duty of erecting and maintaining certain public works and certain public institutions which it can never be for the interest of any individual, or small number of individuals to erect and maintain . . .". In this category we should include schools, hospitals, roads, bridges, and so on. Thus although Smith, writing in an age of paternalistic government, felt the interference of governments in their economies should be ended, he did not exclude government provisions of social services and aids to industry.

Smith's ideas caught on very rapidly and provided philosophic support for relaxation and repeal of the government's control of the economy. They were, of course, popular because they reflected the needs of the mercantile and manufacturing classes for the greater freedom of enterprise. There was a second reason; Smith's teaching seemed to be compatible with that of Nonconformist Christianity, which was followed by many business leaders of the period. Nonconformists shared with Smith a belief in the individual—a passionate belief that moral and economic progress could only come from individual self-discipline and self-sacrifice. In both these spheres all the government was expected to do was hold the ring.

Entrepreneurs, Inventors, and Technology

Earlier books tried to explain the changes in Britain primarily in terms of the achievements of a small group of inventors whose names have become as well known to school children of to-day as those of kings and queens were to their grandparents. However, it is not difficult to see even without a knowledge of history that this interpretation is over-simplified. Most of the under-developed countries of the world would like to enjoy the wealth and power that industrialisation brings, but few have been able to make much progress, even though they have access to the latest techniques of production. The reason is, of course, that they lack capital, or a sufficiently large market to justify investment, or—even more frequently—the enterprise necessary to organise new production and plan the difficult transformation from a traditional rural society to a modern urban industrial society. Under-developed countries (like eighteenth-century Britain) need entrepreneurs, capital, and markets as well as "know-how" in order to industrialise.

In the particular case of Britain there are other reasons for scepticism about the importance of the role of the "great inventors". One is that some of the most important new ideas were already in use on the Continent, while there is serious doubt about the technical originality of several of the great names—Sir Richard Arkwright and Lord ("Turnip") Townshend, for instance. And in general, "in iron as in textiles, small anonymous gains were probably more important in the long run than the major inventions that have been remembered in the textbooks". The significant technological advance was often made by a *community* of artisan inventors, working in centres of industry as we have already noticed.

Some inventors became entrepreneurs, though not all with equal success; but in other ways the contrast drawn between the entrepreneur and the inventor is not so great as at first appears. It is not difficult to appreciate the originality of an inventor because his patent specifications or models of his machinery, or some other evidence, is usually accessible. But the changed times have concealed the originality of the entrepreneur's contribution in organising new techniques of production in a traditional society. He had to choose between competing techniques, find reliable partners or other sources of capital, secure sites by overcoming the suspicions of landowners, recruit a labour force from workers not used to discipline or direction and train them, open up transport connections, build his own machinery, and defeat the prejudices of his customers against goods manufactured on new principles. The "magnificent energy" that directed this kind of development demanded at least as much ability as that required of the inventor. The industrial revolution got off the ground because the technological breakthrough in several industries was joined to organising genius of two generations of dynamic entrepreneurs. Many successful partnerships between inventor and entrepreneur show that they were complementary to each other.

Unfortunately the great majority of the entrepreneurs of the industrial revolution are shadowy or quite anonymous figures and it is not easy to discuss their rise as a class. In most industries only modest capital was required so that firms were typically small and often short-lived. The vast majority have left no record of their existence beyond an entry in a trade directory. But the statistics of patents registered provide an index to the activity of inventors and evidence from other sources confirms that the peak periods for registering patents coincided with investment booms. Consequently this graph is an approximate guide to the phases of industrial investment.

The really difficult problem is to explain why the acceleration in innovation—by inventors and entrepreneurs—came about when it did. Economic historians are still searching for a solution, but it is worth discussing two important theories that have so far been put forward. One theory seeks to associate the radical approach of the innovators with the radicalism of those who dissented from the orthodoxy of the Church of England. The Dissenters (or Nonconformists) grew in numbers and importance after the religious settlement of 1689. There is no doubt that, in proportion to their small numbers (perhaps 5 per cent. of the total population), they played a very important part in the enterprise of the industrial revolution. An American estimate suggests that almost half the principal British entrepreneurs of the period were Nonconformists, and case studies of particular industries (iron and worsted spinning, for instance) have focused attention on the leadership of interrelated Nonconformist families.

The link between eighteenth-century Nonconformity and industry and commerce can best be appreciated by a study of the life of eighteenth-century chapels and meeting houses. Their membership was predominantly urban and middle class, and towards the end of the century they became centres of progressive political, social, and economic, as well as theological, ideas. The most famous Nonconformist figure of the period was Joseph Priestley, who is now most often remembered for his discovery of oxygen, but in fact was a parson

Plate 11.4. The interior of the Octagon Church, Norwich, dating from the mid-eighteenth century.

whose genius penetrated politics and economics as well as science and religion. The many-sided interests of Priestley were characteristic of educated people of his day, for both pure science and the social sciences were still in their infancy and it was possible to pursue progress on both fronts simultaneously. As a minister in Leeds, and then Birmingham, Priestley was surrounded by a circle of leading merchants, manufacturers, and professional men, several of whom made a vital contribution to industrial expansion. In other towns ministers like Dr Richard Price (London), Rev. George Walker, F.R.S. (Nottingham), and Dr Philip Doddridge (Northampton), could parallel the catholic interests of Priestley.

A second theory about the origins of the innovators takes us back to Sir Isaac Newton. Newton's discoveries gave an enormous impetus to scientific research and the scientific method began to be practised by a few leading and educated industrialists. "Everything yields to research" was a well-known saying of the famous potter, Josiah Wedgwood. The importance of technology in the Industrial Revolution compels us to consider the possibility that the successful application of science to industry provided the investment opportunities exploited by entrepreneurs on the grand scale at the end of the eighteenth century; this subject is considered later in this chapter.

The Domestic and Overseas Market

The craftsman in a pre-industrial country often excels in making fine quality and durable wares, but the excellence of his standards is only achieved by the sacrifice of an extensive sale. The quality and cheapness of the greater variety of goods produced in modern industrial countries is attained by factory production, in which workers and machinery are highly specialised and the output mass produced. The investment of capital in land, machinery, and buildings can only be justified by the existence of a large group of consumers with adequate purchasing power. Most under-developed countries face the problem of industrialising with a small and poor population. The problem is to discover how eighteenth-century Britain, with a population of less than ten million in 1780, found a market sufficiently large to justify industrialisation. Some writers on the subject have attributed change primarily to the strength of the domestic market, others to the growth of the overseas market.

The most important characteristic of the British home market was that it was growing. The increase in population gave rise to increasing demands for basic commodities: food, clothing, housing materials, and tools for work. Moreover the steady growth of industry in the seventeenth and eighteenth centuries generated incomes for working families that were the best in Europe, as many Continental travellers noticed. The statistics are, unfortunately, deficient, but one series illustrating the rise of working-class incomes is given on p. 164 (Fig. 1). The English domestic market, furthermore, was more homogeneous in its tastes than that of any other country in Europe. Distinctions between the social classes and between the different regions of the country were slighter than existed on the Continent. The social structure produced "a buying pattern favourable to solid, standardised, moderately priced products"[1] whose sale was energetically pushed, in the days before modern shop-keeping was developed, by a corps of pedlars who had their rounds from hamlet to hamlet. The good natural communications of the country had no doubt played their part in the creation of this more homogeneous social pattern, and the improvement of communications (see Chapter V) served to quicken the levelling processes already at work.

There was, of course, an important and expanding domestic market for luxury and fashion goods—fine clothes, furniture and furnishings, pottery and glassware, silver and jewellery—to mention a few examples. The growth of a sophisticated urban

market had been a feature of the economy from the sixteenth century, when the nobility began to build fine houses in London. The great country houses of the eighteenth century bear eloquent witness to the lavish expenditure of a fortunate minority. In 1760 Joseph Massie calculated that the incomes of the aristocracy, gentry, and rentiers amounted to some 14 per cent. of the whole national income; Gregory King had arrived at a similar figure in 1688. The significance of the expensive purchases of the wealthy was that they invited imitation by those on lower social rungs, and presented a challenge to the entrepreneurs of the Industrial Revolution to reproduce goods with social status in cheaper imitations. Not a few of those who made fortunes based their success on selling the tastes and fashions of the rich in a popular market. Later on we will discuss examples from the fine metal, pottery, and lace industries.

Overseas trade is a better documented subject than domestic trade, mainly because of the records of generations of customs officials. The traditional British export was wool and woollen cloth; but in the eighteenth century British commerce became concerned with an increasing variety of goods. Britain was able to improve her trade with Europe (easily the richest overseas market until well into the nineteenth century) because her trade with the Orient, the Americas, and Africa gave her access to raw materials which could be sold directly on the Continent, or worked up for sale. The earliest example of this kind of trade was the notorious slave trade, which was established in the Elizabethan period. Toys and weapons were exchanged on the west coast of Africa for a hold full of slaves, which were carried across the Atlantic to the West Indian plantations. The slaves were exchanged for a cargo of sugar, tobacco, dyestuffs, or hardwoods, which was processed in London, Bristol, Glasgow, or one of several other ports. The import of Indian cotton became the basis of the Lancashire fustian industry and the Nottinghamshire cotton hosiery trade, and imported Indian calicoes were re-exported to Europe and America. Oriental silks, carpets, brassware, and porcelain invited emulation, and in time became the foundation of a British industry with overseas markets.

By this means the eighteenth century saw the establishment of a multilateral trading system which was increasingly based on and financed from London. Successful merchants frequently took to

---

[1] *The Cambridge Economic History of Europe*, Vol. VI, *The Industrial Revolution and after* (1965).

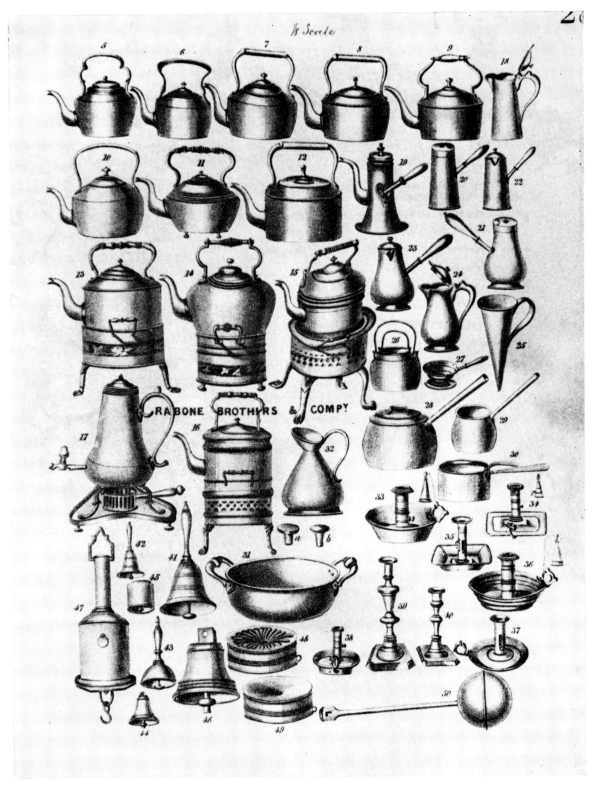

Plate II.5.   This page from a typical nineteenth-century sales catalogue, produced by a Birmingham export merchant who specialised in South and Latin America, shows that hardware production was orientated to the domestic market.   (*Rabone Bros Ltd.*)

pure finance, and a whole network of bankers, insurance companies, and shipping underwriters evolved as the century advanced.

Some of the profits from trade were directed into mining and manufacturing industry, not to mention the purchase of country estates and their subsequent improvement. London and Bristol merchants contributed capital to the development of the South Wales coal and iron industry, Liverpool and Glasgow merchants brought capital to the cotton industries of their respective regions, and even industrial Shropshire, remote from the sea, benefited from the capital that Abraham Darby drew from his trading partners at Bristol. But for all these—and other—examples, it remains true that fortunes made in trade usually found their way to finance rather than direct industrial investment.

Capital

We should explain the legal framework that governed investment. The present-day shareholder's rights did not become general until the passing of the Limited Liability Acts of 1855-62. Up to this time a business company could only be incorporated by a special Act of Parliament, and each partner in an unincorporated business, whether active or "sleeping", was liable for the debts of the business to his last penny, however small the amount he had invested in it. Furthermore, the Bubble Act of 1720 restricted the number of shareholders in any one business to eight. Some large enterprises, particularly turnpike, canal, and railway companies, did secure their own Act, but this was unusual. Practically all manufacturing industry was conducted by family businesses or partnerships. Where partners could not be found in the family they were often recruited at the chapel, where the bonds of mutual trust were strongest, and where moral rectitude and self-discipline were constantly preached and discussed.

The capital which financed the Industrial Revolution was contributed from all classes of British society. The interest of the aristocracy and gentry were not limited to the development of their own estates. In textiles, for instance, Arkwright found some of his most energetic supporters and imitators among the gentry who constituted his neighbours in Derbyshire; in the West Riding Lord Dartmouth invested in mills on his estates, and in Lancashire

the Earl of Derby opened a cotton mill at Preston. Some of the gentry, including Sir Joseph Banks, President of the Royal Society, were among the pioneers of mechanised worsted spinning, and the Earl of Dudley opened one of the first carpet factories at Kidderminster. The merchant classes contributed much to the development of manufacturing, as we should expect, though in some industries they were more active than in others. In textiles they were less active than in the expansion of the iron industry. The professional classes made a valuable contribution. Doctors like Roebuck, clergy like Dawson and Cartwright, and the schoolmaster Samuel Walker were leaders in their chosen industries. Craftsmen and small traders, though men of little capital, found it possible in many instances to husband their limited resources and plough back their profits to build up firms quite as substantial as those which had begun with more ample means. Capital was drawn from every conceivable source of savings; indeed, even the popular working-class friendly societies, meeting at public houses to contribute a few pence a week to cover the contingencies of sickness, unemployment, and death, often invested their funds in mills and mines.

In discussing the generation of capital it must not be overlooked that industry and commerce were expanding more or less continuously for two centuries before the Industrial Revolution. The gradual accumulation of capital in the hands of landowners and overseas and domestic merchants was not always squandered on conspicuous consumption. In the middle classes in particular the presence of sober habits (partly born of commercial experience, partly of Nonconformist belief) assured the retention of profits for sensible expenditure. When a favourable moment arrived this accumulating wealth was available to invest or (as more frequently happened) to provide credit to manufacturers.

All the evidence suggests that the initial cost of fixed assets could be modest. It was possible to begin small and work up; a famous nineteenth-century economist once compared British industry to a forest in which the many trees (firms) differed in size according to their age, and all began as seedlings. Up to the middle of the nineteenth century technology was still so much in its infancy that machinery was simple and cheap to construct. The subsequent chapters of this book will provide several illustrations of this point and for the time

Plate II.6.   Cressbrook Mill, near Tideswell, Derbyshire. The building to the right appears to be the original Arkwright mill of 1779.

being it will be sufficient to provide only an example or two. The early cotton mills were simple functional buildings, at first modelled on Arkwright's second country mill at Cromford, Derbyshire, which was built in 1777. The mill building, the machinery and water-wheel, and the stock (including raw materials and work in progress) were insured only for £1,000 each, or £3,000 in all. This common type of mill is illustrated by many surviving examples in all parts of the country.

In the iron industry the largest firm in the north of England at the end of the eighteenth century was that of the Walkers of Masborough, near Rotherham. The business was begun in 1741 by two brothers, Samuel and Aaron Walker, in an old nailer's smithy at the back of Samuel's cottage. Five years later, the first valuation of the firm's assets amounted to £400. The brothers nursed the business with great care until it grew into lusty adolescence.

Plate II.7.   Maythorn Cotton Mill, near Southwell (Notts), built c. 1786.

At Samuel's death in 1782 the capital was reckoned at £100,000. The Walkers' story of perseverance and sacrifice for their business is better documented than most, but typical of business histories at this period.

If the fixed capital could only be built up by hard work and abstemious habits, there were easier ways to acquire the necessary working capital. The wealthy merchants in London and the provinces were generally ready to provide three or six months' credit to manufacturers, which was quite sufficient to enable them to be paid from the receipts from the sale of the finished product. The London banks, and a growing number of country bankers, provided similar facilities.

Labour for Industry: the Population Explosion

There are no infallible statistics before the first government census of 1801, but various authoritative estimates (see Fig. 2, p. 165) though differing in detail, all point to rapid population growth in the second half of the eighteenth century. Clearly this is highly relevant to the economic changes of the period. An increase in the population of a country is likely to help industrialisation in two ways. First, it creates an increase in demand for goods commonly purchased—popular foodstuffs, clothing, and housing materials, for instance. (In Britain the growth of London had given an important stimulus to regional specialisation as early as the seventeenth century. Not only Kent fruit and hop growers and East End market gardeners, but Gloucestershire clothiers, Nottinghamshire hosiers, and Lancashire fustian makers benefited from this huge urban market.) Secondly, the growth in numbers produces the larger potential labour force that is quite essential for industrial expansion. The labour requirements of agriculture were limited, and were indeed reaching saturation point in late medieval Britain, from which time the surplus began to find an outlet in manufacturing industry and has continued to do so ever since.

Conversely, industrial expansion can stimulate the growth of population. Increasing production gives rise to more jobs, perhaps encouraging earlier marriages and the migration to the industrial areas of a young labour force, the potential parents of the next generation. An increased output of manufactured goods may, in different ways, help to make healthier lives. In Britain, rising production of bricks and slates helped to displace the less healthy mud and thatch, while more abundant and cheaper coal supplies helped to make warmer homes. Cheap cottons made clothing more healthy than the traditional woollens, difficult to wash and heavy, iron holloware was cleaner and more convenient than the spit, and glazed pottery was a great improvement on wood and pewter. An improved transport network gave rise to a better organisation of food supplies to the towns and a better chance of minimising the effects of local shortages. More jobs and better wages enabled more people to buy these goods, and the rise in total national wealth made more money available (via poor rates and taxes) for drainage, sanitation, water supply, and slum demolition schemes. The beginnings of many of these improvements can be discerned in the eighteenth century. Thus, although we have not yet disentangled cause from effect, it is clear that at the industrial revolution population and industrial growth were heavily inter-dependent.

Close links between industrialisation and population growth are emphasised by a study of regional and local variations in rates of growth. The counties in which industry and commerce were centred saw a more rapid growth in population than the predominantly rural counties. Because of the location of the new industry there was a shift in the centre of gravity of population from south to north and Midlands, as a result of high fertility of growing industrial areas, recruited from the surplus of the surrounding country-side. At the same time London easily maintained its position as the largest city and continued to attract the largest flow of immigrants from the surrounding counties, and further afield. The agricultural counties did not see a loss of population during the Industrial Revolution, but the growth rate was much lower.

The question is sometimes asked: was population growth a cause or a consequence of the economic changes of the eighteenth century? All we can say at the moment is that two theories command support. One school of thought attributes population growth to a rise in the birth rate induced by economic changes calling for an increased labour supply and leading to earlier marriage and higher fertility. A second school of thought places emphasis on the decline of the death rate as a result of economic and social factors such as improved food supply, the provision of washable cotton clothes, better housing and domestic equipment. Improvement in the field of medicine can also be cited, particularly in regard to the feeding of children and (in spite of what has been said to the contrary) in regard to the work of hospitals and especially dispensaries. More recently attention has been turned to the importance of inoculation against smallpox which became widespread after 1760 and contributed to the decline in the virulence of epidemics which had retarded population growth in the first half of the century. In general, though it would appear that the upturn of population from 1750 took place before the period of rapid economic expansion and helped to stimulate the early phases of the Industrial Revolution, we can have no doubt that it was sustained and encouraged by factors operating both on the death rate and the birth rate. The example of Ireland, where population growth took place in the absence of industrialisation, and ended in a crisis of starvation and misery, underlines the interdependence of economic and demographic factors in England. Of one thing we can be certain: if there had been a return of a deadly epidemic such as the bubonic plague the Industrial Revolution would have been brought to a halt, since an increased number of workers and consumers was a necessary condition of the continued advance of machine economy.

The Application of Science to Industry

In considering the application of science to industry it is essential to make an initial distinction. In the last chapter we pointed to the development of craft invention and gave an important illustration of it. Craft or (as it is sometimes called) empirical invention was no doubt a reflection of the "spirit of improvement" which pervaded British life and literature in the eighteenth century. However, the development of science and its application to industry has its own distinct pedigree of discoveries which can be traced back to the brilliant group of Englishmen associated with the foundations of the Royal Society in 1662. From this period until recent times empirical invention and science-based

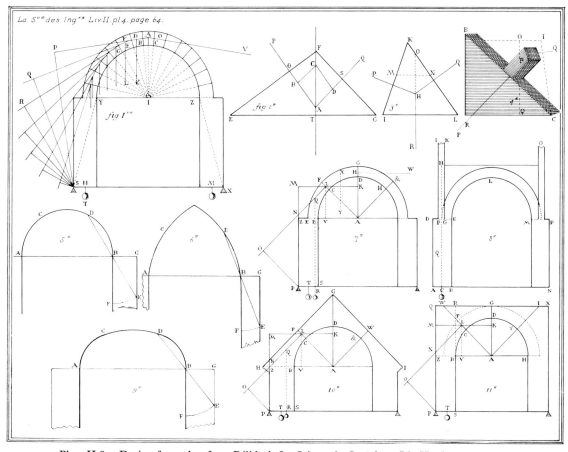

Plate II.8.   Design for arches from Bélidor's *La Science des Ingénieurs*, Liv II, pl. 4, p. 64.

discoveries were both significant elements in industrial progress.

The Royal Society was concerned with the practical problems of industry at its foundation (in 1662) but for reasons not clearly understood its interest in technology languished in the eighteenth century. Its technological function was assumed by the Royal Society for the Encouragement of Arts, Industry, and Manufactures at its foundation in 1754, but before this time the Scottish universities had taken the lead, possibly because of their closer links with the Continent. The first attempts to apply the principles of mechanics and hydraulics to practical tasks in a systematic manner were made by eighteenth-century French engineers. This development originated with the special corps of military engineers (*Corps des ingénieurs du Génie militaire*) which was founded in 1675. The French *Génie* officers were given a scientific education with special emphasis

on mathematics, and their expertise was soon being employed on civil as well as military contracts. One of the most outstanding of them, B. F. de Bélidor, wrote two textbooks, *Science des Ingénieurs* (1729) and *Architecture Hydraulique* (4 vols., 1737-53), which were the best available in any language in the eighteenth century. Continental engineers were a long way ahead of their British colleagues until at least the 1790s.

During the course of the eighteenth century the most important industrial achievements of the advance of science were in mechanical and civil engineering, and in laying the foundations of the modern chemical industry. Scientific notions were beginning to creep into other industries, such as pottery and porcelain, glass-making, brewing and distilling, and tanning, by the end of the century. But, generally speaking, industrial practice continued to be empirical, and even the foremost engineers

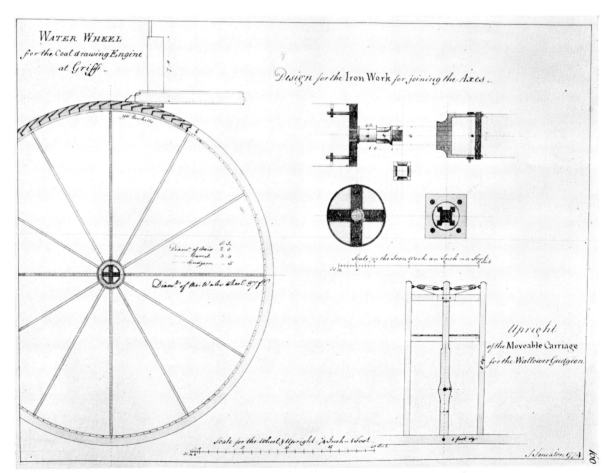

Plate II.9. John Smeaton's design for a water-wheel to power winding gear at Griff Colliery, Warwickshire, 1774. (*Royal Society of London.*)

and scientists working in industry combined calculations with shrewd guesswork and trial and error methods.

Water power and steam power occupied an important place in the scientific mind throughout the eighteenth century. As early as 1704 a Frenchman, Antoine Parent, calculated the efficiency of undershot (or paddle) water-wheels and thus initiated scientific discussion of the subject. In England the engineer John Smeaton experimented with models of water-wheels and demonstrated that an overshot (or bucket) wheel was twice as efficient as a paddle wheel of the same size. The results of his researches were published in the *Philosophical Transactions of the Royal Society* for 1759, and became common knowledge. For the next thirty years Smeaton spent a good part of his professional life travelling the country improving old water mills by substituting breast wheels for paddle wheels. He designed water-wheels for great industrial concerns like the Carron Ironworks at Falkirk (Scotland) and Strutt's cotton mill at Belper (near Derby) and for pumping out collieries, like that of Sir Roger Newdegate at Griff, near Coventry. The advantages of the breast wheels were so considerable that these mills were extensively copied. By the time that the great era of mill-building that followed Arkwright's success was reached, mills were seldom driven by traditional craft-made wheels, but were accurately designed machines based on Smeaton's scientific ideas. "In a country of limited water power, like England", a recent writer observes, "the gain in efficiency may have been crucial in expediting the Industrial Revolution."[1]

Despite Smeaton's success in demonstrating the relevance of scientific inquiry to industrial progress, most of those who designed and erected water-wheels during the Industrial Revolution were millwrights with a practical rather than scientific training. The millwright, according to an early nineteenth century member of the craft, "was the engineer of the district in which he lived, a kind of Jack-of-all-trades, who could with equal facility work at the lathe, the anvil, or the carpenter's bench . . . Generally, he was a fair arithmetician, knew something of geometry, levelling, and mensuration, and in some cases possessed a very competent knowledge of practical mathematics", perhaps particularly in Scotland

where the educational system was superior to that in England. Towards 1800 there are references to leading millwrights reading Bélidor and continental textbooks, but on the whole they picked up the fruits of scientific progress at second hand.

There are, however, some important exceptions to this generalisation. The development of river navigation in England in the early and middle part of the eighteenth century (see Chapter VI) created a small profession of civil engineers with a national, rather than merely local reputation. Most of these men became associated, in 1717, in the first Society of Engineers to be founded in Britain. The Society's members are often referred to as the "Smeatonians" because of the decisive influence that John Smeaton had on the infant profession, but for want of biographical details it is hardly possible to make a categorical statement on the scientific approach of these pioneers of civil engineering.

The connection between science and industry can be demonstrated much more clearly in the lives of James Watt and John Rennie, two Scots who played a pre-eminent role in the Industrial Revolution. Watt was responsible for the most sophisticated and useful mechanism devised during the period covered by this book, the steam engine. Early in the eighteenth century a Dartmouth wholesale ironmonger, Thomas Newcomen, had contrived an atmospheric engine to pump water out of lead and coal mines. The first to be erected was near Dudley, on the South Staffordshire coalfield, in 1712. Others were put up at mines from Cornwall to Northumberland. The engine was extravagant with fuel, but an economic proposition where there were ample supplies of coal to hand. Smeaton improved on it in detail, but the decisive improvement was made by James Watt while he was working as a mathematical instrument maker at Glasgow University. In 1763 he repaired a model Newcomen engine used at the University and became interested in its construction and defects. His experiments during the next few years resulted in the perfection of the separate condenser, a device to minimise the heat losses of the Newcomen engine by condensing the steam in a vessel outside the cylinder. It is said that Watt obtained the theory which helped him to devise the separate condenser from the discovery by Dr Joseph Black of the phenomenon of latent heat of steam. Black was a friend of Watt's,

---

[1] D. S. L. Cardwell, "Power Technologies and the Advance of Science, 1700-1825", *Technology and Culture*, Vol. VI (1965), p. 194.

[continued on p. 35]

Plate II.10. An undershot wheel working in 1967 at Kendal Snuff Mill in Westmorland. This type was replaced first by the breast wheel (Plate II.11) and later by the overshot wheel (Plate II.9).

Plate II.11. Foster Beck Mill at Pateley Bridge, showing the breast wheel (one of the largest in the country). Note this example of the siting of industry in the heart of the country.

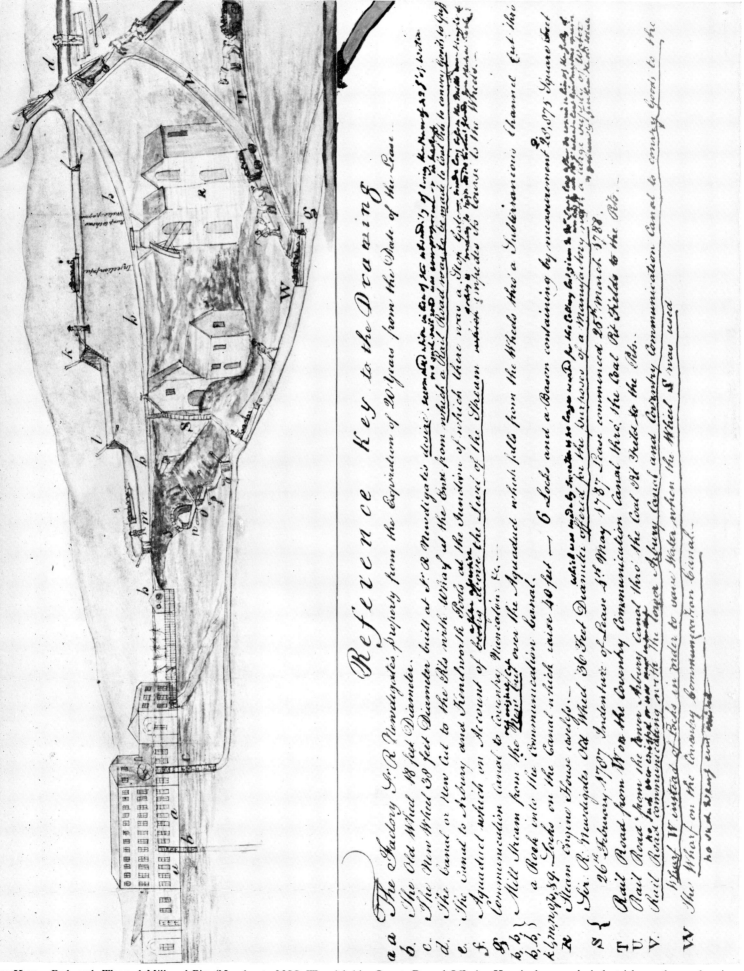

late II.12.   Bedworth Worsted Mill and Pits (Newdegate MSS, Warwickshire County Record Office).   Here is shown early industrial complex, and various stages, such as the modification and addition of water-wheels, can be seen.   (*Reproduced by permission of F. A. M. Fitzroy-Newdegate, Esq.*)

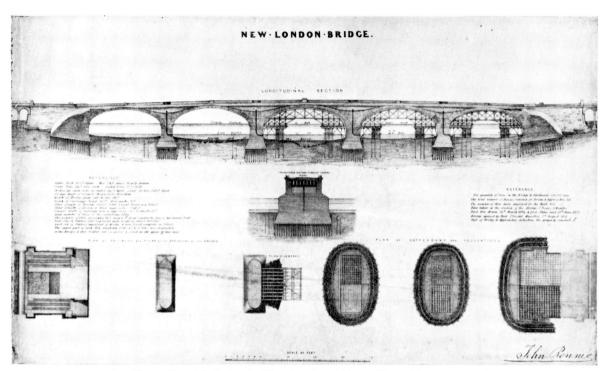

Plate II.13.   Rennie's design for New London Bridge.   (*Port of London Authority.*)

Plate II.14.   Telford's single-span design for London Bridge, which was rejected.   Compare this "Iron Bridge" with
Plates VI.6 and 7.   (*Port of London Authority.*)

and professor of chemistry at Glasgow University at this time.

Rennie came from a better-off home than most of his Scottish contemporaries, and after training as a millwright on his family's estate went to Edinburgh

careers of Rennie and Watt. In surveying the origins of the chemical industry in Britain this influence is even more striking. A group of industrialists who were at Edinburgh or Glasgow University at about the same period were responsible for several of the

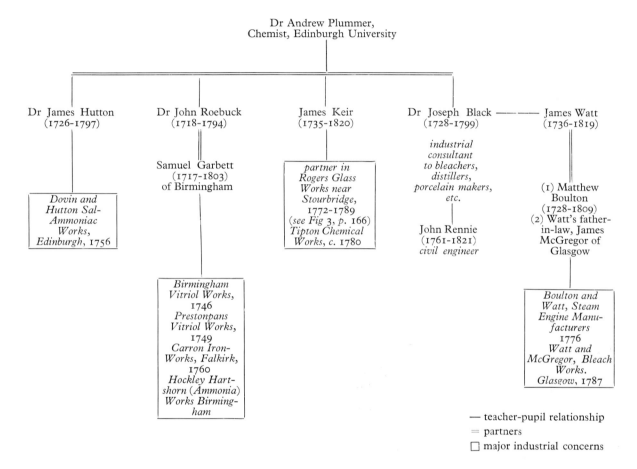

University for three years (1780-3) and then undertook his own version of the "Grand Tour" by visiting many British engineering achievements of the day. The training in both theory and practice was practically unique at the period, but the superiority of Rennie's work illustrated its advantages in a striking manner. Engineering was not specialised at this time and Rennie achieved distinction with his canals, roads, and bridges, as well as machinery and power units. Through his friendship with Professor Robison of Edinburgh, Rennie's work provided the illustrations for the first original textbooks in English.

The benefits conferred on British industrial progress by Scottish university education have already been referred to and illustrated in the

pioneer chemical works as well as other important enterprises. The names and firms of some of the most important of these pioneers are summarised in the above diagram.

Hutton, Roebuck, Keir, and Black were all pupils of Dr Andrew Plummer, a physician who became a professor of chemistry at Edinburgh University. Black was one of his successors at Edinburgh, but previously taught at Glasgow University where (as we have noticed) he was a friend of James Watt. The various industrial enterprises listed here will be examined at greater length in Chapter IV.

In the last two or three decades of the century interest in physical sciences and their applications was widespread among the middle classes. This was partly the consequence of the work of schools and academies that began to adopt curricula with optional science subjects (mathematics, mechanics, astronomy, and so on) about the middle of the century. The dissenting academies were the celebrated leaders of this initiative, but the older grammar schools were not so slow to adopt the "modern curriculum" as was at one time supposed. The most important means of satisfying the growing appetite for science were the philosophic societies that sprang up in most centres of industry. The most distinguished of these societies was the Birmingham Lunar Society, an informal group that brought together scientists and industrialists like Watt, Keir, Roebuck, Garbett, Dr Joseph Priestley, and Josiah Wedgwood, the potter, who travelled down from Burslem for the monthly meetings. Another famous society was the Manchester Literary and Philosophic Society, which was founded early in 1781. The Society arose out of informal meetings held at the home of Dr Thomas Percival, M.D. (Edin.) F.R.S., a pioneer of the public health movement. One of the secretaries of

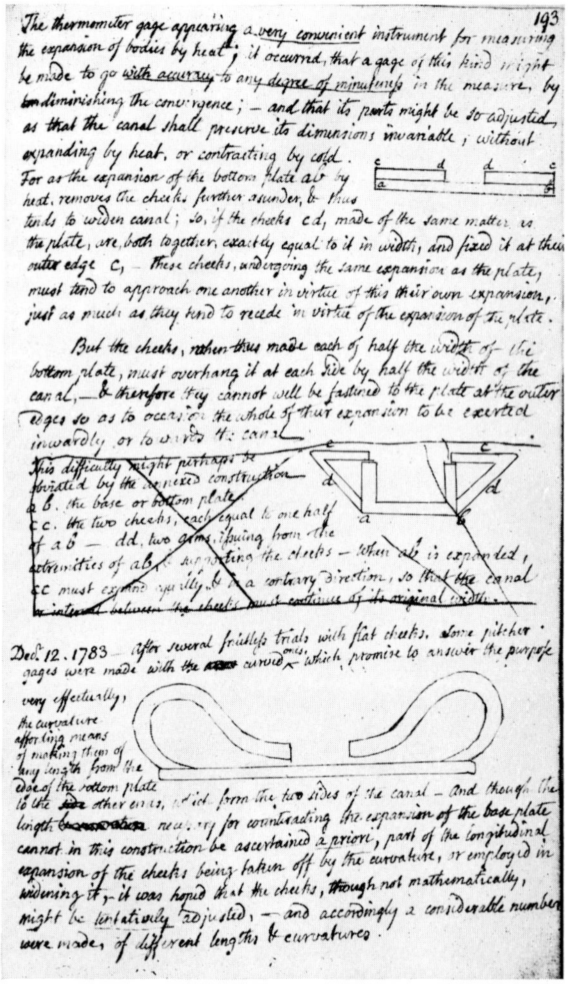
193

The thermometer gage appearing a very convenient instrument for measuring the expansion of bodies by heat; it occurred, that a gage of this kind might be made to go with accuracy to any degree of minuteness in the measure, by diminishing the convergence; — and that its parts might be so adjusted, as that the canal shall preserve its dimensions invariable; without expanding by heat, or contracting by cold. For as the expansion of the bottom plate ab by heat, removes the cheeks further asunder, & thus tends to widen canal; so, if the cheeks cd, made of the same matter as the plate, are, both together, exactly equal to it in width, and fixed it at their outer edge c, — These cheeks, undergoing the same expansion as the plate, must tend to approach one another in virtue of this their own expansion, just as much as they tend to recede in virtue of the expansion of the plate.

But the cheeks, rather than made each of half the width of the bottom plate, must overhang it at each side by half the width of the canal, — & therefore they cannot well be fastened to the plate at the outer edges so as to occasion the whole of their expansion to be exerted inwardly, or towards the canal.

This difficulty might perhaps be avoided by the annexed construction — ab. the base or bottom plate. cc. the two cheeks, each equal to one half of ab — dd. two arms, issuing from the extremities of ab & supporting the cheeks — when ab is expanded, cc must expand equally & in a contrary direction, so that the canal be intended between the cheeks must continue of its original width.

Decr 12. 1783 — After several fruitless trials with flat cheeks, some pitcher gages were made with the curved ones, which promise to answer the purpose very effectually, the curvature affording means of making them of any length from the edge of the bottom plate to the other ends, fixed from the two sides of the canal — and though the length necessary for counteracting the expansion of the base plate cannot in this construction be ascertained a priori, part of the longitudinal expansion of the cheeks being taken off by the curvature, or employed in widening it, — it was hoped that the cheeks, though not mathematically, might be tentatively adjusted, — and accordingly a considerable number were made, of different lengths & curvatures.

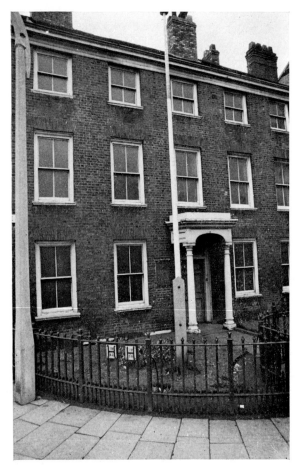

Plate II.15. A page from Josiah Wedgwood's Experiments Book, in which he recorded his results. Several of the members of the Lunar Society kept similar records of their scientific inquiries. (*Josiah Wedgwood and Sons, Ltd.*)

the Society was Dr Thomas Henry, F.R.S., a successful manufacturing pharmacist who gave lectures on the chemistry of bleaching, dyeing, and calico printing. Another philosophic society was that at Nottingham, one of the founders of which was Rev. George Walker, F.R.S., a mathematician educated at Glasgow University who was an active partner in an early worsted mill and became an authority on the steam engine. Other early groups were established at Edinburgh, Dublin, Northampton, Leicester, Newcastle-on-Tyne, and several other large provincial towns.

Plate II.16. Warrington Academy, where Joseph Priestley was educated.

III

The Transition to the Factory System of Production

Since some of the most spectacular changes of the eighteenth century took place in textiles, we must therefore begin with some account of developments in this industry. On the face of it, it is surprising that mechanisation occurred first in cotton which, though growing rapidly, was small compared with Britain's traditional woollen industry. Part of the answer lay in the nature of the raw material, which lent itself to mechanisation far more readily. There was a much larger potential market for cotton than wool, for the mass of people were dressed only in heavy, coarse woollens; the comfort and cleanliness of underwear and the bright patterns of fashion printed fabrics (calicoes) were reserved for the rich. Moreover, the unexploited markets of the Orient and the Tropics cried out for cheap light fabrics appropriate to their warmer climates.

Although no figures are available for the total output of the British cotton industry during the early years of the industrial revolution, the statistics of the imported raw material provide a guide to the growth of the industry (see Fig. 5, p. 168). They show quite clearly the sudden and explosive growth in the industry after 1781, when factory production began in earnest.

The Evolution of Factory Production

Four characteristics distinguish the factory system from the domestic system of production. Manufacture takes place in one building provided by the entrepreneur, instead of being dispersed round the homes of the workers. The work is regulated and supervised by the factory owner (or his manager or overseers) in order to meet the precise demands of his customers; the quantity and quality of production is no longer left to the discretion of the worker. The factory owner is the sole proprietor of the plant and stock, ensuring that his authority is complete. Fourthly, mechanical power drives specialised machinery.

The earliest known factory was the Derby Silk Mill, illustrated in the print overleaf. It is particularly notable for being the first iron-frame building of any size. The mill was built in 1719-21 by Sir Thomas Lombe, a London silk merchant, following a successful mission of industrial espionage to Leghorn (Italy) by his half-brother, John Lombe. It is said to have represented an investment of £30,000 and employed some 300 workers. The Derby Mill served as a prototype for others, particularly at Stockport and Macclesfield. However, the silk mills were few compared with the cotton mills at the end of the century, so that their main importance in the evolution of the factory system is that they provided a precedent for the scale and organisation of Arkwright and Strutt's cotton mills, and their numerous imitators, in the last twenty years of the century.

Much less ambitious concentrations of labour were the germ of the factory idea. Although the great number of weaving looms and stocking frames stood in workers' cottages, a few of them were concentrated in workshops at the warehouse of the merchant clothier or merchant hosier, sometimes to meet special orders, but increasingly to prevent embezzlement of the wool, cotton, silk, or linen being worked. In the East Midlands most merchant hosiers had their "home department" of frames for special orders, and a number of master framework knitters employed as many as a dozen frames. In the West of England and the West Riding of Yorkshire concentrations of up to a dozen looms appear to have been common. Surviving buildings in

DERBY.

Plate III.1. Derby Silk Mill: a contemporary engraving in Derby Public Library (see p. 37).

Trowbridge (Wiltshire), built about 1800, suggest as many as fifty to one hundred workers in one workshop.

In Lancashire and in Coventry the introduction of the Dutch "engine loom" resulted in comparable concentration of workers and capital. The engine loom, which originated on the Continent in the late sixteenth century and came to Manchester via London in the seventeenth century, wove up to a dozen tapes or ribbons at a time. Unlike most of the looms commonly in use it was a relatively expensive machine, almost beyond the reach of the ordinary weaver who, in the seventeenth century, usually owned the loom on which he worked. On account of their cost the Dutch looms tended to be grouped in the workshops of a superior class of master weavers, who employed a permanent class of wage-earning journeymen on a collection of three to twelve looms in workshops apart from the workers' cottages. By 1750 there were at least 1,500 Dutch looms in use in the parish of Manchester. However, the greatest concentration of wage earners in workshops were found in the silk throwsters' shops, in Spitalfields and the adjacent parts of East London. As early as 1694 workshops with 500, 600, and 700 workers, men, women, and children, are reported. The close supervision of workers in workshops, and the concentration of capital in the hands of a few merchants or manufacturers, was clearly taking place in all important regions.

The other focus was the water mill. As the various processes of production increased in size and complexity it became necessary to make use of mechanical power. In the middle ages the process of fulling (or pounding the cloth with heavy wooden hammers to shrink and felt it) had become water-powered. Fulling was still the most important process to be operated by power up to the last years of the eighteenth century, but the source of power had long attracted other operations to itself. By the eighteenth century water power was being used to grind logwood for dyes, often on the same site as the fulling mill. The twisting mill (a machine to twist the warp threads) became power-operated in the early eighteenth century, again often utilising the same waterwheel as the fulling process. Silk reeling was sometimes found on the same site. In the West Country the fulling mill attracted the clothier's house to its side, and the two buildings always formed the nucleus for the spinning and weaving mills that sprang up later in the century. In the West Riding the fulling and scribbling (or carding) mill was

frequently the original building in the growth of first cotton spinning and then worsted and woollen mills by the Pennine streams. Crump and Ghorbai, in their *History of the Huddersfield Woollen Industry*, map something like 130 factories built on the site of fulling and scribbling mills within a six-mile radius of the town. The factory can thus be seen to be the outcome of a long evolutionary process that began to accelerate as the eighteenth century advanced. The addition of roller-spinning and carding in the last thirty years of the century was a continuation, but on an unprecedented scale.

It is interesting to notice here that the later factory buildings have not completely overlaid the evidence of the original industrial development on many of the sites. Leats and mill ponds abound in the old clothing districts, while exploration of a

Plate III.2.   An early Fulling Mill at Dursley, Gloucestershire.   (*Dr Jennifer Tann.*)   The mill house can be seen in the background.

cluster of industrial buildings in Gloucestershire or Wiltshire will sometimes reveal a fulling mill or clothier's house on the site. The remoter parts of the Pennines and Wales offer abundant evidence, in the form of deserted buildings, of the earlier textile industry.

Crisis in the Textile Industry: Hargreaves and Arkwright

The widespread adoption of Kay's "flying shuttle" in Lancashire and Yorkshire in the 1750s enabled the handloom weavers to keep pace with a growing market for cotton and woollen goods, but, for the time being, there was no corresponding innovation in spinning and it proved increasingly

Plate III.3. Peel's Mill at Burton-on-Trent, an early mill complex owned by the family of the future Prime Minister, Sir Robert Peel. The early corn mill can be seen on the right, and later a cotton mill (on the left) was built to take advantage of boom conditions in that industry. The complex has now reverted to its original function of grinding corn.

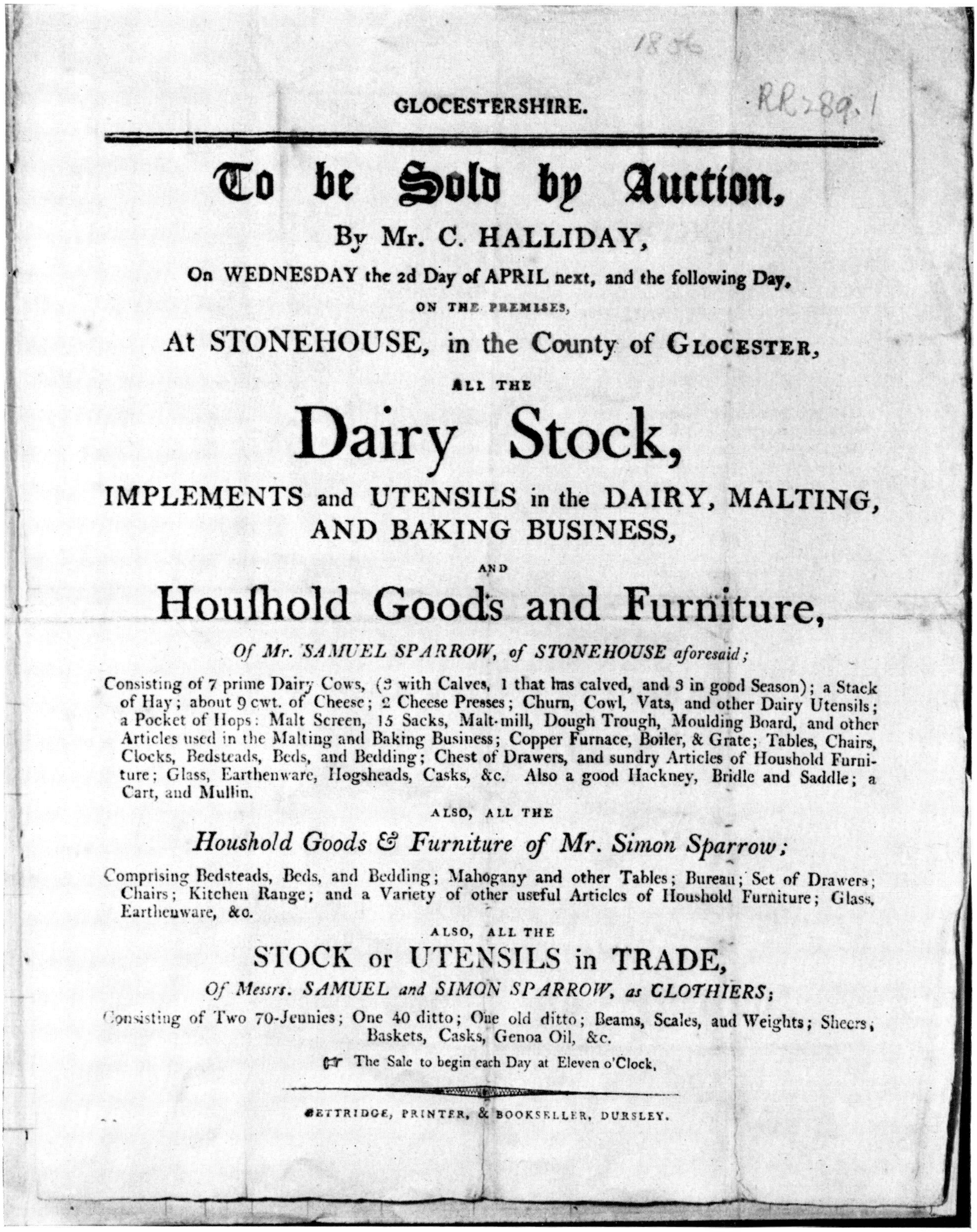

GLOCESTERSHIRE.

To be Sold by Auction,

By Mr. C. HALLIDAY,

On WEDNESDAY the 2d Day of APRIL next, and the following Day,

ON THE PREMISES,

At STONEHOUSE, in the County of GLOCESTER,

ALL THE

Dairy Stock,

IMPLEMENTS and UTENSILS in the DAIRY, MALTING, AND BAKING BUSINESS,

AND

Houfhold Goods and Furniture,

Of Mr. SAMUEL SPARROW, of STONEHOUSE aforesaid;

Consisting of 7 prime Dairy Cows, (3 with Calves, 1 that has calved, and 3 in good Season); a Stack of Hay; about 9 cwt. of Cheese; 2 Cheese Presses; Churn, Cowl, Vats, and other Dairy Utensils; a Pocket of Hops: Malt Screen, 15 Sacks, Malt-mill, Dough Trough, Moulding Board, and other Articles used in the Malting and Baking Business; Copper Furnace, Boiler, & Grate; Tables, Chairs, Clocks, Bedsteads, Beds, and Bedding; Chest of Drawers, and sundry Articles of Houshold Furniture; Glass, Earthenware, Hogsheads, Casks, &c. Also a good Hackney, Bridle and Saddle; a Cart, and Mullin.

ALSO, ALL THE

Houshold Goods & Furniture of Mr. Simon Sparrow;

Comprising Bedsteads, Beds, and Bedding; Mahogany and other Tables; Bureau; Set of Drawers; Chairs; Kitchen Range; and a Variety of other useful Articles of Houshold Furniture; Glass, Earthenware, &c.

ALSO, ALL THE

STOCK or UTENSILS in TRADE,

Of Messrs. SAMUEL and SIMON SPARROW, as CLOTHIERS;

Consisting of Two 70-Jennies; One 40 ditto; One old ditto; Beams, Scales, and Weights; Shears, Baskets, Casks, Genoa Oil, &c.

☞ The Sale to begin each Day at Eleven o'Clock.

BETTRIDGE, PRINTER, & BOOKSELLER, DURSLEY.

Plate III.4.   Handbill advertising sale of goods of a West Country farmer-clothier, 1806.

Plate III.5. A deserted mill in North Wales.

difficult for weavers to procure sufficient yarn to feed their looms. In the summer months clothiers sometimes found themselves scouring the district for miles around to obtain sufficient yarn to begin their day's work, for the women and children who did most of the spinning could obtain better paid work on the farms at this time of the year. The yarn spun at a distance was collected by agents who were mostly shopkeepers, and the quality of the hanks varied enormously as the agent would not offend a shop customer by refusing her work. Collecting yarn was not only time-consuming but hazardous in an age when highway robbery was widespread.

In the East Midlands a crisis of a rather different kind was developing. The merchant hosiers imported their cotton ready spun from India. In Tewkesbury (Gloucestershire), an isolated centre of the hosiery industry, the hosiers discovered that their local women spinners, who were accustomed to handling the long-staple wool of the Cotswold sheep, could adapt their art to the spinning of cotton. The women of Nottinghamshire and Leicestershire, accustomed to short-staple wool, were quite unequal to the task which the hosiers suddenly brought to them. Though the Tewkesbury spun cotton was quite inferior to the Indian, the difference was difficult for the customer to detect in the completed garment, and the Nottingham hosiers foresaw a disastrous contraction of their trade. Frantic experiments were made to spin cotton by machinery, and every artisan in Nottingham and its district knew that a fortune could be earned by the first to achieve success. The significance of the careers of Hargreaves and Arkwright was that they were able, after some initial difficulties, to mobilise financial support to break the bottle-neck in the supply of yarn. Natives of

Lancashire, both men had long been familiar with all the endless trouble and expense involved in securing regular supplies of good quality yarn. The sudden crisis gave them an opportunity they were not slow to exploit. Hargreaves's "Jenny", which was invented some time between 1764 and 1767, was a device to duplicate the work of the domestic spinner so that she could operate up to eight spindles at once, instead of only one. A replica of the original jenny, as it is described in the patent specification of 1770, has recently been constructed, and is shown in the photograph. It is manually operated, and from its size it is clearly a machine that could readily be accommodated in the existing domestic environment of the clothing and hosiery industries. However, within a decade of the original invention, "verticle wheel" jennies were being built with up to 120 spindles each, and the much greater size of these machines compelled their owners to install them in workshops outside the workers' homes. Moreover, the increased output of yarn drew more looms to the clothiers' warehouses, accelerating the tendency for more work to be concentrated there. The jenny was soon adapted to the spinning of wool and widely used in Yorkshire and the West of England. In due

Plate III.7. A whim gin at Shibden Hall Folk Museum, Halifax, similar to those used to provide power in early textile factories.

course it made its way to Scotland, Wales, and East Anglia. In all these regions it served to accelerate a trend towards concentration of production which was already at work.

The roller spinning process proved too heavy for manual power. The machinery of the first mill which Arkwright and his partners built at Nottingham was powered by a team of horses walking round a capstan. By 1772 the mill employed 300 children as well as a number of adults, a labour force as large as that of the Derby silk mill. But Arkwright was an ambitious man and, like other industrialists of the day, dreamed of a country seat and a social circle drawn from the county families. Nottingham, with its oligarchic corporation, austere chapels, violent party spirit, and internecine conflict between hosiers and framework knitters, was too parochial for him. Before the Nottingham mill had reached its optimum size he moved to Cromford, a lead-mining village in the Derbyshire dales, remote from the centres of the texile industry, but near to the fashionable watering place of Matlock Bath. Arkwright's first mill at Cromford, which was completed in 1771, differed from the Nottingham mill in that its machinery was driven by a water-wheel. A second mill was opened in 1777, and then a rapid succession of others, first in other parts of Derbyshire (at Bakewell, Wirksworth, Rocester, near Ashbourne, and other places), and then in Lancashire (Chorley in 1779 and Manchester in 1783), in Yorkshire (Keighley 1778), and finally Scotland (beginning with New Lanark in 1786). Some idea of the extent of Arkwright's industrial empire is given in the diagram (see Fig. 6, p. 168).

Plate III.6. Spinning Jenny, reconstructed from Hargreaves' Patent Specification of 1770 by Messrs Textile Machine Makers, Helmshore, Rossendale, Lancs.
(Chapman.)

Plate III.8.   Aysgarth Mill in Wensleydale; a mill of the Arkwright era.

Even before Arkwright had fully established himself at Cromford, his success began to attract a number of imitators. It is true that his roller spinning process was protected by a patent of 1769, but infringers were numerous. From 1777 he began to grant a number of licences to use his patent, but the enormous cost of a licence encouraged infringement. A long legal battle was fought over the Arkwright patents during the years from 1781 to 1785, but an initial decision in favour of the Lancashire manufacturers made the new process available to everyone.

The Impact of Mechanised Cotton Spinning on the Silk, Woollen, and Linen Industries

The enormous development of cotton spinning was a serious menace to the silk, woollen, and linen industries. The new techniques of spinning made cotton much cheaper, so that it was able to displace the more traditional textiles in popular clothing. In particular, the cheap production of muslins and calicoes in imitation of expensive Indian imports enabled the working and lower middle classes to imitate the dress of their superiors. This popular adoption of the fashions of the few provided the main market for the growing cotton industry.

While cheap cottons flooded the clothing market, the woollen industry was slow to respond to the possibilities suggested by the new textile inventions. After three-quarters of a century of rapid expansion (see Fig. 8, p. 170), the output of the British woollen industry grew less rapidly than the population in the last quarter of the eighteenth century. The implication is that home purchases of woollen goods per head of population actually declined during these years. The more detailed statistics of the silk industry point to a similar conclusion. The

Plate III.9.   Norwich Mill built for worsted spinning and weaving in 1833-6.

first response of the merchants and manufacturers dealing with silk, wool, and linen was to divert capital into cotton. A number of mills were opened by silk merchants at Stockport, Macclesfield, and Derby, by Glasgow linen yarn merchants and manufacturers, and by "stuff manufacturers" (worsted piecemakers) in the West Riding. Norwich also started a cotton spinning industry, but on the whole the old-established centres of the woollen industry in the West Country and East Anglia, remote from developments in the north of England, made little response to new developments.

Worsted was the first fibre after cotton to be spun by power in mills. (It should perhaps be explained that worsted yarns are obtained by combing the raw wool to remove the short stable fibres.) Arkwright had tried to adopt his warp frame to worsted but without success. However, after some experiments several firms in the hosiery districts of the East Midlands opened worsted mills in the late 1780s. A Leicester merchant hosier, John Coltman, assisted by his foreman, Joseph Brookhouse, appears to have been the first to make mechanised worsted spinning a commercial proposition. However, Leicester Corporation was so alarmed by the riots which followed the popular discovery of the invention that they banned the use of the labour-saving machine from the town. Bradford was shortly able to seize the initiative with the "throstle", a manually operated machine based on the principles of Crompton's mule and, like that machine, adapted to the use of power in the 1820s.

The West Riding woollen industry became factory-based almost a generation later than did worsted. It is true that Benjamin Gott, a Leeds merchant, built a large steam-powered scribbling and fulling mill near the town in 1792, but only two or three other merchants followed his lead. The centres of change were not the traditional cloth marketing centres of Leeds and Wakefield, but the new towns of Halifax and Huddersfield, and their neighbourhood. Change was much slower than in cotton or worsted spinning and most of the enterprise was provided by the independent clothiers (or manufacturers). Again transition started with the slow grouping of processes round the fulling mill. Scribbling (a process of separating the fibres to produce a continuous fleece) succumbed to mechanisation first, followed by the subsequent processes of carding (working the wool into slivers) and slubbing (a kind of course spinning). The jenny only gave way to the automatic mule very slowly; much woollen yarn was spun on the jenny by weavers' families down to the 1860s. The power loom was only adapted to woollen weaving between about 1840 and 1860.

The West of England clothing industry resembles the West Riding's, except that Yorkshire's proximity to Lancashire usually put it one step ahead with technical innovations. There is much evidence to show that the established clothiers of the West were more cautious and conservative than the rival clothier-manufacturers of the north.

The Importance of Mechanised Cotton Spinning

A number of writers have wondered whether economic historians have devoted too much time to the textile industry and, in particular, to cotton

Plate III.10.   The Piece Hall, Halifax (1779), once the centre of the West Riding worsted trade.

spinning. In so far as the genesis of factory production has claimed more space in the textbooks than changes in the iron or engineering industries the criticism may be justified. What is important is to recognise the novelty of the economic changes introduced in the era of Hargreaves and Arkwright. We may group these under three headings: the increased scale of production in textiles inaugurated by Arkwright, the wide geographical dispersion of cotton mills, and the attractiveness of the investment opportunity to many classes of British society. In all three respects mechanised cotton spinning brought something new to the developing economy.

The increased scale of production associated with Arkwright's successful adoption of water power to spinning and carding can be illustrated more readily from field work than from the very few surviving engineers' and architects' drawings. The traditional fulling mill, as Plate III.2 shows, was a small functional building constructed of local materials (like stone and thatch). The larger size of even the earliest cotton spinning mills is too obvious to need lengthy description. The cotton mill of the 1780s was typically a building of three or four storeys, often about 75 ft by 25 ft with an improved type (breast or overshot) water-wheel at its centre, and frequently inheriting a mill race from an earlier corn or grist mill on the site, or occasionally from a fulling mill. The mill was often surmounted by a cupola with a bell to summon the operatives to work. In the 1790s these rural mills began to give way to steam-powered mills of two, three, or four times the size, often erected on the banks of newly-cut canals. In the Pennines and Scotland and on the Cotswold scarp water power was displaced only very slowly; a few firms on reliable streams continued to rely on water power alone up to the first world war.

The geographical dispersion of cotton mills refutes the popular error that the early factory

The Factory System of Production

system was confined to the Pennines, and mostly to Lancashire. Nottingham and Mansfield, the Derbyshire dales and adjacent parts of Staffordshire, the Pennine flank of Lancashire and Cheshire, the Yorkshire dales (particularly about Keighley), and the Clyde valley, rapidly became the rural home of a lively new mechanised cotton spinning industry. A search for new sites led the industry northwards into Cumberland and Westmorland, southwards into Leicestershire, Warwickshire, and Northamptonshire, and westwards into North Wales. By the 1790s there were cotton mills at places as far apart as London, Exeter, Bristol, Norwich, Carlisle, Darlington, and Dublin, and an important industry in the Lagan valley of Ulster. Although most of the mills outside the traditional centres of the cotton industry did not survive the Napoleonic Wars, the redundant fixed capital of the industry (buildings and power units) helped to secure the future advance of the

factory system. As Lancashire asserted its lead over its rivals, the mill buildings of other regions were turned over to alternative uses: to woollen and worsted spinning and weaving in the West Riding, to the manufacture of lace in Nottingham, and to the linen industry in Ulster and the Scottish lowlands.

Investment in mechanised cotton spinning was popular in all social classes. There were few landowners who would have agreed with the Duke of Rutland that "it was not for the interest of his estates to encourage manufacturers upon them". The increased rental generated by industrialism was very welcome to most and in Scotland the landowners were one of the principal groups of investors. A recent analysis of the previous occupations of the entrepreneurs of over eighty Midlands cotton and worsted spinning mills made by one of the authors emphasises the diversity of their backgrounds. A large number

Plate III.11.   An eighteenth-century fulling hammer in use at Otterburn Wool Mills, Northumberland.

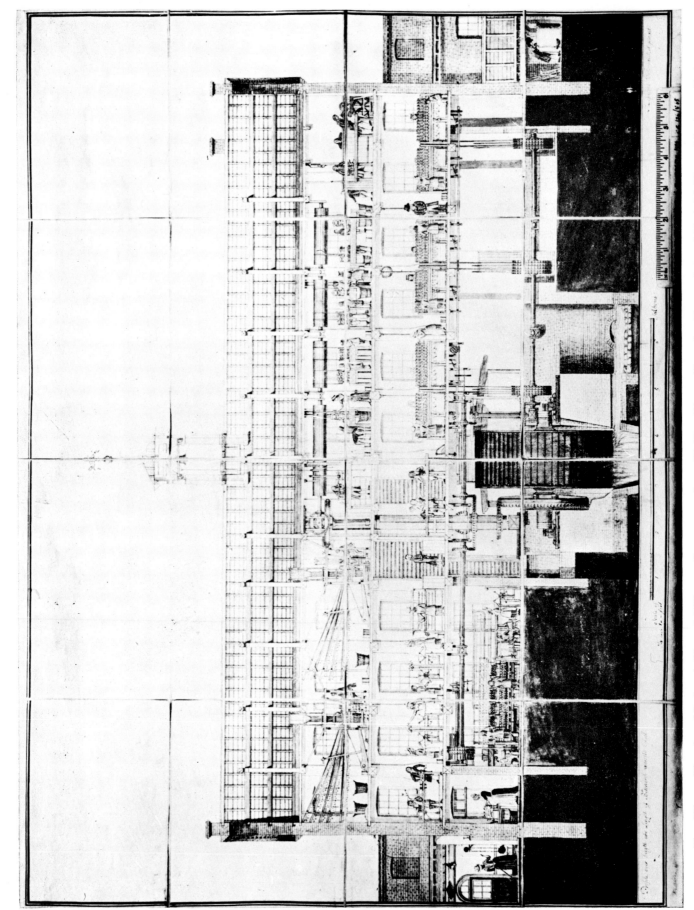

Plate III.12. Elevation of Bedworth Worsted Mill, near Coventry, c. 1800. Cf. Plate II.12. (Reproduced by permission of F. A. M. Fitzroy-Newdegate, Esq.)

were drawn from merchants who had operated the domestic system and their connections (mercers, drapers, bleachers, etc.), but about a third had no previous experience of the textile industry; some came from contracting industries (such as pottery and the Derbyshire lead and iron industry), and others were speculators drawn from retail trade, the building trades, brewing, and a variety of other occupations. An analysis of the origins of capital raised by one particular firm, Cardwell, Birley & Hornby, Blackburn (spinners and weavers), reflects similar diversity. There were ninety-seven investors in the firm between 1765 and 1812, among whom were numbers of widows, spinsters, local clergy, trustees, and friendly societies.

In Lancashire and the West Riding merchants played a rather less important role in cotton mill enterprise than they did in the Midlands. The main reason appears to be that they were generally unfamiliar with manufacturing processes and unable to assess the value of new techniques brought to their notice. They were trained, and spent most of their time, in the mercantile, rather than manufacturing side of industry, and it is a fact that most of the innumerable innovations of this period, both in textiles and other industries, originated with the mechanics who operated or built the machinery. Peter Drinkwater, a merchant who became the first owner of a mule factory in Manchester (in 1788), was totally ignorant of everything connected with cotton spinning and seldom visited his mills, according to his manager, the future utopian socialist, Robert Owen. Benjamin Gott, who has already been referred to as the pioneer of factory industry in Leeds, confessed "I was brought up as a merchant and became a manufacturer rather from possessing capital than from understanding the manufacture. I paid for the talents of others in the different branches of manufacture." Thus although merchants did play a part in the transition to the factory system their lack of enthusiasm allowed others to seize the initiative. In Lancashire and the West Riding small independent manufacturers provided most of the enterprise, while in the Midlands, the West Country, and East Anglia, where the structure of industry gave little opportunity for mechanics to become factory owners, the region suffered a relative decline which can be partly explained in these terms.

Cotton was the first of several industries of the time to offer opportunities for artisans and small tradesmen to climb the social ladder to factory ownership, and it is interesting to see how this came about. In Lancashire, roller spinning factories did not displace jenny workshops immediately, as they did in the Midlands. It was found that Arkwright's techniques produced thread more suitable for the warp, while machines built on Hargreaves's method produced thread for the weft, so that the two kinds of machine proved complementary. (In the Midlands hosiery district only one thread was used by the framework knitters, and this could be produced most cheaply in warp frames.) The jenny was a very cheap machine to build, and could be purchased second hand for as little as £1 each. Hargreaves's patent of 1770 soon proved ineffective. High wages were earned by the workers in the domestic cotton industry during the years from 1788 to about 1803, and many artisans found that they could set up on their own by purchasing one or two jennies. They could then extend their interest by acquiring first carding and slubbing machines, and finally the more expensive warp frames. Cottages, barns, and farm out-houses were often converted for manufacturing purposes during these golden years of the small cotton manufacturer. As Crompton's "mule"—a machine which incorporated the best features of the jenny and warp frame—gradually came into use, the "little masters" were often able to adapt themselves to the technical progress of the industry. Moreover, they soon began to extend their interests into merchanting, opening stockrooms among the crowded courts of Manchester. Thus in Lancashire the factory masters of the new cotton industry originated as weavers of the old industry (very often with an hereditary interest in farming), joiners and "clockmakers" who built the machinery, and others with a less relevant past such as shopkeepers, hatters, and carters. This class of entrepreneurs displayed the vigour, energy, and drive so characteristic of the Industrial Revolution in Britain; for it was only by untiring effort, mechanical skill based on close intimacy with the machinery of the industry, and a tight rein on personal spending that the artisan could hope to become an independent manufacturer.

In the West Riding of Yorkshire, the ranks of the new manufacturers were also swelled by men of humble origins who had the ability to keep pace with the technical evolution of the industry and extend their interests from manufacturing to mercantile activities. This social movement was also encouraged by the tradition of economic co-operation that existed among the small clothiers of the Dales. During the course of the eighteenth century these manufacturers had built the cloth halls of Leeds, Wakefield, and Halifax, where they had their stalls and bargained with the merchants for the sale of their cloths. From the introduction of power-operated machinery the Dales manufacturers united to erect mills, first for the fulling process, and then in turn for other processes as they in turn were mechanised. One of these mills might have from ten to fifty partners, with shares of £25 each or more.

The Decline of the West Country and East Anglia

The period between the end of the Napoleonic Wars (1815) and the middle of the nineteenth century saw the decline of the West Country and East Anglian clothing industries. This is not easy to explain. References to climatic factors (notably humidity) will not do as Norwich was almost as damp as Leeds; and lack of mineral resources is not an adequate reason either, as Stroud had direct access to the Forest of Dean coalfield from the opening of the Stroudwater Navigation in 1778. A proper account will take us back to the origins of Yorkshire success.

In the eighteenth century the West Riding produced the cheaper cloths, such as serges and plain worsteds. The worsted manufacture began round about 1700 because many of the long wool fleeces used by the established Norwich manufacturers came from the Dales. During the first three-quarters of the eighteenth century the expansion of the West Riding was probably based on cheaper labour, an "absence of that corporate conservatism which is often found among the workers in an established *industrie de luxe*" and (in worsted) local supplies of the raw material.

Mechanisation brought the decisive advantages to the northern centre of the industry. Proximity to Lancashire and a cotton industry of her own gave the West Riding the stimulus to mechanise. The presence of coal and iron together were the pre-requisites of the textile engineering industry which was established in Leeds in the 1790s. While the Yorkshire worsted industry was following hard on the progress of Lancashire cottons in the period between about 1795 and 1815, the merchants of Norwich were suffering from the closure of their markets by the Napoleonic blockade, and were obviously reluctant to enter the factory age. After the Wars the cheaper and more varied worsted cloths of Bradford ousted both the traditional and relatively expensive broadcloths of the West and, increasingly, the fine worsteds of Norwich. The decline of Norwich and the West was certainly not precipitate, as the survival of remnants of the industry at Trowbridge, Stroud, and Witney illustrates. It was much more a case of the wearing down of the older industries by the energy of entrepreneurs determined to succeed. The following

Plate III.13. West Harnham (Salisbury) Fulling Mill (early eighteenth century). (*Batsford Ltd.*)

Plates III.14-16.   Stanley Mill, Stroud, Glos.   An early iron-frame mill (1813), still in use.   Compare Plate IV.14.   (*Photo by F. C. Peckham; reproduced by permission of the photographer and the Peckham Studio, Stroud.*)

Plate III.17. Early eighteenth-century cloth weavers' houses at Bradford-on-Avon, Wilts. Weavers' windows can be seen on the topmost storey.

(*National Buildings Record.*)

figures, taken from the directories, are an index to the decline of the West of England industry:

Year of Directory	Number of Gloucestershire Clothiers
1783	75
1820	116
1830	82
1839	54
1849	37

Hosiery and Lace

Arkwright's partners in his early factories at Nottingham and Cromford, Samuel Need and Jedediah Strutt, had made their fortune by catering for the tastes of the upper and middle class in worsted, silk, and cotton hosiery. Strutt was responsible for the commercial success of the first major innovation in the hosiery industry since Lee's invention of the stocking frame. The "Derby Rib" pattern (1758) in the stocking rapidly became fashionable and its success triggered off innumerable attempts to vary the plain stocking stitch with different attachments to the frame. The experiments of knitters and framesmiths produced a ferment of ideas, numbers of which materialised in some new fashion article. In the long run the most profitable achievement was the knitting of lace-net on the frame, which was first made a saleable commodity by the Hayne brothers about 1776. The net was hand embroidered by domestic workers for miles around Nottingham.

The Hayne's achievement precipitated another phase of experimentation, this time to imitate the motions of the cushion-lace workers of Devon, Buckinghamshire, and other southern counties. The break-through was finally made by John Heathcoat, a Nottingham framesmith, who, capitalising on the efforts of his fellow artisans took out the first "twist-net" patent in 1808. Though Heathcoat took his firm to Tiverton (Devon) in 1816, the lace industry fulfilled the promise of its early and vigorous growth in Nottingham. Heathcoat's patent was for a fast hexagonal net, in silk or cotton, and experiments were soon being made to introduce a pattern to the ground. Though patents were being taken out for the addition of a pattern of spots to the net before Heathcoat's patent had expired, it was not until the 1840s that Hooton Deverell (another Nottingham mechanic) adapted the Jacquard principle of forming patterns to the lace machine. Meanwhile the lace machine became steam powered and housed in factories in the 1830s.

The lace industry presents a particularly interesting case of the stimulating high fashion catering for mass production for a popular market. The ceaseless experimentation of Nottingham mechanics and the energy of lace merchants transformed this expensive luxury article to an adornment for every woman and every Victorian parlour.

The Power Loom

The application of power to the handloom was achieved alone by a clergyman of mechanical genius, Rev. Edmund Cartwright. Unfortunately, Cartwright

PREMISES OF MESSRS, HINE, MUNDELLA, AND CO.

Plate III.18.   Hine and Mundella's factory in Station Street, Nottingham.   Built in 1851, it was the first in the town to use steam power to manufacture hosiery.   (*By courtesy of the City Librarian, Nottingham.*)

was less of an entrepreneur than an inventor and his Doncaster factory had only a short life. His brother, Major John Cartwright (better known as "the father of English Radicalism"), was little more successful. A Manchester firm's attempt to install 400 of Cartwright's looms was frustrated by the concerted opposition of the handloom weavers.

In the first years of the nineteenth century the initiative moved to Stockport, where William Radcliffe and Horrocks made important improvements. A number of leading spinners, like the Strutts and Peel, began to apply their steam engines to weaving but progress in replacing the handloom was slow until the early 1830s.

The cause of this was partly the imperfections of the early looms, and partly the determined opposition of the handloom weavers. This opposition will be discussed in more detail in Chapter VII.

Increasing Specialisation

The rapid expansion of the cotton industry after 1780 was at first accompanied by an increase in the range of activities controlled by the entrepreneur. In the 1780s the firms that sprang into existence in the wake of Arkwright undertook—or tried to undertake—all the processes of manufacture from buying the raw cotton at the ports to selling woven cottons through agents all over the country and abroad, as well as building their own mill and machinery. There were of course many small firms whose activities were confined to spinning in a narrow range of gauges, but their expectation was that, in the course of growth, they would open an office in Manchester and extend into merchanting and other branches of manufacturing. In the meantime the purchase of raw cotton and the sale of yarn was undertaken for them, not by specialists, but by larger non-specialised manufacturers.

However, in the 1790s the manufacturers began to discard some of the more troublesome functions to a new corps of specialists. A race of middlemen dealers known as cotton brokers emerged to buy cotton from Liverpool merchants and transmit it to Manchester and other locations of the industry, while banks (many of them founded on fortunes made in cotton) began to provide specialised credit services for the industry. The sale of yarns and fabrics was taken over by specialists and Manchester became the national and international market for cotton goods. The technically more advanced manufacturers in Manchester began to leave the coarser and less remunerative spinning to the country spinners of rural Lancashire, Derbyshire, and Nottinghamshire. The building of machinery was undertaken by a series of small firms engaged on specialities like spindle-making, roller-making, and card-making, so that the so-called machine builders of the industry were able to concentrate on the design and assembly of constantly improving plant. The building of steam engines and the costing of parts for textile machinery was undertaken by iron founders. The early calico printers (like Robert Peel of Blackburn, grandfather of the Prime Minister), were also spinners, but from the 1790s calico printing became a speciality. Bleaching became another branch industry when the use of chlorine superseded the ancient technique of bleaching by sour milk and sunlight in the 1790s. It would be tedious, if not impossible, to enumerate the other branches and sub-divisions; some idea of their extent is given in Fig. 10 (p. 172). Before the end of the century the new entrant to the cotton industry did not even have to provide his own factory space or steam engine power, for speculators and bankrupts' assignees began to provide rooms and power in mills to rent. (This practice enabled "small men" to continue to represent an important part of the enterprise of the industry.) In the 1830s and 1840s the mechanisation of weaving began to create new specialisms in the cotton industry.

A little later a similar process accompanied the rise of Leeds as the national centre of the woollen industry, Bradford as the home of the worsted industry, and Nottingham the centre of the lace trade. It is not possible to trace these developments in detail here, but this is hardly necessary if the fundamental process at work is appreciated.

Metallurgical Industries and Pottery

The use of power and the concentration of capital and labour began in the textile industry as early as the thirteenth century with the use of the fulling mill. In the metallurgical industries and in the manufacture of pottery the employment of water power came later, but it pre-dates the industrial revolution by perhaps two centuries. Water-wheels were commonly used for rolling and slitting sheets of metal, and for driving grinding wheels, before the Civil Wars. In pottery water-wheels were used for grinding flints and bones (a constituent of the raw material) in the seventeenth century, if not before.

During the second half of the eighteenth century a number of large firms developed whose capital investment, number of workers, and size of premises paralleled those in cotton and worsted spinning. The developments began in Birmingham and Burslem (Stoke-on-Trent) more or less simultaneously, so that although the metallurgical and pottery industries survived in some other towns and districts, our account can reasonably be concentrated in the two leading centres of the respective industries. In Birmingham and the Potteries there was no simple standardised product like spun cotton, or cotton cloth, and the process of mechanisation, compared with that in textiles, was much slower. Birmingham was the home of the earliest successful rotary steam engine (built by Boulton and Watt); but although steam power played an important role in the transition to the factory system, the earliest motive for factory investment was commercial rather than technical.

To follow up this point we may examine the careers of the two leading industrialists of Birmingham and the Potteries. Matthew Boulton (1728-1809) was a button, buckle, and "toy" maker who inherited a business from his father said to have been worth £20,000. Boulton's first experience of power-operated machinery was a rolling mill at Yardley, near Birmingham, which he opened sometime before 1756. Marrying in 1760, he received a dowry worth

Plate III.19.   Sarehole Mill, Birmingham, once owned by Boulton.   (*Dr Jennifer Tann.*)

£28,000. Two years later he entered into partnership with John Fothergill, a merchant, to build a factory at Soho. Boulton explained the reasons for building the Soho manufactory in a memo to his partner. The document contains no word about mechanical power. The important matter in his eyes was to have the workpeople "under our eyes and immediate management . . . every day and almost every hour". The Soho enterprise was a necessary part of Boulton's plan to build up the business he had inherited by improving the quality and quantity, and increasing the novelty and variety of the goods he made. In order to extend his market he had to by-pass the merchants and middlemen who separated the Birmingham artisan from the world of fashion, and establish higher standards of design and artistry. He thus assumed direct control and immediate supervision of the manufacturing processes and (with the aid of his partner Fothergill) controlled the distribution and sale, both at home and abroad, of the output of his works. With Boulton and Fothergill it was sensitivity to the demands of increasingly discriminating customers that prescribed centralised factory production.

Boulton's close friend was Josiah Wedgwood (1730-95), of Burslem in the Potteries. Like Boulton he was brought up to the traditional craft of his district, but his conception of design and standards of workmanship soon acquired him markets beyond his own region. In 1768 he entered into partnership with Thomas Bentley, a Liverpool merchant, and the following year the partners opened a factory at Etruria, on the banks of the newly opened Trent and Mersey Canal, near Hanley. Wedgwood's motives for building at Etruria were similar to those of Boulton at Soho. The Potteries were already moving towards greater specialisation by the middle of the eighteenth century, but the process was accelerated by Wedgwood's initiative. He foresaw that the only possible method of improving the quality and variety of his products was to organise his works in such a way as to press division of labour to the point of optimum efficiency, with each distinct process and technique defined and separated. His organisation "aimed at a conveyor belt progress through the works: the kiln room succeeded the painting room, the account room the kiln room, and the ware room the account room, so that there was a smooth progression from the ware being painted, to being fired, to being entered into the books, to being stored". The specialisation of the labour force was linked with a careful gradation of wage payments, which ranged from forty-two shillings a week for the most skilled modeller to

Plate III.20. Potbanks at Stoke.

though (as we saw in Chapter I) there was a fairly universal tendency to try to secure a more immediate control over the production and delivery dates by buying up domestic machinery or concentrating the finishing processes at the warehouse. With Wedgwood and Boulton this increasing control was so accelerated as to change the whole concept of the entrepreneur's functions. They were not content to purchase raw materials through the traditional channels, but subscribed to the development of turnpike roads and canals. Wedgwood established turnpike connections with the Liverpool and London roads (1762-5) and in 1777 was one of the prime movers of the Trent and Mersey Canal, a 93-mile artery which opened up the landlocked Potteries to better supplies of raw materials (particularly china clay from Cornwall), to domestic markets, and to the ports. Boulton was a principal promoter of the Birmingham Canal (1768-72) which linked Birmingham to the Black Country coal-pits

one shilling a week to a woman who was described as a "painter of pins" for the gloss ovens. Everyone was a specialist. Such a direction of labour, as a student of the Etruria works has pointed out, "did not destroy skill: it limited its field of expression to a particular task, but within those limits it increased it".[1]

Boulton and Wedgwood were friends and there is no doubt that they borrowed each other's ideas where they could be applied to their own work. On the commercial side they show striking similarities. Both of them were constantly experimenting with new techniques and new forms of organisation to extend the markets for their products. Under the domestic system the merchant's functions were generally limited to buying and distributing the raw material and disposing of the finished work,

[1] N. McKendrick, "Josiah Wedgwood: an Eighteenth Century Entrepreneur in salesmanship and marketing techniques", *Economic History Review*, XII (1959-60).

Plate III.21. Stuart Crystal Works, at Kingswinford: the glass cone.

Plates III.22-41. Division of Labour in the Pottery Industry (from *Enoch Wood's Manufactury*, 1827), from a copy held by the British Ceramic Research Association, Penkhull, Stoke-on-Trent.

Plate III.22.

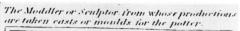

Plate III.23.

Plate III.24.

Plate III.25.

Plate III.26.

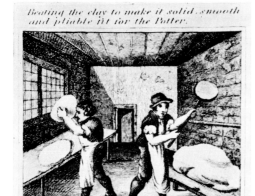

Plate III.27.

Plate III.28.

Plate III.29.

Plate III.30.

Plate III.31.

Plate III.32.

Plate III.33.

Plate III.34.

Plate III.35.

Plate III.36.

Plate III.37.

Plate III.38.

Plate III.39.

Plate III.40.

Plate III.41.

and provided an outlet to national and international markets. As we have seen, neither Wedgwood nor Boulton were content to leave it to their workmen to continue their traditional craftsmanship. They concentrated the ownership and control of the manufacture in their own hands by training their own labour for specialised tasks in which original skills could be acquired. Boulton set up his own drawing school at Soho, while Wedgwood set about making "Artists . . . of mere men".

Only by this considerable advance were they able to give decisive direction to the development of their respective industries. In marketing, Wedgwood and Boulton showed the greatest originality and supported their manufacturing achievements. In this respect they went further than Arkwright, for

they would not leave the sale of their products, dependent on changing fashions, to the control of independent wholesalers. They established their own warehouses, salerooms and showrooms, travelling salesmen and agents, trade catalogues and extensive newspaper advertising. They obtained the lion's share of the market in their different lines by securing the patronage of royalty (both British and Continental) and of the nobility and wealthy gentry. By this, they won a special distinction for their goods, which they turned to profitable account by giving wide publicity to their patronage. Advertising brought the larger turnover that made the cultivation of the eminent worth the time and trouble. In other words, the advances of the industrial revolution were by no means confined to mass production or shoddy production. More efficient production certainly played its part, but just as important was the response of shrewd, sales-conscious business men to the increasingly discriminating demands of a growing urban market.

The enterprise of Boulton and Wedgwood presented a challenge to their competitors. Their products and organisation were carefully studied and quickly imitated. In this way the functions of the entrepreneur and the structure of the two industries were soon changed. Specialisation and attention to public demand became general, and it became as important to have a sound knowledge of the quirks of the markets as of those of production.

Plate III.42. The Wedgwood Catalogue of Queensware, 1774. Queensware was Jos. Wedgwood's earliest successful mass-produced design. The catalogue helped the quality product to find an extensive sale. (*Jos. Wedgwood & Sons, Ltd.*)

IV

Raw Materials, Iron, and Engineering

The processes of industrialisation surveyed so far necessarily required increasing supplies of raw materials. In the reign of the early Tudors the universal raw material of industry was timber, used alike as a structural material for building, power units (water mills and windmills), and machinery, and as a fuel in all industries from pottery, paper, and brewing to the smelting of metals. In the next century timber formed the foundation for the infant chemical industry, for its potash content was the essential ingredient of soap, glass, bleach, and gunpowder. For centuries the clearing of virgin forest had been a double gain to the landowners, providing timber and opening up land to farming, but already in the sixteenth century a crisis of timber supply in London compelled industrial users to recognise the value of the accessible sources. A search for cheap substitutes for timber began. The next two centuries saw a gradual transition from wood fuel to coal; and iron, brass, and brick supplanted wood as a structural material.

In Chapter I we saw how the shortage of fuel in London gave rise to the Newcastle coal trade, and how coal was substituted for timber fuel in one industry after another, finally winning over the iron industry in the last decades of the eighteenth century. Coal was also the means of averting a power crisis in the second half of the eighteenth century. Despite improved designs of water-wheels and the use of Newcomen engines to replenish reservoirs, water power was clearly a limited natural resource. It was, moreover, an irregular and unreliable source of power, unsuited to the exacting delivery schedules which eighteenth century customers were calling for. Arkwright scoured the country searching for suitable locations for new cotton mills, and the remote sites seized upon by his competitors indicate that they had no less of a problem. The metallurgical industries evidently faced a similar crisis. Already in 1700 all possible sites within a five-mile radius of Birmingham were being exploited. The impasse was broken by Watt's development of the rotary-steam engine which, for all its economy of fuel, relied on cheap coal supplies.

Metal increasingly took over from wood in building and engineering. The new techniques of the textile industry called into existence a machine-building industry whose need for accuracy and rigidity (particularly as mechanical power was adopted) compelled the engineers to substitute metal (particularly iron) for wooden parts. The larger machinery had to be housed in bigger and bigger factories, so that Jedediah Strutt's multi-storey iron-framed factory at Derby (built 1792-3) soon became the prototype for all textile mills. The growth of communications produced iron bridges, aqueducts, railroads, locomotives, barges, and (in due course) ships. The initial stimulus was invariably the growing demand for coal; so it was that iron served coal as coal was serving iron. In this way the Industrial Revolution in textiles leaned heavily on cheap metal and coal supplies, which in turn served each other. Thus were built up the "great staples" of nineteenth-century Britain—coal, iron, and textiles.

The textile and iron industries depended on producers of raw materials other than the coal industry. The heavy chemical industry supplied sulphuric acid for metal refining and for soap, bleach, and starch in the textile industries, as well as glazes for pottery and soda for glass-making.

Plate IV.1. Token coinage (used when copper coin was short) from Coalbrookdale, nucleus of Abraham Darby's industrial empire. On the left is the famous Iron Bridge and on the right the inclined plane at Ketley. The engine drew up a loaded set of wagons to the top, and they, now empty, ran down of themselves. Alternatively, the plane could be used to make loaded wagons (descending) pull empty ones to the top of the slope. (*Chapman.*)

The organic sources proved inadequate to meet the ever growing demand for chemicals and scientific research suggested mineral sources that were shortly to be profitably exploited.

The iron industry was, of course, not merely a producer's industry. During the eighteenth century the foundry masters produced an increasing variety of consumer goods—cast iron grates, cooking pots, pipes, railings, balustrades, and ornaments among many others. The role of iron in the process of economic change was so fundamental that some scholars consider that it has at least an equal claim with cotton textiles to be considered the "leading growth sector" in the Industrial Revolution. Its contribution to the national income was certainly as great and it exhibited characteristic features of modern capitalistic enterprise from the time of the introduction of the blast furnace in Elizabeth's reign. If

Plate IV.2. Iron bridge of 1827 on the Birmingham Canal.

Plate IV.3. Hebburn Colliery, 1844, with ventilating shaft *left*, and screens *right*. (From Hair's *Coal Mines*.) Corves
are being raised by winding engine (left).

the growth of the iron industry was less spectacular than that of the textiles it was only because its period of evolution was longer.

Coal

In the mining of coal, unlike the spinning and weaving of cotton and woollen fabrics, there were no impressive changes of technique or spectacular increases of output. The eighteenth and early nineteenth centuries saw a steady and persistent increase in output (see Fig. 11, p. 173). Mining remained a pick and shovel operation and the increased quantities of coal were obtained by opening more pits and exploiting deeper and deeper seams.

For most of the eighteenth century the coal-mining industry was under the direct or indirect control of large landowners who were also the owners of the minerals that lay under their estates. Aristocrats like the Dukes of Argyll and Hamilton in

Scotland, the Dukes of Devonshire in Derbyshire, the Dukes of Norfolk in Sheffield and South Yorkshire, the Lords Middleton in Nottinghamshire, and the Lords Dudley in South Staffordshire, were prominent in mining for three centuries or more.

The gentry and smaller landowners played a role proportionate to the mineral endowment of their estates, and indeed wherever coal lay accessible to markets the proprietors of the soil were busy drawing the profits or royalties. The exploitation of the coal measures was for them just another branch of the management of their estates, and some employed a bailiff to manage the pits for them, while others contracted the work out to small capitalists for an agreed royalty.

The largest and most technically advanced pits were to be found on the Great Northern Coalfield (Tyneside and Wearside) and in Cumberland until the coming of the canals and railways. These fields had direct access to the sea, the greatest highway of eighteenth-century Britain, and hence to the

Plates IV.4 and 5.   Pre-Industrial Revolution techniques still survive, even in mining.   These photographs were taken in 1966 at Elsden Mine, near Otterburn, Northumberland.   *Top,* the pit-head; *bottom,* the main adit.   The mine is privately owned. Access to the mine is provided by a ladder.

urban markets. The scale of colliery enterprise is suggested by the fact that, in the north-east, collieries over 600 feet deep were being sunk after about 1790 at a cost of from £15,000 to £40,000. On the Cumberland coalfield, Isabella Colliery at Workington cost £80,000 to open up in the years 1808-22. The northern pits employed a labour force as large as that of most cotton mills—in 1829 forty-one Tyneside collieries employed 12,000 men, or an average of 300 each. The land-locked inland coalfields generally operated on a much more modest scale, and pits employing no more than a dozen men were common until the railway age.

The growth of the coal industry was accompanied by the rise of professional colliery agents and managers, known in the north-east as mine viewers, and it was these men who were primarily responsible for the introduction and diffusion of new techniques. The earliest member of this class of whom we have any real knowledge was Huntingdon Beaumont, who came of a gentle family with mining interests at Coleorton, Leicestershire. Beaumont gained experience at his family's pits, became the agent of Sir Percival Willoughby's mines at Wollaton (Nottingham) and, when this venture failed to fulfil expectations, moved to Blyth on the north-east coast to venture £6,000 in supplying the London market. Beaumont's concerns were a commercial failure, but he pioneered the idea of running coal wagons on wooden rails or guides, both at Wollaton and Blyth, and introduced iron boring-rods to assess the depth and thickness of coal seams without the necessity of sinking trial shafts. This method of prospecting for coal was still

in common use at the end of the nineteenth century. Beaumont also grappled with the perennial problem of mine drainage, though in this instance his methods are not known.

The techniques of mining, as we have already noticed, changed only very slowly during the Industrial Revolution, and indeed work at the coal-face was still almost entirely manual in 1914. The traditional method of extracting the coal was known as "bord and pillar" working. The miners dug out aisles of coal from the seam, leaving huge pillars to support the roof. This saved subsidence but left a large proportion of the coal underground. About the middle of the seventeenth century the more economical "longwall" system gradually began to spread from Shropshire. All the coal was taken out and the roof supported by long walls made from the "spoil" from the mine to form a series of tunnels and cavities. In some parts of the country the bord and pillar system was still in use this century.

As the mines became deeper the problem of flooding and explosions of inflammable gases became graver. In hilly country a good deal of capital was invested in excavating soughs (or drainage channels) but this solution was not practicable everywhere. The seventeenth and eighteenth centuries saw a long series of experiments with machines to drain the mines. Bucket chains and horse-driven pumps were only of limited value, so that the first real measure of success was achieved by Thomas Newcomen of Dartmouth with his atmospheric pump, which is illustrated on p. 7. The trustees of Lord Dudley erected the first Newcomen engine at

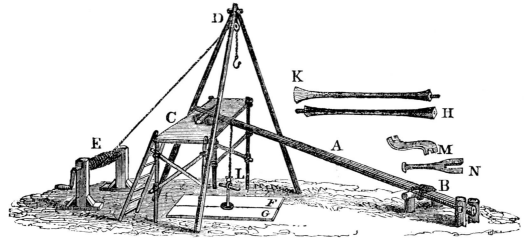

Plate IV.6. Boring equipment (from Holland's *Fossil Fuel*, 1835). (*Durham Co. Local History Society.*)

Plate IV.7. A chaldron wagon running on rails, 1778 (from Morland *L'art d'exploiter les mines*). (*Durham Co. Local History Society.*)

Plate IV.8. Miners' lamps: left to right, an early Davy lamp, a late nineteenth century safety lamp, and the extremely dangerous "midgy" lamp. (*Durham Co. Local History Society.*)

Tipton, on the South Staffordshire coalfield, in 1712. Within half a dozen years the famous ironmasters, the Darbys of Coalbrookdale, were supplying sets of iron castings for "fire engines". The problem of fire damp was not solved until Sir Humphrey Davy and George Stephenson simultaneously invented the miner's safety lamp in 1815.

The deeper mines and more extensive workings also created problems of shifting hewn coal to the surface. The early practice was for women and children to drag the corves (wicker baskets) of coal to the foot of the shaft and then hump it to the surface on their backs up long ladders or winding stairways. In some coalfields—notably Lancashire—women were still working as "drawers" for the miners when the first government inquiry, the Mines Commission of 1842, presented its report. In the course of the eighteenth century, horse capstans, known locally as "gins", replaced ladders and stairways for raising coal to the pit-head. The

application of water power to winding followed, but both this and the adoption of steam engines came only very slowly. The "little gin-pits", as D. H. Lawrence called them, could still be seen in the East Midlands and on the South Staffordshire coalfield up to the period of nationalisation of the coal industry (1946). Our photographs show that the earliest and most primitive techniques of mining can still be found in privately operated mines in remote parts of the country.

The most important development in the transport of coal was, of course, the introduction of the rail roads. These were soon extended underground, and also stretched many miles across the face of the countryside in mining districts. By 1700 wagonways already carried coal as many as ten miles to the Tyne and Wear. The 103-ft Tanfield Arch (1727) illustrated here, makes clear the magnitude of some of these early transport undertakings. The line it carried was built to carry coal from Colonel Lyddal's collieries at Tanfield to the Wear, five miles away.

Plate IV.9.   Tanfield Arch.   (*Frank Atkinson, F.M.A., F.S.A.*)

Its course included embankments a hundred feet high and cuttings of half a mile or more in length, as well as several arched stone bridges. When Richard Reynolds of Coalbrookdale introduced grooved iron rails (1768) it became possible to move large quantities of coal with ease and efficiency.

The contracts and conditions under which the coal seams were exploited varied considerably from one field to another. It was never easy to recruit labour for the hard and dangerous toil of mining so that in the north of England men were engaged on long contracts of up to a year at a signing wherever possible. The longer contract often suited the needs of the miners for whom it offered regular employment and immunity from the press-gang. In Scotland a system of serfdom for the miners had been established at some remote point of time as a result of which they were bound to the colliery for

life, and an Emancipation Act was not passed through Parliament until 1774. Even at the end of the century many colliers remained unfree, because they had failed to qualify under the terms of the Act, which required them to establish a claim in a Sheriff's court.

In the Midlands, coal was usually mined under the collective contract system. The colliery proprietor did not mine the coal himself, but contracted out to a number of miners with a small but sufficient capital to exploit a small working. The gang of miners was represented in bargaining by a leader often known as a charter master, or butty, in the Midlands. (The system may be compared with the merchant capitalism of the domestic system of industry.) The terms of the contract would of course vary with the size of the pits that it was necessary to make. A printed form of contract for

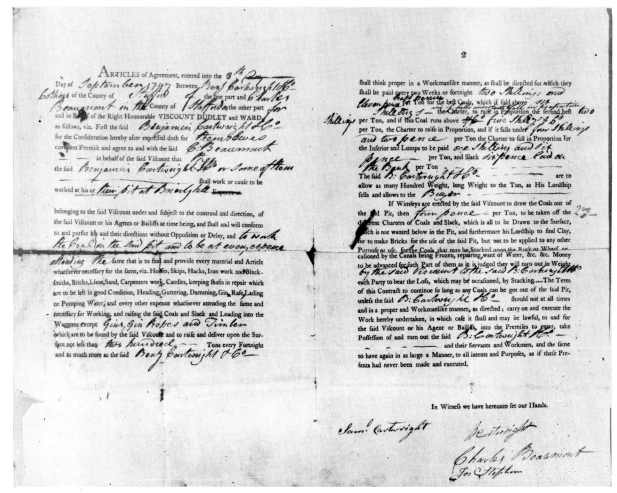

Plate IV.10. Printed form of contract prepared by Charles Beaumont for Lord Dudley's charter masters. (*Public Record Office.*)

Iron, and Engineering

Viscount Dudley's pits is reproduced here. The Dudley family estates encompassed a large part of the famous Staffordshire thirty-foot seam, much of which lay near the surface and could be readily obtained with a minimum of equipment. Lord Dudley therefore only found it necessary to provide gins, gin ropes, and timber for raising the coal to the surface.

During the course of the eighteenth century the structure of proprietorship of the coal industry began to change. As coal was increasingly used for the smelting of iron, the ironmasters began to buy estates containing coal and iron ore in close proximity. A handful of large landowners participated in the trend towards integrated coal and iron companies, but most of the capital came from the ironmasters. This is a subject that can best be illustrated and examined in the next section.

Iron

We have already noticed that the iron industry was dominated by large landowners and wealthy merchants for several generations before the Industrial Revolution, and that its entrepreneurs were capitalists in the fullest sense. Great ironmasters like the Crowleys, Foleys, and Lloyds owned the capital for and conducted all the processes of the industry from excavating the ore (or importing bar-iron) to selling a whole variety of finished metal goods, employing and directing wage-labour

Plate IV.11. Eighteenth-century smelting furnace at Coalbrookdale.

Plate IV.12. Black Country iron works, about 1830.

Plate IV.13. Trip-hammer at Wortley Forge.

71

Plate IV.14. Tutbury Gypsum Mill. Formerly a cotton mill. The construction shows the partial substitution of iron for masonry and wood. Tutbury represents a half-way stage between traditional construction and full iron-framing. Compare Plates III.15 and 16.

at all stages. The iron industry was thus less open to those spectacular changes in leadership and structure that transformed the textile industries. Nevertheless, important changes in techniques brought revolutionary changes in the size, output, and location of the industry.

The changes in the techniques of the industry occurred at approximately the same period as those in cotton-spinning. The attempt to substitute coal for charcoal in the smelting process had engrossed many able minds in the seventeenth century, but without success. The break-through was finally made by Abraham Darby, the Coalbrookdale iron-master, in 1709, but for various reasons the method was not generally adopted for another three-quarters of a century. Darby succeeded where others had failed because the sweet "clod" of the Shropshire coalfield was particularly suited to coking for iron smelting. Moreover, the quality of metal that was produced by this process in the early days was suitable only for the poorer quality cast-iron wares, which at this time was much

Plate IV.15. Spademaker, Swindells & Co., Netherton.

72

inferior to the wrought-iron branch of the industry. Darby himself specialised in the casting of cooking pots which he sent down to the Severn to be sold in Bristol. It was not until steam-powered blasting was introduced by the ironmaster John Wilkinson (about 1775) that coke smelting became as efficient a process as charcoal smelting. The difference was made by the application of Boulton and Watt's engines to the blasting process.

Finished iron goods may be formed by either casting (running the molten metal into moulds) or forging, *i.e.*, shaping the wares under the continuous impact of the hammers. Darby's technique gave the foundry an advantage over the forge which it retained in the eighteenth and early nineteenth centuries, and an increasing range of cast-iron goods was produced, displacing wrought iron and other metals. Cheap iron made possible, on the one hand, the modern hardware trade of Birmingham, with its incredible variety of metal goods, and, on the other hand, all the infinite possibilities of construction in iron. Architects incorporated iron pillars and girders, iron vaulting and fanlights, not merely in the basic structure of factories and warehouses, but also in the design of churches, shopping arcades, markets, theatres, and proud new railway stations. Engineers rejoiced in the freedom that the

Plate IV.16. Bath. An elegant Regency terrace with effective use of cast-iron railings.

Plate IV.17. Puddling iron at a furnace in the Black Country. A photograph taken about 1905. (*Dudley Public Library.*)

strength of iron lent them in the construction of bridges, viaducts, and harbours. Cast-iron balustrades and verandahs are still the most striking feature of the attractive Regency houses of Brighton, Bath, and Cheltenham, and middle-class residential districts of London, Bristol, Liverpool, and other towns built at the period. At its best the incorporation of iron produced results no less graceful than the most elegant masonry. The old charcoal iron industry was finally killed by Henry Cort's puddling and rolling process, which dates from 1783-4. Cort's achievement was the separation of the earthy impurities to make bar iron of as high a grade as that imported from Sweden and Russia or obtained from British charcoal furnaces. The white-hot molten metal was "puddled" or raked through apertures in the furnaces to coagulate the slag, the lumps of which were beaten out of the raw metal under the forge hammer and by being passed through rollers. Cort's patents were soon disputed and, in 1789, confiscated as a result of a financial scandal for which his partner was solely responsible. His technique was quickly adopted by other ironmasters, particularly in the rapidly expanding industry of South Wales, and resulted in a rapid increase in pig iron production, as the following estimates show:

NUMBER OF FURNACES AND OUTPUT OF PIG IRON IN
GREAT BRITAIN

Year	Furnaces	Output (tons)
c. 1760	—	30,000
1788	85	68,000
1796	121	125,400
1806	221	250,400

Imports of bar iron fell away and in 1797 Britain began to export. During the period of the French Wars (1792-1815) the demand for armaments further stimulated the industry.

The widespread adoption of Cort's process gave rise to fundamental changes in the location, organisation, and products of the British iron industry. Now freed from "the tyranny of wood and water" it rapidly moved from its dispersed locations to concentrate on the coalfields. The foundries were no more tied to remote forests and fast streams; the tall blast furnaces were soon to be found crowded together in the Black Country, South Yorkshire and its Derbyshire borders, Glamorgan, and the Scottish lowlands. The ironmasters' aspiration was now a "mineral estate", the control of ample supplies of coal and ore in immediate proximity to each other.

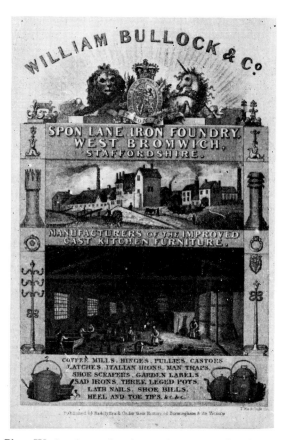

Plate IV.18. An early nineteenth-century advertisement for cast-iron kitchenware. Note the engraving of an ironworks.

The pursuit of minerals was already taking English capitalists into Scotland and Wales in the 1760s. The Welsh industry originated with the enterprise of Anthony Bacon who began his career exporting coal from Whitehaven to Dublin and won his fortune on government contracts for victualling troops in the colonies, particularly during the American War of Independence. In 1755 he leased the mineral rights of some thirty square miles around Merthyr Tydfil, then an undeveloped area, for a mere £200 a year. He constructed a turnpike road to Cardiff and built foundries and forges. Like other ironmasters of the period, he found government contracts for cannon particularly profitable. When Bacon withdrew from his Welsh interests in 1782 he was drawing a clear £10,000 a year from this source. His interests were taken over by the Crayshaws of Staffordshire who, benefiting from Cort's discovery, were able to accelerate the exploitation of these once green and sparsely populated valleys. This pattern of development was repeated in

Plate IV.19. Locks and tunnels on the Birmingham Canal.

ironworks, near Wrexham (North Wales), from their father about 1761. It was a good time to take over an ironworks as the Seven Years War (1756-63) was bringing prosperity to those who could fulfil government contracts for ordnance. The brothers built up the prospering works until it was reported, in 1789, as the largest in Europe. John Wilkinson's two marriages brought him an ample fortune which, it is said, enabled him to buy a second ironworks at Broseley near Coalbrookdale. It was here that he perfected the art of smelting with coke, perhaps with the help of workmen from the nearby Darby ironworks. His success drew him to the rich coal and ironstone reserves of South Staffordshire, and he opened the first furnace there about the time the Bilston-Birmingham Canal was cut, in 1769. Birmingham lay off the coalfield and depended on the new route for vital supplies of iron and coal; at Bilston, Wilkinson saw his opportunity. However, the Black Country had very little water power, and it was not until after 1775, when Wilkinson was able to use a Boulton & Watt steam engine to provide a blast, that the Bilston works began to expand rapidly. The three Wilkinson ironworks were much more than foundries; they were in fact general engineering works, making cannons and steam engine cylinders (by a new boring technique), boilers, vats, iron pipes, barges, and indeed any article in iron for which the Wilkinson brothers could secure an order. At Bilston, John Wilkinson had twelve Boulton & Watt engines by the end of 1791, which were applied to boring, rolling metal, and forging (*i.e.*, hammering out the pig iron), as well as providing a blast. Like many industrialists of his age, Wilkinson acquired interests in warehouses, canals, banks, and landed estate (see Fig. 13, p. 175). He held shares in lead and copper mines and works, while his brother William appears to have been a partner in an early (1782) cotton mill at Cark, in Cumberland. John Wilkinson was said to have been a millionaire before his death in 1808.

Most of the industrialists of the Industrial Revolution were *nouveaux riches*, but in coal and iron a handful of aristocrats retained their leading position. This can be illustrated from the rising fortunes of succeeding holders of the title of Lord Dudley. The Dudley estates covered a large part of the Black Country. The heavy topsoil was not much valued for farming, but the presence of the famous South Staffordshire "ten-yard" seam just underneath was

many other Welsh valleys: London iron merchants provided the bulk of the capital, with some support from Midland ironmasters (see Fig. 12, p. 174).

The first major ironworks in Scotland was opened at Carron, near Falkirk (20 miles from Edinburgh) in 1760. The entrepreneurs were Samuel Garbett and Dr John Roebuck, who were already in partnership in a chemical works in Birmingham and at Prestonpans. The Carron Company pioneered Darby's process in Scotland and, after some initial financial difficulties, achieved fame and fortune with "the carronade", a cannon made by the method pioneered by the ironmaster, John Wilkinson.

The use of coal and steam power enabled the ironmaster to concentrate all the processes of manufacture on one site. Crowley had tried to do this at Newcastle in the 1690s; but was able to only by importing his bar iron from abroad. The interest of ironmasters increasingly embraced smelting, refining, manufacturing, and selling. The earliest examples of the ironmaster with all-embracing interests is provided by the Wilkinson brothers. John and William Wilkinson inherited Bersham

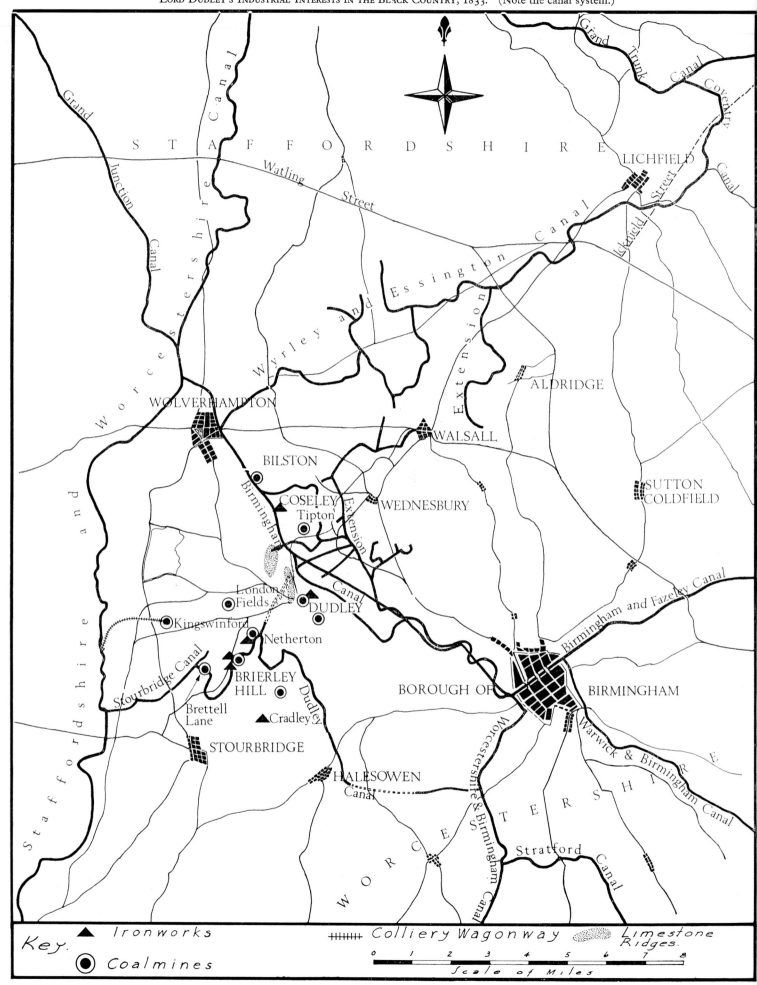

LORD DUDLEY'S INDUSTRIAL INTERESTS IN THE BLACK COUNTRY, 1833. (Note the canal system.)

STAFFORDSHIRE

Grand Junction Canal

Worcestershire Canal

Staffordshire Canal

Watling Street

Wyrley and Essington Canal

Extension Canal

Grand Trunk Canal

Coventry Canal

Lichfield Street

LICHFIELD

ALDRIDGE

WOLVERHAMPTON

WALSALL

BILSTON

Birmingham

COSELEY
Tipton

Extension

WEDNESBURY

SUTTON
COLDFIELD

London
Fields

DUDLEY

Canal

Kingswinford

Netherton

Birmingham and Fazeley Canal

Dudley Canal

BRIERLEY
HILL

BOROUGH OF

BIRMINGHAM

Staffordshire and Worcestershire Canal

Stourbridge Canal

Brettell
Lane

Cradley

Warwick & Birmingham Canal

STOURBRIDGE

WORCESTERSHIRE

Worcestershire & Birmingham Canal

HALESOWEN
Canal

Stratford Canal

WORCESTERSHIRE

Key. ▲ *Ironworks* ⊕ **Coalmines** ┼┼┼┼┼ Colliery Wagonway Limestone Ridges.

0 1 2 3 4 5 6 7 8
Scale of Miles

Plate IV.20. Limestone works at Wren's Nest, near Dudley, about 1905. (*Dudley Public Library.*)

ample compensation. There were, moreover, associated ironstone and limestone deposits, with clay suitable for making fire bricks. According to Dud Dudley's *Metallum Martis* (1665), the family also operated several charcoal ironworks from the early seventeenth century. A survey of the family estates made in 1701 showed that Lord Dudley was already operating three collieries in the neighbourhood of the town, as well as renting land for "butty" mining in the fields below Dudley Castle. At the beginning of the eighteenth century the income from coal-mines, iron-mines, and limestone quarries amounted to almost half the annual income of the estate. By 1740, when the next estate accounts occur, the charcoal iron industry was largely dispersed from the Black Country. The family's interests in iron were reduced to renting Cradley Ironworks (a forge and slitting mill near Stourbridge), and selling the lessee charcoal and

ironstone from Pensnett Chase where Dud Dudley's ironworks had once stood. Viscount Dudley first leased land and mineral rights for coke furnaces at Coneygre (Tipton) in 1782, hard on the heels of John Wilkinson's pioneer enterprise. At the end of the eighteenth century, the cutting of the Dudley and Stourbridge Canal (1776), the enclosure of common lands, and the appointment of Charles Beaumont as mine agent in 1797 led to further opportunities for profit.

A survey of the estates of the first Earl of Dudley— the family titles appreciated with their fortunes— after his death in 1833 showed that he operated ten collieries, three limestone works, and an engineering yard (to make and repair steam engines for the mines), and owned six ironworks. The latter were leased to local firms of standing, like Gibbons, the Kingswinford nail merchants, and Isons, the West Bromwich pioneers of the holloware industry.

77

The mineral workings were directed by the Earl's Mine Agent and his subordinate mine bailiffs. Two-thirds of the Earl's annual income (£55,000 just after his death) arose from his mines and other industrial concerns; the total capital value of the estates must have been in excess of £1,000,000. Moreover, the estate was certainly not fully exploited at the time, as the appointment of Richard Smith as Agent was to show.

Smith was really the first professional Agent retained by the Dudleys (Beaumont had been dismissed after a few months) and his long period in office (1836-64) coincided with the most vigorous period of development of their Black Country estates. The position in 1852 may be summarised as follows:

INDUSTRIAL INTERESTS OF THE FUTURE 2nd EARL OF DUDLEY, 1852.

	No. of Concerns. Operated by the Dudleys' Agent.	No. of Firms Paying Rent or Royalties.
Coal- and iron-mines	24	30
Ironworks	3	7
Limestone works	1	6
Claypits and brickworks	1	16
Stone quarries	1	—
Pumping engines (power rented)	3	—
Railway lines	3	4

The figures conceal large differences in the scale of enterprise in mining; coal royalties ranged from a few shillings a week to the £17,450 a year tribute of the British Iron Co. The map shows the state of the estates in 1833.

Steel

Until the introduction of the Bessemer process in 1856 steel was a valuable metal that was only made in small quantities for cutlery and tools. Even so, some important advances in the techniques of steel-making, with corresponding changes in the location and structure of the industry, took place during the Industrial Revolution. In particular, the period saw the rise of Sheffield to the status of Britain's premier steel town. An attempt to survey the origins of this development must involve some explanation of the process of making steel in the early eighteenth century.

Steel is an alloy of iron (96%) and carbon (4%), the exact proportions varying with the use for which the metal is required. Until the 1780s most British steel was made by the cementation process, which involved heating bars of wrought iron with finely ground charcoal for six days. The bars were converted into steel as they absorbed carbon from the charcoal. The industry was first in the district about Stourbridge, whence Sir Ambrose Crowley took it to Newcastle. It did not become well established in Sheffield until the second half of the eighteenth century, when successive improvements of the Don Navigation brought Swedish bar iron cheaply to the growing town.

The great rise of Sheffield dates from the invention of Benjamin Huntsman's process of making steel. Huntsman was a Doncaster clockmaker who began his experiments to find a better steel for clock springs. He succeeded in producing a superior quality steel by bringing cementation steel to a molten state in clay crucibles with a flux which freed the metal from particles of slag which spoiled the quality of English steels. Huntsman's steel was no cheaper than that made by other manufacturers, but its quality matched that of imported steels. The inventor tried to keep his process a secret but it leaked out when Huntsman gave some details to members of the Royal Society. Information was purchased by Walkers, the Rotherham ironmasters, who built their own steel refinery in 1750. The concentration of the cutlery trades in Sheffield gave the refined steel an immediate market, and the secrecy which covered the new process ensured its retention in the district for some years.

Huntsman himself worked with only two workmen and the early firms that adopted his technique also worked on a small scale. It was from these small beginnings that the captains of the nineteenth-century steel industry worked their way to fortune. It was not until the 1840s that the great Sheffield steelworks were built by men like Mark Firth, Samuel Fox, and John Brown.

Copper, Lead, and other Metals

Apart from iron, the main metals for which demand expanded during the Industrial Revolution were copper and brass, the latter being an alloy of copper with zinc. The great expansion of the Birmingham metal trades throughout the eighteenth century, and of machine building at the end of the century produced an unprecedented demand for brass, while copper was in great demand for sheathing

Plate IV.21. Leadworks near Reeth, Swaledale.

Plate IV.22. The end of a flue, 1½ miles long, from leadworks in Allendale, Northumberland.   These were necessary to get rid of the poisonous fumes.

wooden sailing ships. Most of the copper was mined in Cornwall and sent by water to Swansea, where cheap coal was available for smelting. New sources were opened up when extensive deposits were discovered at Ecton (Staffordshire) in 1739 and in Anglesey in 1761.

The exploitation of the Anglesey ores produced one of the most outstanding careers of the Industrial Revolution. Thomas Williams of Llanidan was a country solicitor in Anglesey with no industrial interests until he became employed in litigation over the ownership of the open-cast copper workings. He emerged from the legal struggle as managing partner of the Parys Mine Co. (1778) and extended his activities by setting up smelting and manufacturing works in Swansea, St Helens (Lancashire), and Holywell (Flintshire), when he found it difficult to sell his ore to the established smelting firms, who acted in concert. Williams shortly (1785) obtained control of the Mona Mine Co., the other company working the Anglesey ores. An agreement with the Cornish Metal Company in 1787 made him the virtual monopolist of British copper for five years. Dr J. R. Harris, Williams's biographer, says that "in 1799, when his power was considerably reduced, his various copper concerns had a capital of £800,000; with his other industrial and banking interests the total capitals he controlled may have been little short of a million".

There was no rapid expansion of the lead industry

in the eighteenth or early nineteenth centuries, but there were changes in technique which largely followed those in coal mining. In the Pennines a good deal of the lead was mined close to the coalfields of the north-east and of Yorkshire and Derbyshire, and some proprietors had interests in both materials. Lead-mine workings were generally quite small but in the northern Pennines there were several large concerns operating. The London Lead Company concentrated its interests in the Alston Moor and Teesdale area and over the period 1815-65 employed an average of 865 miners. The Beaumont Blackett Company controlled most of the mining in Allendales and Weardale, Co. Durham. Both companies emerged in the 1690s when lead began to be smelted with coal, and both managed their extensive concerns by employing engineer-agents whose functions paralleled those of the mine viewers in the adjacent coalfields.

The Chemical Industry

Although the British chemical industry can be traced back to the reign of the first Elizabeth, when oil of vitriol (sulphuric acid) began to be manufactured for commercial use, the application of the fruits of laboratory research to industrial problems was still in early adolescence at the end of the period covered by this book. It is necessary to make this initial point

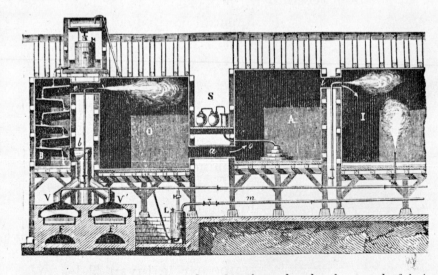

Plate IV.23. The lead-chamber methods of making sulphuric acid. (*Chapman.*)

Fig. 201.—Ancienne disposition des chambres de plomb pour la fabrication de l'acide sulfurique.

because histories of science and technology all too often impress the reader with chapter after chapter of chemical discoveries without giving due acknowledgement to the gap between the laboratory and the workshop, and to the perpetuation of effective traditional processes and continued use of natural products. In the 1780s and 1790s chemistry became a popular hobby among the educated middle class (doctors, clergymen, merchants, and some manufacturers), and at the literary and philosophic societies where experiments were often demonstrated the industrial implications might be discussed. But the calico manufacturer who, for instance, saved time by using sulphuric acid in the bleaching process would still go on making the traditional "iron liquor"—a solution of rusty iron in stale beer—as a mordant, and use cow dung for bringing out the colours after the printing process. Such a mixture of traditional and novel processes within an industry is a striking characteristic of this period of British economic history.

The famous German chemist, von Liebig, wrote in 1851 that "we may judge with great accuracy of the commercial prosperity of a country from the amount

Plate IV.24. Frontispiece from Berthollet's *Elements of the Art of Dyeing*, translated by William Hamilton, London, 1791.

of sulphuric acid it consumes", and the number of times his remark has been quoted in the scientific press indicates the measure of support for his recognition of the central importance of the manufacture of this product. Apart from its direct use in bleaching cotton, linen, and paper, in dissolving dyestuffs, metal refining, tanning, and glass-making, it was the active agent in the manufacture of an increasing variety of inorganic compounds serving several other industries. The key development was therefore the establishment of a cheap process of making the acid, and a study of some of the details illustrates the relative roles of chemical knowledge and business acumen in the emergent chemical industry.

The discovery that sulphuric acid could be made by burning a mixture of sulphur and nitre in an enclosed vessel containing water was made by two Frenchmen in 1740, but the commercial exploitation of this technique was at first confined to laboratories. Dr John Roebuck, whose medical education included

Plate IV.25.   Stove House at Frogmarsh, Gloucestershire.
(*Dr Jennifer Tann.*)

lectures on chemistry, recognised that there would be an economy of scale in production in lead chambers rather than glass jars and, in partnership with Samuel Garbett, a thrusting entrepreneur who had made his way up from being a brass worker, erected a pilot plant of thirty lead chambers, each 8 ft × 6 ft × 4 ft, in Birmingham in 1746. Birmingham was still a land-locked town at this time, so the partners extended their operations by building a new plant of 108 chambers at Prestonpans, near the Firth of Forth, three years later. The new site enabled the essential raw material, sulphur, to be shipped from Sicily without the expense of overland transport and, moreover, bulk purchase would also keep prices low. (The surviving account book of a late eighteenth-century sulphuric acid manufacturer, Thomas Farmer of London, shows that he commonly laid out £800-£1,000 when a supply ship came to port.) In the process of manufacture the problem of heat build-up during the reaction soon determined an upper limit for the size of the lead chamber, so Roebuck devised his chambers so that the reactions finished in a sequence and the handful of workmen were fully occupied. Roebuck and Garbett's plants proved to be the prototype for many others, bringing down the price of oil of vitriol from 2s. per lb. to little more than 2d. per lb. at the close of the century, and reducing the duration of the souring process in bleaching (*i.e.* immersion in sour milk, or lactic acid) from between two and six weeks to twelve to twenty-four hours.

This innovation was a vital contribution to the competitive strength of the British linen and cotton industries, but not to the woollen and silk manufactures. Animal fibres did not respond favourably to immersion in sulphuric acid, and this was an additional reason why cotton gained so much ground at the expense of rival textile materials in the Industrial Revolution. Wool and silk continued to be bleached in sulphur dioxide fumes in ventilated towers erected for the purpose. Hikers in the West of England clothing districts still pause to wonder why the occasional surviving stove house (such as that illustrated here) was placed at such a distance from the mill buildings to which it belonged.

When the Frenchman, C. L. Berthollet, demonstrated the bleaching properties of chlorine in 1785, the commercial implications of the discovery were immediately recognised by several firms in the different textile regions, Gordon Barron & Co. in Aberdeen, James Watt and his father-in-law, James MacGregor of Glasgow, Dr Thomas Henry in Manchester, and

Robert Hall, a Nottingham cotton spinner. But chlorine gas weakened the cloth, did not give a permanent white, and poisoned some of the workmen, and only the most determined pursued their experiments into its use. Robert Hall, a keen student of the works of the Continental chemists, experimented to obviate the use of the poisonous chlorine gas and found that when it was dissolved in a mixture of lime and water the resulting solution had powerful bleaching properties. However, it was left to Charles Tennant of Glasgow to discover the properties of bleaching powder and manufacture it on a considerable scale at his St Rollox chemical works. The high court refused to recognise the validity of Tennant's 1799 patent when Hall's earlier work was proved, but St Rollox nevertheless became the leading chemical works in the century.

The key to Tennant's success was the earlier discovery of the cheap method of manufacturing sulphuric acid, which he improved upon after innumerable experiments. Roebuck and Garbett synthesised their acid by a batch process, *i.e.* a process in which the product was drawn off after a cycle of operations lasting a month, when the process was begun again. Tennant modified Roebuck's method to make it one of continuous production, so that acid was being drawn continuously from the lead chambers. Readers interested in the technical aspects of this development can study the illustration (Plate IV. 23) from a mid-nineteenth century textbook of chemical engineering.

The other major development in the chemical industry was in the manufacture of alkali for soap-making and other industrial uses. Here again the growing needs of the textile industry acted as a major stimulus and, ultimately, the discovery of a Frenchman and the availability of cheap acid provided support for a new development. In the eighteenth century soap was made by boiling natural fats (olive or palm oil, wax or animal fats) with soda alkali obtained from the ashes of certain plants. The growing needs of the soap industry resulted in an intermittent rise in prices, which induced a search for synthetic substitutes to the vegetable alkalis. The most popular line of research was into the decomposition of common salt, and Dr Joseph Black, Dr Roebuck, James Watt, and James Keir wrestled with the problem for several years. The most important outcome was the foundation in 1780 of Keir's alkali works at Tipton, in the Black Country, an inland location that would have insulated him from fluctuations in the price of imported vegetable alkali.

The reason for the flagging of these experiments was not so much lack of scientific ability as the competition of imported natural alkali when the country was at peace and the high excise duty on salt. The cheap method of manufacture, which consisted in the addition of sulphuric acid to common salt to make Glauber's salt (sodium sulphate), followed by the addition of this compound to chalk to produce the required sodium carbonate, was made by Nicholas Leblanc in 1791, but it was not adopted in Britain for another quarter of a century. The innovating entrepreneurs were Tennants of Glasgow, Doubleday & Easterby of Tyneside, and James Muspratt of Liverpool, all engaged in the making of sulphuric acid. The last two had access to cheap supplies of salt and Muspratt had the additional local advantage of the Merseyside soap industry, which had been growing rapidly under the stimulus of Lancashire cotton. Muspratt was not an inventor, but an entrepreneur who recognised the needs of the Merseyside soapboilers and established the manufacture on an unprecedented scale, justified only by the size of the local market. The boldness of his enterprise was appropriately rewarded, and Muspratt shortly succeeded Tennant as the leading manufacturer of heavy chemicals in the kingdom.

Engineering

The engineering industry, like the chemical industry, was created by the growth of other industries, whose growing demand for steam engines and machinery of all kinds has already been noticed. Even before the industrial revolution, engineers with a considerable capital were not unknown, particularly in London. The large London millwright employed smiths of various sorts, founders for his brass work, plumbers for his lead work, and a class of shoemakers for making leather pipes. About 1750 it was estimated that he needed at least £500 to set up in business. Apart from London the greatest concentration of these men would be in the lead-mining districts of the Pennines and Cornwall. Thomas Newcomen, of Dartmouth, might be counted the first of this race of engineers, though for most of his life he was in business as a merchant ironmonger.

There are two overlapping phases in the development of engineering. The earlier phase was dominated by the building of improved power units, particularly water-wheels and steam engines. All the great engineering names of the second half of the eighteenth century had some interest in this development; even those usually remembered as civil engineers, like Smeaton, Brindley, Rennie, and Telford, had a prior interest in water power. The engineers in Manchester in the early 1790s were at first primarily concerned with the design and building of power units, for the building of textile machinery was only just becoming a specialised occupation; in London the growing colony of engineers on the South Bank thrived on the power needs of breweries and paper mills, as well as dozens of other demands of the metropolis.

Historians used to think that the engineering scene at this period was dominated by the patentees of the superior separate-condenser steam engine, Boulton and Watt, of Birmingham. Watt's patent was extended by Parliament for a second term, so that he and his partner held the monopoly from 1776 to 1800. The monopoly was less important than a first impres-

sion suggests because water power was cheap and sites common in the north of England, and the Newcomen engine's extravagance with fuel was of little consequence where coal was available in abundance, as it was on the flanks of the Pennines where the new textile industry was growing so rapidly. Boulton and Watt's engines, though efficient, were expensive and the distance that separated the firm from most of its potential customers on the coalfields and in the textile districts often gave the decisive advantage to the local firms of engineers. Before the Boulton and Watt patent had expired a number of steam engine manufacturers had come into being, waiting for the day when their improved "common" engines could be converted to Watt's design.

Boulton and Watt's reputation, and their need for agents in different parts of the country, enabled the firm to recruit some of the most able mechanics living at that time. The agents had to understand

Plate IV.26.   Part of the machinery at Boston Spa Flint Mill, Lincs.   Note the mingling, characteristic of the earlier part of our period, of iron and wood.

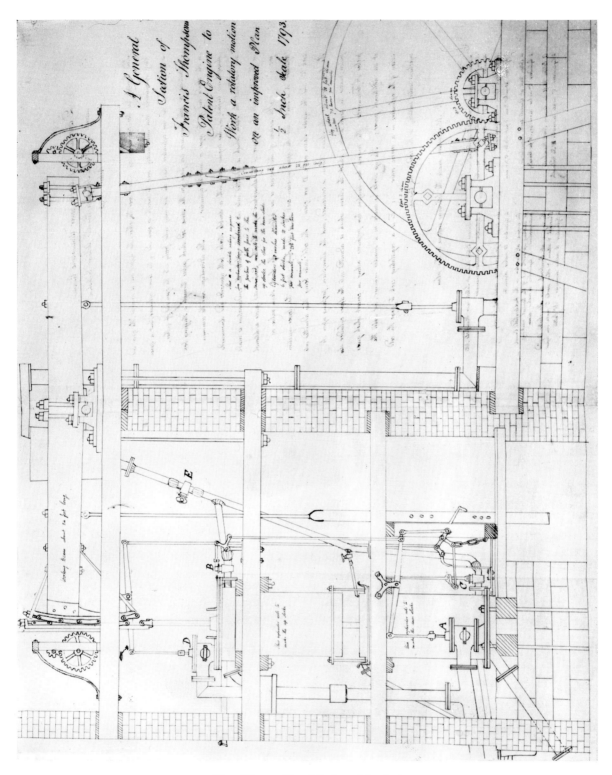

Plate IV.27. (*Royal Society of London.*)

Plate IV.28. A Newcomen engine. Ison's were makers of holloware. (*Royal Society of London.*)

and work to draughtsmen's drawings and standards of precision that were rare at this time. Some of the agents were already in business on their own account and others shortly became independent, so

that Boulton and Watt's standards became adopted in different parts of the country. An interesting illustration of the exactitude needed is the mistake of George Lowe of Nottingham, a millwright whose

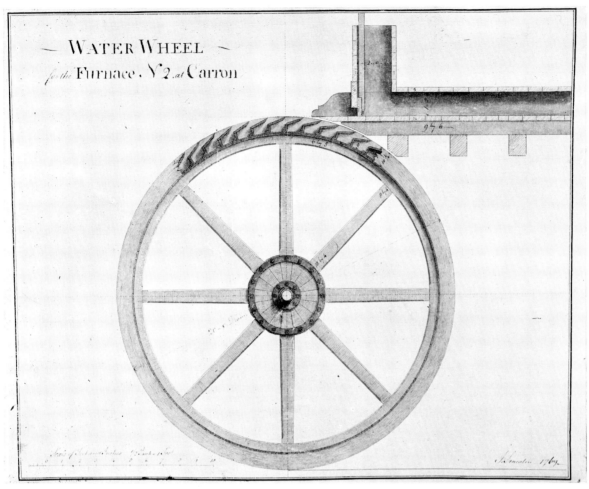

Plate IV.29. John Smeaton's design for a water-wheel at Carron Ironworks, Falkirk, 1769. (*Royal Society of London.*)

early connection with Arkwright made him "in demand in every part of the kingdom where a cotton factory had to be built". The first Boulton and Watt engine that he erected, which was for a cotton mill at Nottingham in 1785, did not work because Lowe used a framework of timber that was too green and consequently warped. However, the mistake was rectified and in due course Lowe erected most of the Boulton and Watt engines in the East Midlands cotton and worsted spinning industry, as well as some of the spinning machinery.

The entrepreneurs of the new engineering industry were drawn from three principal sources. Iron founders, particularly in Lancashire and the Midlands, extended their activity from the casting of iron components to the building of machines, particularly steam engines. The Birmingham directory of 1777 claimed that the chief advantage to the town of its cast iron foundries "had been in supplying the manufacturers of this place with many of the engines, tools, &c., they require...". The best known firm in Lancashire was Sherratt & Bateman, of Manchester, who probably erected more steam engines for the north-west than Boulton & Watt. In the East Midlands the pioneer firm was Ebenezer Smith & Co., of Chesterfield (founded 1778), who were able to supply pumping engines for the Yorkshire, Nottinghamshire, and Derbyshire coalfield, as well as machine parts for the Midlands and West Riding textile industries.

Secondly, the millwrights: the enormous growth in demand for mechanical power during the industrial revolution gave these craftsmen unprecedented opportunities for developing their small businesses. From the design and erection of water-wheels they turned to the building of steam engines and textile

Plates IV.30 and 31. The Elsecar engine, Yorkshire, and, *below*, its piston.

machinery. Thomas C. Hewes, who came to Manchester in the 1790s as a millwright, employed 140 to 150 men in 1825, a labour force that he had recruited from cabinet-makers and clock-makers.

A third source of engineers was the body of skilled craftsmen who worked at the textile mills of the Midlands and north of England. In the pioneer days of the mechanised spinning industry the mill owners had to build their own machinery by recruiting a team of smiths, carpenters, clock-makers, and other workmen, and a few firms (like, for instance, Strutts of Derby) continued to build their own machinery until after 1825. But textile machine building was becoming a specialised occupation in the 1790s. An interesting example of this development is provided by Matthew Murray, who after seven years working as plant engineer and supervisor of machine building with John Marshall, the pioneer of flax spinning in Leeds, opened his own business in the town in 1795.

Thomas Hewes's firm at Manchester was by no means the largest built up in this period. In Manchester the largest firm, Peel & Williams, iron-founders and engineers, "may well have been employing several hundred men" by 1820. The largest concentration of engineering workshops in the country was on the South Bank of the Thames, between Waterloo and Blackfriars bridges, where the biggest firms employed something like 200 men each at their works. The district contained a large colony of Scots, including some famous names like John Rennie and David Napier, who in 1808 founded the famous engineering firm that still bears his name.

The pioneers were necessarily versatile men, constantly ready to adapt themselves and take the initiative in the rapid development of technology. They were ready to apply their skills to whatever new machinery the advance of industry suggested. In the 1830s and 1840s some of them began to

Plate IV.32.   An eighteenth-century engineering shop, Wortley Forge.   Note the two tilt-hammers.

turn to the manufacture of railway locomotives, cranes, presses, and steam ships. In the railway age the ranks of the engineers were swelled by new firms of locomotive and carriage builders like Robert Stephenson & Co. of Darlington (1823) and Stephenson & Tayleur (1831) of the Vulcan Foundry, near Warrington, Lancashire.

Though the industry served the needs of mechanised industries, the techniques of the pioneers were primitive, and the power units and machinery it built were for long constructed by traditional hand tools to individual orders. At the beginning of the nineteenth century the file was still the principal and final tool of precision in the heavy metal trades. The backwardness of technique in the industry can be illustrated from the experience of Fairbairn & Lillie, a famous firm of Manchester engineers. When the firm received their first major order for millwork in 1818, they had only one machine in their possession, a lathe which they had just built themselves and which was operated by "a muscular Irishman".

Plate IV.34.   Chain-making at Cradley Heath, Staffs.

Plate IV.33.   Use of pole lathes at Birmingham Brass Works, about 1830.

The lathe was considered to be of "considerable dimensions" as it was capable of turning wooden shafts of from three to six inches diameter. Nevertheless, Fairbairns was soon designing and building water power units for the biggest cotton mills in the country. But soon afterwards, as Fairbairn himself related, the techniques of engineering began to change very rapidly. In the second phase of development, we see the beginnings of the adoption of power-operated precision machine tools.

It was appropriate that the first advances should be made in Birmingham. By 1770 Matthew Boulton was using two of his water-wheels to power some of his lathes at Soho, and also to give power to polishing and grinding machines. The idea was so popular by 1783 that a gun manufacturer called Charles Twigg advertised steam power to let for turning lathes and boring guns at his factory in Snow Hill, Birmingham.

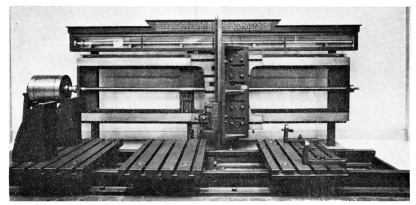

Plate IV.35. Slide rest in Birmingham Science Museum.

Boulton and Watt's early business associate, John Wilkinson, invented and built a boring mill (1775), in effect a giant lathe for boring cannon and (later) the cylinders of steam engines. Despite this early progress the use of power was slow to catch on, even in Birmingham. In 1830, the Eagle Foundry, one of the largest in Birmingham, still did all its drilling by hand. Martineau & Smith, perhaps the largest firm of brass founders in the town, were still using pole lathes at this time, as the engraving shows.

The application of power to tools was, however, only one side of the picture. The more significant innovation was the achievement of *accuracy* in the manufacture of machine parts. The vital first step in this direction was made by building lathes, and later other machines, in metal instead of wood, which greatly increased their rigidity and hence accuracy.

The second essential step was the substitution of a mechanically directed cutting tool for the vagaries of the human hand and eye. This was achieved by Henry Maudslay's introduction of the slide rest to the lathe. The rest is made to travel along the bed of the lathe by the slow rotations of the long screw under the bed. In the evolution of this machine we can recognise the achievement of accuracy in the motions of a tool cutting either in a straight line or a circle. Maudslay made the lathe an instrument of precision. A former workman of Joseph Bramah's who had in turn worked with Boulton and Watt, he used a micrometer of his own making which was accurate to 0.001 inch, and in his factory in Lambeth he instilled his insistence on accuracy into a whole generation of workmen, many of whom came to own works of their own. Among the more famous of his workmen were Richard Roberts, of Manchester, who

Plate IV.36. Steam hammer in Birmingham Science Museum.

perfected the self-acting mule in 1825, James Nasmyth, who is remembered as the inventor of the steam hammer (1839), and Joseph Whitworth, who established standardised screw threads which are still used in the engineering industry.

Maudslay was also connected with an early and successful attempt at mass-production. Sir Samuel Bentham was promoted Director of Naval Dockyards in Britain because of his original ideas on the introduction of mechanisation. He employed Maudslay to build a set of forty-four machines to mass-produce standardised blocks for the Royal Navy's sailing ships. With this machinery, which took six years to build, ten unskilled men were able to do the work of 110 skilled ones. It was not long before Manchester engineering firms were mass-producing textile machinery.

Before the middle of the nineteenth century the British engineering industry had attained the ultimate achievement in mechanical engineering, the mass-production of standardised machine tools for engineers. The responsibility for this important development lies with a number of firms, among which the most prominent were probably Nasmyth and Whitworth. Nasmyth established his own firm in Manchester in 1834 and before long was employing 300 men at the Bridgwater Foundry (1837). He made lathes, planing machines, drilling, boring, and slotting machines, steam engines and, after 1839, steam hammers and railway locomotives, all of which are illustrated in their printed catalogues. The works were run on assembly line principles, so that castings coming out of the foundry went directly to the machinists, then to the fitters and filers, and finally to the erectors. The eighteenth-century craftsman's manual versatility began to disappear; his sons used more and more standardised machine tools, and took one part only in the assembly of the new machinery—machinery whose purpose was to produce in great quantity an increasing variety of identical products.

V

Agriculture and the Supply of Food

In his famous book, *English Farming Past and Present*, Lord Ernle wrote that the changes in British agriculture in the eighteenth century which we call the Agricultural Revolution were, broadly speaking, identified with four great pioneers: Jethro Tull, Lord Townshend, Bakewell of Dishley, and Coke of Norfolk. Lord Ernle's book was itself a pioneer work. It was of such high quality that it was immediately regarded, and still remains, a classic of agricultural history, and no student can afford to ignore it. Work of later students, however, especially in the last twenty years, has had the effect of changing the emphasis of Lord Ernle's brilliant account in a number of ways, and perhaps particularly in the degree of importance which is now attached to the work of the four famous pioneers. It is now seen that their contribution must be examined in the light of other factors of long standing and that to "identify" them with the changes of the eighteenth century is both to do them too great an honour and also to do less than justice to predecessors and contemporaries whose contributions were hardly less important. The eighteenth-century pioneer-improvers were standing on the shoulders of other men whose work can be traced back to a much earlier period. It is also related to underlying changes in the social structure of the English farming community dating from the later middle ages when the class of yeoman farmers rose on the ruins of the manorial system and laid the foundations of commercial agriculture. It would be wise, therefore, to forget the great figures of the eighteenth century for the present and sketch in the background on which they played their part—a relatively modest part —in the transformation of English farming that took place in the century of revolution, 1750-1850.

England is one of the best farming countries in the world. The climate is mild enough to enable the farmer to continue the operations of farming through the greater part of the year and the variety and fertility of the soil have permitted the combination of arable and animal husbandry—mixed farming—in almost all parts of the country for many centuries. The chief element in the farmer's capital is the fertility of the soil, and in this respect England was well favoured, especially in regard to sheep pasture. The mild damp climate gave England a great advantage in pasture farming, and wool was exported to the continent from a very early period. A native cloth industry existed in Roman times and its development in the fifteenth century in the form of the "putting-out" system represents the first stage of industrialisation in England.

The foundations of English leadership in farming— especially in wool—were laid by Nature before the earliest settlers arrived: and our Germanic ancestors, already highly skilled as farmers according to the standards of the time, quickly discovered and developed the natural advantage of soil and climate which they had not enjoyed in the harsher lands they had left behind. They built up thriving communities of farmers, and villages whose names, ending in -ham, or -ton, or -by, or -thorpe, reveal the ancestry of their earliest founders. The essential tool which they used was, of course, the plough. Large and clumsy as it appears in our picture, it was nevertheless the most advanced instrument of cultivation in existence at that time. In addition to the two wheels on which the forward end of the plough rested, it possessed three essential components: the coulter which cut a slit in the soil; the share which widened it; and the mouldboard which pushed the

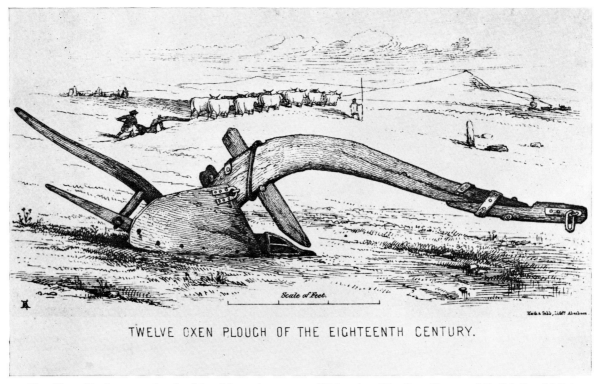

TWELVE OXEN PLOUGH OF THE EIGHTEENTH CENTURY.

Plate V.1. Twelve-oxen plough of the eighteenth century. (*University of Reading, Museum of English Rural Life.*)

soil to one side thus leaving a furrow about four or five inches deep and the same width as the plough share. The effect of the fixed mouldboard was to throw the furrow towards the ridge, which left the land in "ridge and furrow" formation and enabled the surface water to drain away down the furrow. Thus heavy wet soils were brought into cultivation and it became possible to support a relatively dense population on the clay soils—the Keuper marls and boulder clays, as the geologist calls them—of the Midlands.

This form of ploughing had another important effect: it left the soil in strips consisting of furrows laid on either side of the first furrow ploughed by the farmer. The length would be about 220 yards—a "furrow-long" or furlong, and the width would vary from ten to twenty yards representing an area that the oxen would plough in a day. It was called an "acre" but was more usually half an acre according to our measurements. In light soil the oxen would do more in a day than in heavy soil, but it was still regarded as an acre. The strips would be ploughed all in one direction for the purpose of draining the surface water, and would change direction from time to time according to the lie of the land; thus

groups of strips would lie together in different directions and each group would itself be called a furlong and would be given a name such as Hardacre or Skitterpool Furlong.

Each farmer would usually have one or more strips in different parts of each furlong so that the good and bad land should be equally distributed; and the strips in each furlong would be sown with the same crop—wheat or rye or beans as a winter crop, oats or barley or peas as a spring crop. The furlongs in wheat would be grouped together and fenced off with hurdles and would be regarded as the winter wheat field; similarly a spring corn field would be fenced off and a third area over which the village animals would be allowed to graze would be left fallow to recover fertility and to enable the farmer to prepare it for the next crop. Primitive as their arrangements appear to us to-day, they were the most advanced form of agriculture known at that time and are basically the same as are employed on the open fields of Laxton, Nottinghamshire, to this day.

By these methods, the early English settlers were able to produce corn for bread and beer for a rising population and also seed for next year's crop. But

Plate V.2.   Lower Ditchford, Gloucestershire, showing ridge and furrow, and also modern boundaries superimposed on those of the deserted medieval village (see p. 98).   Foundations of houses can clearly be seen.   (*Dr J. K. St Joseph; Crown Copyright.*)

Plate V.3. Ploughing in the open fields at Laxton in 1936. *From J. D. Chambers,* Laxton—A Guide. [*M.A.F.F.
(Publications); Crown Copyright.*]

Plate V.4. An open field system in use to-day. Braunton Great Field, North Devon. (*University of Reading,
Museum of English Rural Life.*)

96

there was another side to their economy which was of the greatest importance but which is often over-looked. They also had to provide food—"fodder"—for their animals during the winter. They had, of course, no "artificials" such as cow cake, and turnips (roots) and clover, sainfoin, or vetch (legumes) were unknown; they had only the grass of the meadow which they cut with the scythe and made into hay. The hay crop was absolutely crucial to the farmer's survival. If it failed, or if the winter was long and hard, the animals might starve. Sometimes they were so weak by the time spring came that they had to be carried out to the pastures on hurdles to recuper-ate. This was a common practice in Scotland and was known as "the liftings".

This was the age of subsistence agriculture when the farmer's object was to provide food and shelter and sufficient surplus over immediate needs to buy necessities such as salt and iron and to pay the dues exacted by the lords. The only way to increase supplies of bread was to take in more land, assarts from the waste, or to convert pasture into arable, and if population continued to grow there was a real danger of famine. This situation arose on the eve of the Black Death in 1348-9 and it may be that the tendency to convert the pasture into arable to increase the bread supply was a contributory factor since it had the effect of decreasing the meat component in the diet of the peasantry. It also decreased manure supply which reacted adversely on the output of the arable land. The agricultural population were involved in a vicious circle of declining subsistence, and failing a revolutionary improvement in agricultural production, famine was inevitable. The circle was cut by the Black Death when at least one third of the population died, but the situation never arose again; there was now an abundance of land and a shortage of men to till it, and farmers could make their own bargains with their landlords. They had found the road which led to improved farming and eventually to the agricultural revolution which removed the danger of famine wherever it was adopted.

There are certain landmarks along this road which we must briefly examine. The first is the change in the social structure of the village which was now no longer based on servile tenure of villeins paying dues in money and weekly labour on the lord's farm (the demesne) but on a free contract of tenants (copy-holders) paying money rents in return for use of the land and the buildings on it. Arising out of this contract between landlord and tenant an

Plate V.5. Broadcasting at Laxton, 1935. (*From C. S. & C. S. Orwin,* The Open Fields, *Oxford University Press, 1967; reproduced by courtesy of Mrs Orwin and The Clarendon Press, Oxford.*)

important practice grew up by which the landlord, in return for the rent, assumed responsibility for fixed capital in the form of farmhouse and buildings and eventually drainage, while the tenant was responsible for stocking and running the farm—the circulating capital. It was a form of partnership between landlord and tenant in which both had an interest in getting the best out of the capital which Nature itself had put into the land in the form of fertility. In the hands of intelligent landlords and enterprising tenants, the arrangement could lead to progressive farming and must be counted as one of the important factors in achieving a position of leadership for English farming in later years.

The basis of this landlord-tenant system began to take shape in the fourteenth and fifteenth centuries when the balance between manpower and capital in the form of land was all in favour of the farmer. The amount of land remained constant but the man-power to till it had been reduced by one third or more as a result of the Great Pestilence; the landlords, therefore, had to be satisfied with low rents; and since wages were relatively high, they could not afford to work the demesne with hired labour and preferred instead to let it out to capitalist farmers or graziers who were looking for profits. This is the point at which the yeoman farmer comes into the picture of the changing English countryside. Many yeoman farmers owned the land they occupied; they were the owner-occupiers we shall meet again in this story; but an increasing number were tenants who were often at an advantage over the owner-occupier since rents lagged behind prices and when prices fell to unprofitable levels they could sometimes persuade their landlords to make reductions or forgo the rent altogether.

The yeoman farmers were a pushful, thriving class. The more successful ones became rich and bought up their neighbours; they sometimes laid field to field and enclosed them with a hedge. The more commercially-minded of the landlords did the same, and since wool prices were higher than either meat or corn prices, there was a great increase in sheep farming, and whole villages disappeared or dwindled almost to nothing in some areas as arable was turned into sheep runs and village fields that had formerly supported—on a near starvation level— large communities, were now peopled by a few shepherds and their dogs. This was the first phase of commercial farming for profit and it was marked by a ruthlessness that was fortunately never equalled again in the history of agricultural development in England. But it showed the way that English farming was to follow, the way of adjusting farming practice to the demands of the market. And the demands of the market were due for another important change.

This brings us to the next milestone on the road to modern farming. The fever of enclosure for sheep farming began to wane when prices fell as a result of the collapse of the foreign market for English cloth in 1551, and the great boom in wool production was virtually over. But as the trend of wool prices moved downwards, that of food prices, especially corn, slowly moved upwards. What lies behind this upward movement of food prices in the century 1550-1650 is not altogether clear; it has been attributed to the influx of

Plates V.6 and 7. V.6, A draining spade from Austwick, Yorks, West Riding. Much shorter than the Fenland type. Compare with the also very short turf-stripping spade in V.7.

silver from Spanish America; but why should this rise be so markedly in favour of food prices, especially corn? The answer seems to be that population was on the rise again and that prices were moving in response to demand. The market was exercising its influence and the structure of English farming consisting of rent-paying tenants and owner-occupiers permitted it to respond by increasing production to take advantage of the rising prices.

What were the methods by which the English farmer of the sixteenth and seventeenth centuries could raise production? The first was by increasing the area under arable cultivation. This could be done by ploughing up some of the land that had been allowed to go down to rough sheep pasture during the wool boom or by taking in more virgin

Plate V.9. (See over.)

Plate V.8. (a) The Old Bedford River and
(b) Winter flooding in the Fens. (*Charles Moseley.*)

land from the forests and marshes. All these methods were adopted: "assarting" in the form of enclosures on the margins of the village, and the draining of drowned land in Lincolnshire and the Fens made large contributions to the area under cultivation. Much of the draining was done by Dutch engineers, especially Sir Cornelius Vermuyden who recovered thousands of acres of drowned lands in the first half of the seventeenth century in Hatfield Chase at the junction of Nottinghamshire, Lincolnshire, and Yorkshire; and the Earl of Bedford followed with the Great Bedford Level reclamation, the dykes and embankments of which can be seen for miles to this day in the area between Wisbech and Crowland.

Except for the Isle of Axholme, which was—and is still—laid out in intermixed strips (but not subject to rights of common) this new land consisted of enclosed fields; and the practice of enclosure was advancing elsewhere too. Farmers found that by allowing old arable to go down to grass and ploughing up land that had been pastured for many

Plates V.9 and 10.   Draining the fens.   When steam engines became efficient they rapidly replaced the old
post windmills for drainage.   These two photographs are of the flywheel and beam of Stretham Old Engine,
Isle of Ely, dating from 1830.

years, they could increase the yield of corn on the new arable, and if they could select the seed with which the new pastures were sown they could also improve the yield of grass and so increase the hay supply. By these means they were enabled to keep a larger head of cattle and so increase the manure supply. The farmer had discovered the principle of "increasing returns", *i.e.* for every increment of capital invested in the land by these "improvements", he obtained a corresponding margin of profit. One seventeenth-century farmer, Robert Loder, has told us how it was done. He was a farmer on the north side of the Berkshire Downs, and the Notebooks which he left behind have been edited by Mr Fussell, who writes about him as follows:

> Before all things he was a business man.... He farmed his land because he wished to make a living and he wanted that living to be as substantial as possible.

That is the keynote of this race of yeoman farmers who were beginning to lay the foundations of modern farming and whose solid farmhouses were becoming a familiar feature of the English countryside. One of the interesting things about the account he gives is that his arable land lay in strips in the open fields but in spite of this he left some of them down to grass and arranged the rotations to suit himself. This shows that farmers in the open fields were not entirely bound by the so-called three field system with its rigid rotation of winter wheat, spring barley or oats, and bare fallow. They were even in the habit of reserving parts of the fallow field from common grazing in order to grow peas or vetches, probably in temporary enclosures protected by means of hurdles. He also seems to have experimented with water meadows, a method of increasing the "bite" of grass that was spreading in many parts of England; and besides using the dung of the farmyard and dovecote, he bought "black ashes" from the neighbouring village of Chilton. The result is seen in the fact that whereas a medieval farmer usually harvested only from four to six times the amount of seed he sowed, Robert Loder's average was more than eleven times the seed; and similarly, the yield per acre was more than twice the medieval yield.

If this was possible in an open field village of Berkshire, we may suppose that still better results were being achieved by farmers on enclosed farms that were spreading especially among the dairy farms of the West and South and along the river valleys of the Midlands. We also know that in the highly cultivated region around London, a market-garden industry was springing up to supply the population with fresh vegetables, and the famous Smithfield Market was developing for the supply of fresh meat which was coming down "on the hoof" along the drove roads from all directions and sometimes from great distances. London had, by this time, a population of 150,000 and by 1700 it had grown to at least half a million, *i.e.* almost one in ten of the population was a Londoner. It was drawing its supplies from many sources, both far and near; cereals came in by sea from coastal ports and also along the river; malt and poultry (on foot) came in from Norfolk; cattle from Lincolnshire and as far north as Scotland and as far west as Wales. A tendency towards specialisation of regions was growing up and wherever the pull of urban markets was felt, there were farmers who were alive to opportunities for improving their methods in order to raise output.

There was no lack of experts--real and self-styled—who were prepared to offer advice. Lord Ernle lists nearly sixty publications on agriculture and stock-rearing between 1600 and 1700. Some of them described the methods they had seen employed in Flanders and Holland during the years of self-imposed exile during the Civil War. They drew attention especially to the use of clover and turnips, to the practice of sowing root crops in rows to facilitate hoeing, and to the importance of a rotation of crops, though their knowledge of agricultural chemistry did not enable them to give the correct reasons for it. Turnips had been known as a garden crop in England from Elizabeth's time and they were being sown in rows as a field crop as part of a rotation in Suffolk from the middle of the seventeenth century; the virtues of clover were also well known and the seed could be bought in a London shop in the 1650s; and William Marshall, writing in 1787, said that the farms of north-east Norfolk "have been kept invariably for at least a century under the following course of cultivation: wheat, barley, turnips, barley, clover, rye grass". The use of "alternate husbandry", *i.e.* corn followed by a ley of clover or sainfoin, or other legume crop, has been traced back on the estates of the Walpoles from 1673 and on those of the Coke family from the 1720s.

It will be noticed that all these examples come from the region of light soils of Norfolk which were unsuitable for continuous cropping for corn under the open field system and were particularly responsive to alternate husbandry of corn and ley with periodical crops of turnips which enabled the farmer to clean the soil by hoeing between the rows, and to feed the soil by heavy manuring. Under soil conditions of this kind—and there were many areas in England besides Norfolk where they prevailed—we may say that the foundations of the new farming had already been laid. The Agricultural Revolution was fully launched by the end of the seventeenth century.

We may now turn to the four famous "improvers" whose work has traditionally been identified with the Agricultural Revolution: Tull, Townshend, Bakewell, and Coke. What importance should we assign to them in view of the new chronology of agricultural change? Jethro Tull, the advocate of the use of the drill for sowing corn and turnips and, in fact, all other farm crops, and of the horse hoe for pulverising the soil and destroying the weeds between the drills, was a populariser rather than an inventor, but the fertility and persistence that he showed in practising his ideas in the face of discouragement and ridicule stimulated an atmosphere of enquiry and experiment among more intelligent farmers.

In some respects he was wildly wrong: he thought that plant food consisted of particles of soil and concluded, logically, from this, that manure was unnecessary: deep ploughing and constant stirring of the soil were his prescription for good husbandry; but by asking these fundamental questions he was performing an important service although his answers were wrong.

In regard to Lord Townshend, little can be said except that he was an ardent exponent of practices that had long been current among leading improvers, and through his social position and political connections gave the ideas of the new farming the prestige of a great man.

Robert Bakewell of Dishley is a more important figure, though perhaps not the giant that he appears in the pages of Lord Ernle. His fame rested upon his work as a specialist pedigree breeder of livestock. He developed the business of letting out bulls and rams for hire at a high fee which made him widely known among the more enterprising farmers and brought him to the notice of Arthur Young. This in itself was enough to raise him to the stature of a national figure,

Plate V.11. Leicestershire ram (Bakewell's "Two pounder", oils, by J. Digby-Curtis, 1790). (*University of Reading, Museum of English Rural Life.*)

Plate V.12. Field Marshal V, bred and owned by King George V. Winner at the Shire Horse Society Show, 1920.

as the writings of Arthur Young were likely to be a subject of discussion wherever farmers met on their business or social occasions; but Robert Bakewell had predecessors and contemporaries whose contributions to the science of stock breeding were no less, and in some respects more successful, than his own. The area around Bakewell's farm at Dishley, according to William Marshall, had "for many years abounded with intelligent and spirited breeders". And his famous herd of longhorns was probably surpassed by that of one of his contemporaries who was equally skilful but less well known.

It should be remembered, too, that the pre-eminence of Leicestershire as a breeding county already had a long history. Defoe had noticed, early in the eighteenth century, that the Leicestershire graziers "are so rich, that they grow gentlemen . . . the sheep bred in the county of Lincolnshire which joins it, are, without comparison, the largest, and bear not only the greatest weight of flesh on the bone, but also the greatest fleeces of wool on their backs of any sheep in England". But in Defoe's day they fattened slowly, owing to the limited supply

of roots and legumes which were still scarcely known among the rank-and-file farmers; but as knowledge of these forms of fodder spread it became possible to keep larger numbers of breeding livestock through the winter and select from these the best specimens from which to breed. The revolution in livestock breeding—the New Leicester sheep, New Longhorns, the modern shire horse—with which Bakewell is associated was itself made possible by the new farming which, as we have seen, has origins going back to the previous century and beyond; and the work of John Ellman of Glynde, Sussex, and the Colling brothers who farmed near Darlington, carried the work of Bakewell and his contemporaries to a level which made Britain the recognised stock breeder for improving farmers throughout the world.

The reputation of Thomas Coke of Holkham should also be seen in the context of the farming history of the region with which his name is so intimately associated. He was an improver on a large scale and of great influence, but he was not in any sense an innovator of new farming practices. The enlightened husbandry methods with which he is

Plates V.13 and 14. Two hand-operated seed drills, ultimately derivative from Tull's ideas, in the collection of the Durham County Museum Service, Bowes Museum, Barnard Castle.

justly credited: long leases, large farms, the Norfolk rotation, the large-scale use of marl, were all more or less standard practice among the best farmers of Norfolk. Like Townshend, he gave them publicity and prestige, and his famous sheep shearings no doubt accelerated the progress of innovation and gave it, as we should say to-day, a status symbol in the eyes of farmers who might otherwise have been slow to move; but he introduced nothing new.

Farming Tools

Whatever the scale on which the innovators worked, they exercised an influence upon two related aspects of agricultural history which have still to be considered: on the evolution of farming tools and on the advance of enclosure. In regard to the former, progress at first sight appears to be surprisingly slow. There were no epoch-making inventions as in the manufacture of cotton and the production of

THRESHING.

Plate V.15. Illustration from *Sketches of Rural Affairs*, Vol. 4, 1845-7. (*University of Reading, Museum of English Rural Life.*)

Plate V.16.   A flail recently used in Austwick, Yorkshire.

iron; there were numerous improvements, but apart from Tull's drill and horsehoe, no genuine breaks with the past; and even in the case of these two much-publicised innovations, the effects were minimised by the reluctance of farmers to adopt them. The drill was too complicated for most village craftsmen to produce and not sturdy enough to stand the buffetings of heavy soil and was easily damaged by careless labourers. Most farmers still preferred to sow broadcast or to dibble their corn with the aid of children who dropped the seeds in the holes made by the labourers with a three pronged dibbler. Labour was cheap and tended to become cheaper after the Napoleonic Wars, and neither farmers nor labourers were anxious to see it displaced by expensive machinery, and the drill did not finally supersede these traditional methods of sowing until the second half of the nineteenth century. Similarly, the threshing machine had a long and chequered history. Tull himself is said to have made a model of one, much to the disgust of the local labourers; and the machine invented by the Lowland farmer, Andrew Meikle, in 1786 made slow progress in England, especially after 1815. It was based on the principle of the revolving drum, which separated the

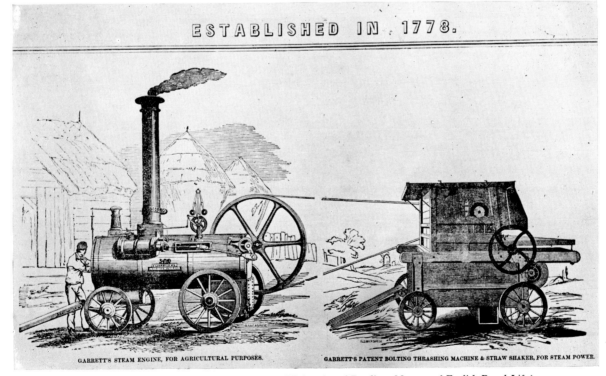

ESTABLISHED IN 1778.

GARRETT'S STEAM ENGINE, FOR AGRICULTURAL PURPOSES.

GARRETT'S PATENT BOLTING THRASHING MACHINE & STRAW SHAKER, FOR STEAM POWER.

Plate V.17.   An early threshing machine.   (*University of Reading, Museum of English Rural Life.*)

grain from the ears and could be driven by horse or steam power. It proved popular and successful in the Lowlands where labour was comparatively scarce, and it spread slowly into the north of England, but owing to the over-population of many villages south of the Trent, its progress was held up, especially after the disastrous revolt of the labourers in 1830, which was largely occasioned by the fear that their traditional winter labour on the threshing floor would be taken over by the machine. It was not

M'Cormick's American Reaping Machine.

THE McCORMICK REAPER OF 1847, ON WHICH SEATS WERE PLACED FOR THE DRIVER AND THE RAKER

Plates V.18 and 19. (*University of Reading, Museum of Rural Life.*)

until the 1850s that the mobile steam thresher moving from farm to farm took the place of the man with the flail on the threshing floor.

This was rapid progress, however, compared with the advance of mechanisation of reaping. Crops continued to be reaped by hand throughout the whole of our period: that is they were cut by scythes and sickles, bound by straw bands and reared up together into stooks. One scytheman and four binders (taking it in turn to work the scythe) and stookers could harvest two acres per day. Carrying and stacking followed and then came the long hours

of threshing, winnowing, sorting, and sacking during the winter months. When it is remembered that both production and productivity were advancing as a result of enclosure and improved methods of husbandry, and that no less than six million acres were under the plough by the end of the eighteenth century, it will be readily realised that the new agriculture called for a larger not a smaller labour force, as is sometimes supposed. The reasons for this slow progress are not in doubt. The technical problems of reapers had been solved by the Northumberland millwright, John Common, in 1812. His

Plate V.20.

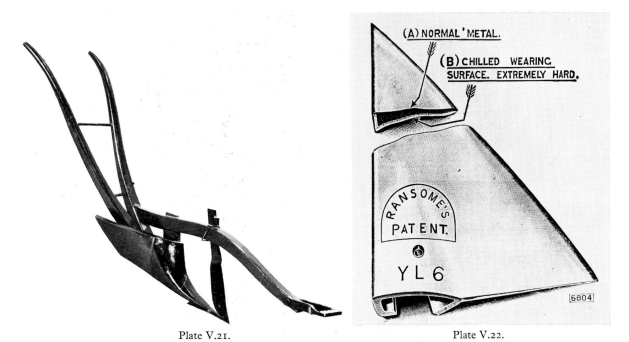

Plate V.21.

Plate V.22.

Plates V.20-22. Ploughs. Plate V.20 is self-explanatory; Plate V.21 is an eighteenth-century Rotherham plough; Plate V.22 shows the Ransome share. (*University of Reading, Museum of English Rural Life.*)

Plate V.23. An extant Kentish turn-wrest plough. (*University of Reading, Museum of English Rural Life.*)

machine was taken up enthusiastically, not in Britain but in America where labour was scarce; and after many years of successful operation on the prairie, it returned to England and re-appeared in the Great Exhibition of 1851 as the famous McCormick reaper.

It will be seen that the Agricultural Revolution had been accomplished without a technological revolution. That does not mean that technical progress was at a standstill, but its importance was marginal to the changes in husbandry practices and the opportunities opened by enclosure. Apart from the threshing machine, the impact of which was slow in making its effect, the most important technical change was the improvements in the plough. The Rotherham plough based on Dutch designs, and patented in 1730, was light and efficient compared with its predecessors. According to an enthusiastic account written in 1766, it could do twice as much work as any common plough and "with only one man and two horses, will perform, even in stiff land, as much as two men and six horses can do in a moderately light soil". It had a curved mould board of iron which put it in a new class compared with the almost entirely wooden ploughs that generally prevailed; and in 1784 the improvement of the curved mould board was taken a step further by James Small who evolved the type of mould board which is in use to-day. In the same year Robert Ransome founded

Plate V.24. Regional variations persisted till late. This is a wooden plough of the nineteenth century in the Bowes Museum, Barnard Castle.

108

Plate V.25. A very unusual pair of "clog" wheels built in Sedbergh in the mid-nineteenth century. It is remarkable to find such primitiveness at a time when wheelwrighting was about to reach the summit of perfection. (*Found by Frank Atkinson and now in the Bowes Museum, Barnard Castle.*)

the famous firm of agricultural machine manufacturers at Norwich and quickly established himself at the head of the industry by introducing his self-sharpening hardened cast-iron ploughshare. He followed this up by organising production on the principle of standardisation of manufacture which made the replacement of parts easily available, and not only ploughs but horse rakes, tedders, hoes, were produced by factory methods. Nevertheless, the wooden plough was still to be seen on some farms in the nineteenth century, and the triumph of the machine in agriculture could not be said to be assured until the second half of the century.

Enclosure

The advantages of enclosure of the intermixed strips and common meadow and the abolition of common rights after harvest had long been obvious to enterprising farmers, and many were already enjoying them. So widespread were the enclosures that by 1750 only half the existing arable remained to be enclosed. The counties of Kent, Surrey, Sussex, Hertfordshire, Essex, and Suffolk had little or no open fields to enclose; most of the land to the west of a line drawn from the Lancashire-Yorkshire border down to Bristol was already enclosed; and the main area of still unenclosed arable was to be found in the Midland and central-Southern counties of England, especially in those areas where the land was for the most part heavy and suitable for regular cropping for corn under the traditional open field system. Elsewhere, the common field had been largely enclosed silently and "by agreement" of the owners; the opposition of smallholders was extinguished by purchase and absorption in the estate of the large owners, and large numbers of "old enclosed" parishes, *i.e.* those enclosed before 1700, were entirely owned by single proprietors.

If the opposition of small owners proved an obstacle, it could be overcome by an Act of Parliament promoted by the owners of three-quarters or (after 1801) of two-thirds of the soil; and as prices rose in the second half of the eighteenth century landlords resorted more and more frequently to this method. Prior to 1750 barely 300,000 acres had been enclosed by Act, but between 1750 and 1850, 4,000 Acts were passed affecting 6,000,000 acres, or one quarter of the total cultivated acreage. They were mainly concentrated in two periods, 900 of them in the period 1760-80, and no less than 2,000 between 1793-1815, the years of the Napoleonic Wars. A closer examination of their chronology suggests that the most important influence behind this movement was the price of wheat.

The connection between wheat prices and enclosure is not difficult to understand in view of the rising population and the demand for white bread which had become the mainstay of the national diet, at least as far as the Trent. The more northern counties continued to rely on oatcake and "meslin", bread made from a mixture of barley and wheat flour; but the price of wheat was the main determinant of living costs for the country as a whole. Moreover, the demand for bread was inelastic, *i.e.* the same amount—no less and no more—was needed whatever the price. Hence a shortfall or surplus in supply, however small, had a disproportionate effect on price because the demand was the same. In the first half of the century, improved methods of farming and the slow—almost stagnant—population trend had combined to keep prices low; but with the rise of population after 1750 there was a gentle upward trend (marked by peaks or troughs in years of good or bad harvest) until 1793-1815 when, owing to a combination of bad harvests, war conditions, and rapidly rising population, prices rose to unprecedented heights. Since imports were limited by war conditions, only the expansion of agricultural production at home stood between Britain and sheer starvation. The nine hundred enclosure acts passed during the war period played an essential part in the national effort.

There were two main economic advantages of enclosure—(1) more compact farms which could be worked as a unit with a proper balance of arable and pasture and with appropriate rotation; (2) the conversion of old worn-out arable to ley or permanent grass and the ploughing of rough or over-grazed common pasture for manuring and cropping. It would not be wise to say that these objects were always attained: a large scale map of a parish will often show a confused patchwork of intermixed ownership even to-day; and farmers were often slow to make the best use of the opportunities that enclosure presented; and there was still the underlying problem of drainage of heavy soils. Enclosure disturbed the age-old pattern of drainage by ridge and furrow method without putting anything in its place: and when wheat prices fell after the war many farmers in these areas were ruined. It was not until the mass-production of underground drainage pipes was made possible by the pipe-making machine patented by Thomas Scragg in 1845 that the necessary equipment became available to overcome this problem.

From the point of view of the landlords, the criterion of success of enclosure was the rise of rents. Between 1750 and 1800 they almost doubled and by 1815 they had almost doubled again. On land that was subject to enclosure the rise was usually still greater. It was a halcyon period for the landlord, and although during the war wages and poor rates rose almost as fast as rents, and taxes much faster, farmers also prospered. The fall of prices after the war ruined many farmers, especially on the heavy soils, enclosed at great expense during the war, and brought the rise of rents to an abrupt halt; but the growth of the urban market kept up prices of meat and dairy produce to profitable levels, and the Corn Law of 1815 did something to protect the wheat farmer from foreign competition. The chief source of competition for the hard-pressed clayland farmers was not the foreign producer but the British farmers on the lighter soils brought into cultivation by enclosure, and although the population of Britain rose from ten to twenty million, the number of people fed on foreign corn rose from roughly one in eighteen to one in fifteen. This achievement had been made possible by bringing two million acres of new land into cultivation and raising the productivity of both new and old land in the form of enclosed farms. By this achievement British farmers answered the gloomy doubts of the economist Ricardo who feared that British economic advance would be brought to an end by the shortage of land from which to feed the rising industrial population.

Without enclosure and improved farming, industrialisation would have been halted.

We may now summarise the economic effects of enclosure and the contribution it made to the Industrial Revolution. By bringing in new land and enabling farmers to make better use of the natural fertility of the soil, it made possible an increase of production that almost kept pace with population growth. Thus only moderate imports were necessary and after 1815 prices tended to fall. It was not necessary, therefore, for wages in either agriculture or industry to rise in order to maintain living standards. This was a great advantage to manufacturers in their competition for foreign markets, and the fears of Ricardo and other classical economists that the industrial advance of Britain would be stopped by rising prices followed by rising wages owing to the shortage of land were proved false. This was especially the case after 1815 when the artificial conditions of war came to an end and agricultural prices and profits fell. Farmers were now compelled to make the best use of their land by adopting the latest improvements and landlords were encouraged, with the help of cheap credit from the government, to undertake extensive drainage works. The Agricultural Revolution had postponed the necessity of heavy imports of food from abroad and provided a breathing space during which British industry could meet the growing needs of the nation by buying the products of foreign farmers in return for cheap manufactured goods. It was only on this basis that Britain could build an economy that could truthfully be called the Workshop of the World.

Social Consequences

The social consequences of enclosure have usually been the object of severe attack. One well-known textbook tells us that the Enclosure Acts "drove the labourers to the noisome towns": another that they "caused the small farmer to disappear from the land". Both these statements are thoroughly misleading. Although many labourers left the villages for the towns, they went not because of enclosure but because the rural population was rising too fast to be absorbed by rural industries. Indeed, some industries such as spinning, and later weaving, were leaving the rural districts altogether; but agriculture was actually expanding its demand for labour and numbers employed continued to rise in most districts

until the 1840s. From that time, the increase of agricultural mechanisation, and the growth of railways, reversed the trend, and in terms of manpower, agriculture became a declining industry.

In regard to the small farmer, the story is a long and complicated one; but though many small farmers were bought up and small tenants squeezed out by the general movement towards larger farming units which enclosure encouraged, in 1831 there were still 130,000 farmers who employed no labour, *i.e.* small family farms for the most part, compared with 144,600 who employed outside labour.

The social structure, and the relations between the social classes, however, had changed for the worse as a result of enclosure. In the old enclosed villages the commons had already been obliterated by the process of enclosure and the Enclosure Acts of the eighteenth and nineteenth centuries failed to take advantage of this opportunity of correcting the injustice. They could—and in common justice should—have set apart land for cultivation or grazing by the resident labourers of the village who had formerly benefited from the use of the commons. Some Enclosure Acts did this, and Arthur Young speaks of the value of this kind of provision by landlords in Lincolnshire where pasture grounds and allotments for labourers were fairly widespread. He found that they were invariably associated with the reduction in poor rate and the increase in the happiness of the labouring families in the villages where this provision was made; but in the great majority of villages throughout the country, the commons were absorbed into the estates of the owners who had common rights over them. Even the smallest *owner* could claim compensation for loss of common rights: but not the tenant or labourer. The latter was now a wage earner, denied the use of the common and with diminishing opportunities of subsidiary earnings from rural industries. The Poor Law, however, came to his assistance, especially after the Speenhamland decision of 1795, but it carried the stigma of pauperism, and the social gap between the labourer and the rest of the rural community steadily widened. When the labourers revolted in 1830, burning stacks and smashing threshing machines, they were put down by Lord Melbourne's government with great ferocity; in 1834 the attempt to form a trade union was brutally suppressed by the arrest and deportation of the Tolpuddle Martyrs; and in the same year the labourers' cup of misery was filled to overflowing by the Poor Law Amendment Act which cut off poor relief for the able-bodied labourers and offered the work-house as the only form of relief for the able-bodied unemployed. They met their family needs by drawing upon the earnings of women and children organised in groups under gang masters, a debased form of labour organisation beside which the regulated factories of the towns could be said to be enlightened and humane. During the period when English farming was climbing to the peak of success, many counties of the east and south were steeped in discontent that was kept silent only by fear.

It should be remembered, however, that the counties north of the Trent were far less seriously affected by these evils. There was no labourers' revolt in the Midlands or the North; although the Chartists were active in these parts, especially among the handloom weavers and frame work knitters, they had little success with the farm labourers, and all the evidence seems to point to a slow but steady improvement in their living standards. In Lancashire and Nottinghamshire, for instance, their wages were nearly twice as high as in Wiltshire or Sussex by the middle of the century. Both farmer and labourer were reaping the benefits of urban industrialisation and new forms of transport. Discontented labourers had greater opportunities of finding alternative employment; and even during the so-called depression after the Napoleonic Wars, the more enterprising farmers found profitable outlets for meat and dairy produce as well as corn in the growing urban markets. The spread of railways at home and steam shipping on the ocean routes gave additional stimulus to urban industry and provided further openings for rural labour, and by the 1850s the tide of national prosperity began to be felt even among the rural labourers of the South. The Agricultural Revolution had now run its course; its success had been bought at a heavy cost for some sections of the rural population; but by enabling agricultural production almost to keep pace with population growth, it had ensured the success of industrialisation and removed the fear of famine from town and country.

VI

The Expansion of Transport and Commercial Services

Plate VI.1. Canal tunnel on the Lancaster-Kendal canal.

The expansion of industry and trade and the growth of towns demanded better transport services to supply industrial and domestic consumers with bulky raw materials (particularly coal) and to extend the market which mass production called for. From the time when Defoe travelled round England onwards there was an accelerating provision of transport amenities of all kinds—roads, bridges, carrier and coach services, river navigation, canals, aqueducts, docks, harbours, and warehouses. The same period also saw the establishment of banks, insurance companies, shipping under-writers, and other bodies providing financial services to industry. The growth in the scale of industry and towns, and the kind of attitude to marketing which was discussed in connection with the careers of Boulton and Wedgwood, brought about a fundamental re-shaping of the pattern of wholesale and retail trade. These three changes are worth looking at separately.

Roads and Bridges

At the middle of the eighteenth century the roads of Britain were merely stone or rubble causeways, invariably so narrow that only one cart could pass at once. Some roads, particularly in the clay belts of the Midlands, were quagmires in wet weather, and travellers wrote of ruts and holes that made travel on horseback dangerous. Traffic moved very slowly, two to three miles an hour being quite normal for any wheeled vehicle. Mule trains were the quickest form of overland transport for goods and walking was usually quicker than coaches.

The cause of the bad roads was partly administrative and partly technical. The responsibility for maintaining the roads lay with the parishes, each of which (by a statute of 1555) were responsible for appointing a surveyor of highways. This official, who would be forced into office at the annual parish meeting, was an amateur who probably had

113

Plate VI.2. Whitehaven Docks.

little interest in transport. The technique of road-making had been lost with the Romans and the parishes were apathetic about the state of the roads since few parishioners were interested in travelling.

The solution to the problem was characteristically found by local enterprise, rather than the central government. Turnpike trusts removed the responsibility for a section of road from the parishes to a group of interested people named in an Act of Parliament. The first turnpike Act was passed in 1663 when the Justices of the Peace of Hertfordshire, Cambridgeshire, and Huntingdonshire sought powers to improve part of the Great North Road. A second Act was passed in 1690, but it was not until 1760 that the Justices' initiative was widely copied, and most of the promoters were merchants and manufacturers, with some support from landowners and

professional people. Between 1760 and 1777, 452 Acts were passed, and there was a second boom between 1787 and 1794. Travellers along the turnpike roads had to pay a toll at the gates which the trustees erected; surviving toll houses can still be seen in many parts of the country. An interesting example, with toll board, is illustrated here.

During the course of the eighteenth century the main industrial towns of Britain became the focus of a growing number of turnpike roads. This gradual development can be illustrated from the experience of Birmingham, whose radiating system is shown on the following page. An early (1726) connection with Walsall and Wednesbury, followed by Stourbridge (1753) and then Dudley (1761), provided the main industrial (as opposed to commercial) links with the town. Many early turnpikes connected coalpits with their markets.

 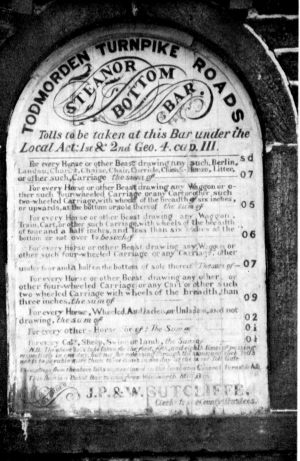

Plates VI.3 and 4. Toll house and board at Todmorden, Lancs.

The growth of a network of turnpike roads inaugurated the age of the stage coach. The coaches were not merely the long distance express trains of their day, but also provided local "omnibus" services to meet the needs of the growing industrial districts. The coverage and regularity of coach services reached its zenith in the 1830s, on the eve of the great era of railway development. The value of the service provided to a major industrial region can be judged from the map of the stage coach services in the West Riding of Yorkshire. There were twelve coaches leaving Leeds for Manchester every day, joining the principle foci of the north of England textile industry, and taking $5\frac{1}{2}$ to 6 hours to cover the 40 miles. Over longer distances the competition of the coaching companies achieved spectacular savings in time, the journey from London to Birmingham falling from two days in the 1740s to 19 hours in the 1780s while from London to Manchester (184 miles) the travelling time was reduced to 28 hours. The stage coaches were responsible for improvements in the regularity, speed, and comfort of travel, whose value to commerce has hardly received adequate recognition.

The turnpike roads did not bring about any immediate improvement in the technique of road-making. Thomas Telford did not begin his work as county surveyor of highways in Shropshire until 1790 and John MacAdam did not begin to work as a turnpike surveyor until 1815. Moreover, the "new" techniques of road-making associated with their names consisted essentially of the Roman engineers' practice of building up a hard surface by packing fine chippings or broken stones into a foundation of boulders.

TURNPIKE ROADS ROUND BIRMINGHAM, 1725-1830

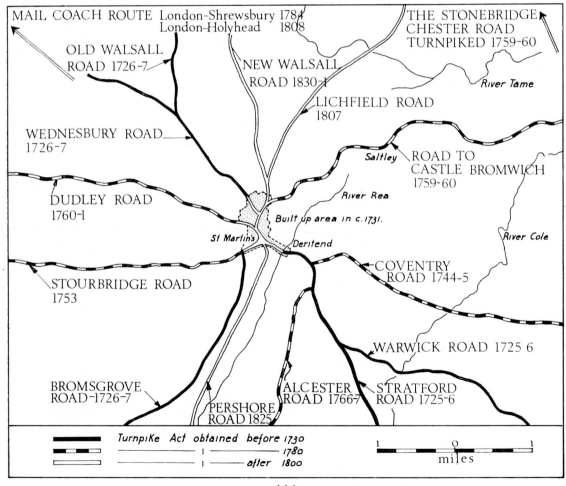

Plates VI.5 and 6.   Transport continued to depend on ancient crafts until the advent of the motor.   These reconstructions, in Shibden Hall Folk Museum, Halifax, show (5) a wheelwright's shop and tools, and (6) a saddler's and harness maker's.

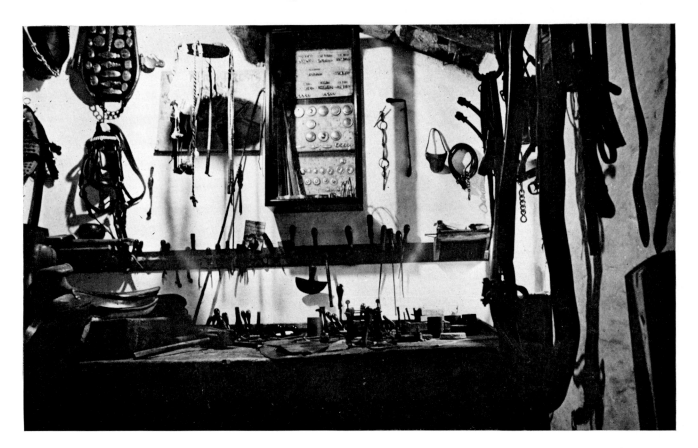

The originality of the civil engineers of the period lies more in the design of their bridges.

At the middle of the eighteenth century, bridge building was not quite the lost art that road-making was, but it is certainly true that practice had not advanced very significantly beyond the achievements of the Romans. The inspiration of British civil engineering can be traced partly to Bélidor, whose books contain material on the theory of the arch and of structural engineering generally, and partly to the cheap production of cast iron that transformed an expensive metal into an economical building material. Abraham Darby's cast iron bridge at Coalbrookdale (1779), even to-day an imposing span, 100 feet across and rising 46 feet above the Severn, is the first and best-known landmark in the history of bridge building in the Industrial Revolution. Telford made this pioneer effort appear an anachronism with his elegant Buildwas bridge (1795) and the spectacular Pontcysyllte aqueduct (1803), carrying the Ellesmere Canal across the Vale of Llangollen in an iron trough. In the north, Walkers of Rotherham, the

Plates VI.7 and 8.   Abraham Darby's Iron Bridge.

and Commercial Services

ironmasters, built the well-known Sunderland Bridge (1796), and in London, Rennie's Southwark Bridge (1819) was an equally noted iron structure. The Industrial Revolution was not all ugliness; the bridges of Telford and Rennie combine elegance with sound construction (see Plates II.13 and 14).

The constant experimentation with new techniques, which is so characteristic of the Industrial Revolution, is nowhere more evident than in the variety of bridges that survive from the period. The early years of the nineteenth century saw some spectacular successes, and disastrous failures, in the construction of suspension bridges. Among the former, Telford's bridges at Conway and the Menai Straits are the best known. Swivel bridges were a popular feature of the docks of the period; Telford's drawings of one built at St Katherine Docks, London, are shown (p. 120). The more traditional form of bridge building, the masonry arch, attained excellence in the designs of John Rennie, whose London Bridge (1824-31), appears in Plate II.13. The precise detailed planning of the great engineers is abundantly clear in their surviving blueprints, an example of which is reproduced overleaf.

River Navigations, Docks, and Harbours

If it had been left to the turnpike trusts and their surveyors there might have been no Industrial Revolution in Britain before the railway age. Fortunately the country enjoyed considerable natural advantages in the proximity of several manufacturing districts to the sea and the abundance of navigable rivers. Until the end of the eighteenth century the sea was the main commercial highway of the nation, with the navigable rivers acting as feeders of the sea routes.

It is not surprising that the first extensive attempts to improve the transport system of the country were a series of projects to extend the length of navigable rivers, or to make narrow streams of commercial use. Broadly speaking, the period between 1600 and 1750 is the main period of river navigation in England. A few schemes were affected by the unanimous agreement of a group of property owners involved, but most required access to the land of other parties and hence could only proceed when they were legalised, either by Letters Patent or a Private Act of Parliament.

A study of the chronology of schemes approved by Parliament suggests that there were three phases

Plate VI.9. The opening of St Katherine Docks, 1828. Oils, by W. J. Huggins. (*Port of London Authority.*)

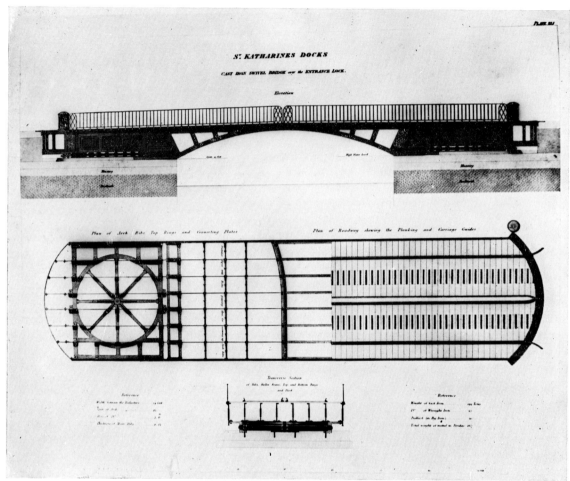

Plate VI.10.   Telford's blueprint for the cast-iron swivel bridge at St Katherine Docks.   (*Port of London Authority.*)

of development of navigation. The earliest period, 1662-5, saw the launching of six major schemes, including the Medway (Kent) and the Stour (Worcs.), which offered the first opportunity of cheap transport from the inland South Staffordshire coalfield. The second phase, 1697-1700, produced eight successful schemes, including the Aire and Calder, in the West Riding, the Bristol Avon, and the Trent Navigation, that extended the head of navigation of the Trent from Nottingham to Burton-on-Trent. A third period, from 1719 to 1721, saw nine successful schemes, among which the Douglas (Wigan coal), the Weaver (Cheshire salt), the Derwent (Derbyshire lead and iron), and the Mersey and Irwell, providing the link between Manchester and Liverpool, were particularly important.

In addition to these twenty-three successful Bills there were at least eight schemes that failed in Parlia-

ment because of the weight of opposition to them. Navigation projects were attacked by a variety of vested interests—towns that expected to suffer loss of trade from the opening up of a new trade route, landowners and farmers who feared flooding, trespass, or other damage to their property, and land carriers, ship owners, mill owners, and others, who saw a threat to their livelihood. The promoters of the schemes, as would be expected, were principally the merchants of the chief river towns, together with a number of country landowners of various ranks. The trustees of the particular scheme were mentioned in the various Acts of Parliament. The Act usually empowered the trustees to borrow money on the security of tolls at a maximum rate of 5 or 6 per cent.

The development of river navigation did not come as the immediate consequence of any new invention or engineering experience. The pound

120

lock, the familiar technique of retaining a flow of water, was widely known on the Continent in the middle ages (the first example that can be dated with certainty was built at Vreeswijk, Holland, in 1373) and in England was employed in excavating a cut on the River Exe in 1564-7. The British were very slow to emulate Continental experience and the early promoters suffered many abortive schemes. Nevertheless, the period after the Restoration saw the employment of a handful of experts who can properly be called consulting engineers, engaged in drawing up schemes for navigable waterways, mills, the supply of water to towns, and the construction of docks and harbours.

The best known of this group of pioneers was Captain Andrew Yarranton, who surveyed the Dee, Avon, Thames, Severn, and Humber, and made the Stour navigable. George Sorocold possessed more originality as an engineer. He pioneered piped water

Plates VI.11 and 12. Pound locks and flights on the Stourbridge Canal.

supply to large towns, beginning with Derby in 1692, designed the power system for Lombe's silk mill at Derby (1718-22), and probably built Howland Dock, the first wet dock at Rotherhithe (1695-1700). His principal assistant in this enterprise was Thomas Steers, engineer of the Irwell Navigation who built the Newry Canal in Northern Ireland—strictly speaking the first canal in the British Isles—and was engineer for the first Liverpool wet dock.

The systematic development of port facilities, like navigable rivers, began in a slow and almost grudging manner. The Howland Dock had to wait fifteen years for a successor, and after Bristol's first dock was opened in 1717, no other docks were built until 1743. However, the improvement of harbours by building piers and quays began in earnest during the early part of the eighteenth century at all places round

Plate VI.13. Dockside warehouses of the eighteenth century at Whitehaven, Cumberland.

the coast. Among the most notable improvements were those at the coal ports of Whitehaven, Maryport, and Sunderland, at the fishing ports of Great Yarmouth and Grimsby, and at Bristol and Dover.

There was a fairly continuous series of port improvements during the middle decades of the eighteenth century, but the cumulative benefit conferred by these improvements is unimpressive compared with that achieved between 1790 and 1815. The spectacular increase in wet dock and basin accommodation is illustrated in the block diagram (see Fig. 14, p. 176); it was paralleled by a considerable increase in harbour accommodation. Between 1796 and 1815 six docks were opened in London, three in Liverpool, and one each at Bristol, Hull, and Grimsby. This investment reflected the rapidly increasing overseas trade of Britain during the period. The trade boom in 1824-5 saw another acceleration of dock building, including Telford's St Katherine Docks at London, illustrated

opposite. They were completed in 1828 at a cost of £1,352,000.

An Act of Parliament was usually necessary to sanction harbour and dock developments. This was expensive, but did result in the setting up of bodies of trustees and commissioners with authority to provide an adequate income and power to administer the port efficiently. By 1830 there were at least thirty harbour and dock trusts and commissions in existence; in 1690 there had only been one, at Dover.

Canals

The construction of the course of the Sankey Navigation (1755-7) provided the link between river improvement and canal building. The "Navigation" was built by widening the Sankey Brook and providing it with a dozen locks for its ten-mile course between St Helen's (Lancashire) and the

Plate VI.14.   Warehouses at St Katherine Docks, London.

Plate VI.15. Canal basin and Customs House at Stourport, built in 1771 at the junction of the Staffordshire and Worcestershire Canal with the River Severn.

River Mersey, near Warrington. The scheme was projected by a group of Liverpool merchants to bring down the price of coal in the town. But the man responsible for projecting and working out this particular solution to the problem of constructing a navigable waterway was Henry Berry, who had succeeded Steers as Liverpool dock engineer.

The better known Bridgwater Canal (1761-3) achieved greater fame; its Irwell aqueduct and underground tunnels to the Duke's collieries created something more than a nine-day wonder. The engineer was James Brindley, a former Leek (Staffordshire) millwright, whose energy was rewarded by many more commissions. Brindley could lay little claim to technical originality, his "contour canals" not bearing comparison with the best Continental canals. Professor T. S. Ashton suggests that "the real secret of his success lay in his gift for organisation. He had had experience as a master millwright and had, no doubt, learnt how to lead and discipline workers . . . . . to control 400 to 600 rough and

turbulent men scattered over miles of country was a . . . . difficult problem."[1]

The spectacular success of the Bridgwater Canal produced a host of other schemes, among the best known of which were those to provide east-west routes across the country (Trent and Mersey Canal, 1777) and north-south routes. As in the case of river navigations, most projects involved a private Act of Parliament; between 1758 and 1802, 165 Bills were approved, more than half of which were connected primarily with transporting coal. Like the navigable rivers, the canals were fed by miles of tramways, linking the collieries with the piers where the coal was tipped into waiting barges. Wigan pier, for long a favourite butt of music hall comedians, was nothing more than a coal-discharging hythe in the Leeds-Liverpool canal, essentially similar to dozens of others on the coalfields. The canals were particularly important to land-locked coalfields and

[1] T. S. Ashton, *An Economic History of England: the Eighteenth Century* (1955), p. 76

124

Plate VI.16.   Five-rise locks at Bingley, on the Liverpool-Leeds canal.

Plate VI.17.   Locks at Brierley Hill, Staffs, on the Stourbridge Canal.

125

industrial regions like the Black Country, the Potteries, central Lancashire, and the Erewash valley (Nottinghamshire-Derbyshire borders).

Canal development attracted wider support than river navigation. Industrialists, merchants, and landed proprietors with direct interest in particular schemes were most active as promoters, but a whole range of people with money to invest—local tradesmen, widows, gentry and nobility, lawyers, bankers, clergy, and others—subscribed capital. Shares were advertised in the local papers, so that, for the first time, investment in its modern sense became popular. In this respect, and in their economic consequences generally, the canals anticipated the effects of the railways, though on a smaller scale.

Railways

The railway in the modern sense has two distinct roots; wooden guides can be traced back to the beginning of the seventeenth century and rails were in common use on all the coalfields within a century; the steam engine, as a commercial proposition, dates from the beginning of the eighteenth century, but it was not until the partnership of Boulton & Watt that it was applied to rotary motion, and the possibility of using it for transport appeared.

William Murdock, Boulton & Watt's foreman, made a working model of a steam carriage in 1784. The early years of the nineteenth century saw a number of engineers at work trying to build a steam locomotive, among which Trevithick, Blenkinsop, Hedley, and Stephenson are the best known names.

George Stephenson was engine-wright at Killingworth colliery, near Newcastle, when he began his experiments with steam traction. His *Locomotion* demonstrated its value on the 27-mile Stockton and Darlington railway when the line was opened in 1825. However, horse drawn coaches and stationary engines continued to be used on the railway, which was operated much like a turnpike road, private users paying tolls for the use of the track. The real historical significance of the Stockton and Darlington line was that it attracted the attention of merchants, industrialists, and engineers, and encouraged other more ambitious projects.

The first line to convey goods and people solely by steam locomotives was the Manchester and Liverpool railway, opened in 1830. The Company both owned and operated the line and its stations. George Stephenson and his son Robert not only built the *Rocket* that convinced the promoters of the value of steam traction, but also established a railway works at Newcastle that provided a series of famous engines.

Plate VI.18.   George Stephenson's "Locomotion", preserved at Bank Top British Railway Station, Darlington.   (*Frank Atkinson.*)

and Commercial Services

The main period of railway development in Britain lies beyond the scope of this work. The appearance of a railway network in the 1840s accelerated the industrialisation of the country both by the direct stimulus it gave to the construction industries (iron, bricks, stone, timber) and engineering, and to the enormous benefit conferred by a faster, more direct, and cheaper form of transport for both goods and people. Only one point about this development can be made here. One school of economic historians, surveying the limited statistical data on British investment in the eighteenth and nineteenth centuries, reach the conclusion that the railway age produced a higher level of investment in industry and commerce than any previous period, and that this period might therefore be considered as the crucial stage of the transition of Britain to a modern industrial economy. The validity of such a conclusion turns on the criteria that are used to identify the course of change. If we think of the Industrial Revolution as a fundamental re-shaping of the national economy that involves every facet of life, then we will want to put the centre of gravity of the transition period quite early. We shall return to these wider issues of interpretation in the final chapter.

Banking and Insurance

The most important financial service that developed in Britain in the seventeenth and eighteenth centuries was banking. There was a developed banking system in Italy in the later middle ages, receiving deposits, making loans, dealing in bills of exchange, and issuing paper currency. When the centre of gravity of European trade moved to the low countries, a similar banking system grew up in Antwerp. The leading merchants trading with the Continent must have been familiar with banking principles from this early period, but it was not until the sixteenth century that British specialists in credit provision appear. In the Tudor period wealthy merchants, goldsmiths, money scriveners (lawyers), and retail brokers (a sort of pawnbroker) all appear as money-lenders to different strata of society, the merchants often providing loans (forced or unforced) for the State.

However, the first group to fulfil the essential banking function of receiving deposits and using them to provide credit were the seventeenth-century goldsmiths. Fearing for the safety of their plate and cash reserves during the uncertain period of the Civil Wars and Commonwealth, landowners and merchants transferred their reserves to the goldsmiths, who had a high reputation for financial integrity. They were, moreover, legally liable for what was deposited with them, and offered interest on deposits. The goldsmith bankers were patronised by provincial merchants (like West Country clothiers) as well as by metropolitan customers. The habit of leaving reserves with the goldsmiths was continued

Plate VI.19.   A banknote of 1799.   The Leeds Bank became one of the constituent banks of the present Westminster Bank. (*Westminster Bank Ltd.*)

after the Restoration, and made profitable by the considerable loans negotiated by Cromwell and the last Stuarts at high interest rates. Discounting bills of exchange came to be an important part of the work of the goldsmith bankers. Goldsmiths' receipts for cash deposited with them, which took the form of written promises to pay the depositor, shortly began to circulate as cash on the endorsement of each successive person through whose hands they passed. In the eighteenth century these printed receipts (or notes) were made payable to any bearer. An example of an early bank note is shown on p. 127.

The expansion of English overseas trade and the example of the Bank of Amsterdam (1619) and other controlling banks on the Continent led to increasing pressure for a central bank in London in the last quarter of the seventeenth century. However, the Bank of England (1694) was only established as a joint-stock corporation because of William III's difficulty in raising loans to continue his Continental wars. The Bank's charter was given in return for a loan of £1,200,000 at 8 per cent.—not a high rate of interest considering the parlous state of the government's credit. In 1708 the Bank of England was granted the privilege of being the only joint-stock bank in the country; no other bank could have more than six partners. This law was not repealed until 1826 (and then only to the extent of allowing joint-stock banks more than 60 miles out of London) so that the Bank of England was necessarily the strongest bank, and came to hold the reserves of all other banks. The restriction placed on the size of other banks made them less stable than they might have been. Despite its title, the Bank of England did not function as a central bank, controlling other banks, for most of the eighteenth century. Its first, and successful, attempt to do so came in 1783, when the Bank damped down a period of rapid inflation by withdrawing credit.

At the middle of the eighteenth century there were not more than a dozen banks outside London, and those that existed were very unevenly distributed; there was no bank in the leading manfacturing centres of Manchester and Birmingham. The work of the banks—the provision of short-term credit—was carried on by merchants, prosperous retailers, reliable innkeepers, and others whose financial integrity was trusted by the local community.

The late eighteenth and early nineteenth centuries saw the opening of several hundred banks in the provinces, notably during periods of expanding trade like 1784-93 and 1797-1810. Dr L. S. Pressnell's *Country Banking in the Industrial Revolution* provides the following approximations of the number of banks in existence in England and Wales outside London, based on the Post Office London Directory:

1750	About	12	1810	..	654
1784	..	128	1820	..	606
1800	..	270	1830	..	628

In 1802 there were said to be fifty-one banks in Scotland. An analysis of the origins of all these concerns suggests that their founders fall into four categories: industrialists, merchants and wholesale traders, lawyers, and collectors of government revenue. The motives for entering banking varied with the occupational grouping of the founders.

Industrialists entered banking because they needed capital for the extension of their concerns, and their factories or forges were often isolated from existing banking houses. Moreover, there was an acute shortage of small coin and low denomination notes in Britain at the time, and many manufacturers were compelled to issue their own token coinage and notes to pay wages and lubricate the wheels of local retail trade. The issue and redemption of token coinage (see Plate IV.1) served as an apprenticeship to banking operations. Some of the best-known banks of to-day were founded by eighteenth-century industrialists—Lloyd's Bank in 1760 by Sampson Lloyd, a Midland iron founder, and John Taylor, a Birmingham toy maker, and Baring Brothers by a family of Exeter clothiers.

While industrialists as a class were debtors to the community, merchants and wholesale traders as a group were creditors. Both overseas and domestic commerce involved the provision of credit due to the hazards of travel and the long period that elapsed between production, finding a market, and securing payment. Merchants bridged the financial gap between production and payment, one of the main activities of the banker. The economic expansion of the eighteenth century brought considerable wealth to the most able traders who, more often than not, gradually shifted their interests from commodity dealing to pure finance. All the main trading centres of the country produced a number of banks of merchant origins; in Liverpool, for instance, ten out of fourteen banks in the town about 1800 had merchant origins. Drapers, mercers, ironmongers, and coal and corn merchants also provided recruits to banking.

In rural areas people often left their money with money scriveners for investment in land and "safe" investments like river navigations, turnpikes, canals, and enclosures. The scriveners commonly became bankers in country towns, but usually in partnership with merchants or industrialists. Government revenue officials held substantial sums of money for periods before they were remitted to the treasury. It is clear that these were often used to finance local industry and trade. The first recorded provincial banker, Abel Smith of Nottingham, was a mercer who acquired experience in handling money as a revenue collector.

Up to the middle of the eighteenth century London banking was supported by government finance, the mercantile needs of the City, and the landowners. In the second half of the century a change in the structure of the London banking system strongly suggests a wider function. New firms were established and new partners drawn into the established banking houses who had more specifically mercantile and manufacturing origins. Leading country bankers like Smiths of Nottingham, Taylor & Lloyd of Birmingham, and Peel & Wilkes of Manchester and Tamworth, opened branches in the City. The most important link of the City banks with the industrial provinces was that the majority of them had agencies for the country banks. However, there is evidence that some City banks advanced money for industrial and transport developments. Glyn, Mills & Co. advanced money to Francis Garbett (a partner in the Carron Ironworks), Childs lent money to the Duke of Bridgwater for canal building, and Staples allowed a £9,000 overdraft to Timothy Harris, a City hosier who opened a spinning mill in Nottingham.

The country bankers were obviously conversant with local financial needs and investment possibilities. This familiarity enabled them to provide a service that would have been less adequately provided by a more centralised system. A more satisfactory legal framework would have allowed the country banks to acquire more stability and hence offer an even better service. In general the banks preferred to offer modest short-term loans (for instance, to cover the time lag between completion of an order and payment of the bill) rather than invest in fixed assets like buildings, plant, and machinery. A balanced picture of a substantial banker's support of industry and trade can be obtained from an analysis of the end of year statements of Smiths, the Nottingham bankers. In 1792, a peak year for the expansion of the Midlands cotton industry, Smiths advanced £29,921 on over-

draft to ten firms engaged in cotton spinning, the largest debit balance amounting to £9,318, the smallest £186. The £29,921 represented 30 per cent. of Smith's total advances to its customers. Several merchant hosiers, two leading lace manufacturers, and a colliery proprietor also had active accounts at the period, but most of the remainder of Smith's customers were local tradesmen and country gentry and farmers, with a sprinkling of professional people.

The development of insurance in several respects followed a pattern similar to that already traced for banking. The beginnings of insurance business are to be found in London in the sixteenth century, and

Plate VI.20. Insurance mark on an early nineteenth century house in East Road, Cambridge. (*Charles Moseley*.)

the capital retained its leadership through the period covered by this book and up to the present day. The earliest underwriters of risks as we understand the term were wealthy merchants, who were prepared to insure ships for a calculated consideration. The losses of these men during William of Orange's wars with Louis XIV led to Parliament approving two joint-stock companies in 1720, the Royal Exchange and the London Assurance Companies. Private underwriting of marine risks was also undertaken by merchants meeting at Lloyd's coffee house, a group that took separate rooms in the Royal Exchange in 1771. The first fire insurance companies were established after the Great Fire of London (1666), beginning with the Phoenix in 1680. The two chartered companies began to register fire and life insurance premiums the year after their foundation.

Outside London only two or three fire insurance companies were opened before 1760, the best known being the Bristol Crown (1718) and the Edinburgh Friendly Society (1719). In the last three decades of the century there was a proliferation of provincial fire offices, but most of the business was still handled by the established London offices, who had agents in most towns and advertised regularly in the local newspapers. Thus the Royal Exchange Company and the Sun Fire Office (1710) took the major part in the risky cotton mill insurance business between 1780 and 1800, despite the existence of the Manchester Fire Office (1771). In 1830 the provincial offices took less than 30 per cent. of the total fire insurance business.

Wholesale and Retail Trade

Wholesale and retail trade provide the essential channels for distribution of the products of industry, and thus serve both the manufacturer and the consumer. In the middle ages surpluses available for exchange were small and most of this work was done in annual fairs and weekly markets, and these popular occasions still carried on an important though diminishing share of trade during our period.

With the exception of London, markets were local affairs, an opportunity for local farmers, fishermen, cowkeepers, and others to sell their small surpluses, as some of them still do in parts of Britain to this day. The stalls and plots of the dealers crowded the streets, offering bread, cheese, meat, fish, fruit, and vegetables for sale in what, to-day, would be regarded as very unhygienic conditions. In market trading no distinction was at first made between wholesale and retail trade; the medieval practice was for both rich and poor to buy in large quantities (in proportion to their means) at infrequent intervals. Only in London, where street markets were held daily, could it be said that people were supplied from day to day. After the Great Fire (1666) four great market halls were built to replace the open-air trading of the congested streets, and this idea was shortly copied in numbers of other towns.

Fairs, unlike markets, were national and sometimes international functions, and originally dealt in textile and metal goods and the more valuable commodities of inter-regional and international trade. Both clothes and tools were expected to last not merely

a lifetime, but were customarily handed on from one generation to the next, so that the trade in these goods was more limited than that in food and drink. The most famous English fair was held at Stourbridge, near Cambridge, and at the beginning of the eighteenth century Defoe described how the finest manufactured goods from all over England and the Continent were exchanged there. By this time, other fairs had become specialised—sheep at Burford, fish at Yarmouth, butter at Ipswich, cheese at Chipping Norton, and so on. As the eighteenth century advanced and commercial intercourse increased fairs lost ground to markets because the latter offered merchants and manufacturers more regular opportunities of meeting.

In the course of time many markets, like fairs, came to specialise and drop their retail trade. The rise of the cloth-making industry was marked by the erection of cloth halls at centres like Colchester, Ipswich, and Witney, though much of the cloth went direct to Blackwell Hall, the international market in London. The West Riding announced its coming of age by building cloth markets at Leeds (1711, 1755), Bradford (1773), Colne (1775), Wakefield (1776), and Halifax (1779). The greatest markets were held in London; Covent Garden, Billingsgate, Smithfield, the Corn Exchange, Blackwell Hall, the Coal Exchange, attracted produce from all over the country, and the first three are still pre-eminent as centres of wholesale distribution.

From the late middle ages a second system of distribution began to overlay that based on markets and fairs. The break-up of the manorial economy and the growth of towns—particularly of London—gave rise to a corps of middlemen dealers, or warehousemen, who bought up the small surpluses of farmers and domestic manufacturers and sold them to other dealers or to manufacturers or retailers. The middleman, then as now, was a much-maligned man, popularly regarded as unproductive and consequently as a parasite on the national economy. In fact the middleman had (and still has) an important economic role, simplifying the process of distribution by allowing the producer to concentrate on his chosen speciality, and ironing out differences between periods of surplus and dearth. In a backward country, with poor communications, this function was particularly useful.

During the seventeenth and eighteenth centuries the numbers of middlemen multiplied and specialisation among them increased. Various examples of middlemen, like wool broggers and foggers, have

Plate VI.21. Leeds Corn Exchange (1860), where farmers still haggle with corn merchants over the price of their "purses" (samples) of grain.

already been noticed in the discussion of the domestic system of manufacture. The trade in grain, meat, fish, coal, metals, leather, and other commodities all had their own succession of dealers, with a vocabulary of titles peculiar to the trade. Thus in the grain trade, the men who bought the wheat from the farmers were known at different times and places as "badgers", "kidders", "laders", "broggers", and "carriers". Other surpluses were disposed of through corn factors, who acted as agents to buyers and sellers and worked on commission. Corn jobbers bought and sold alongside the factors, but did so as speculators on their own account. Buyers, factors, and jobbers sold to wholesalers of various kinds, export merchants, millers, maltsters, brewers, and mealmen for processing or further distribution before the commodity reached the appropriate retail outlets.

The origins of shopkeeping are also to be found in the growth of London. In the late sixteenth and early seventeenth centuries the population of London was increasing much faster than that of other towns. It reached half a million before the end of the seventeenth century, ten times larger than the next biggest English town (Norwich). It became fashionable for the aristocracy to build town houses in and about the capital, spending the season at court and indulging their expensive tastes. The general increase of wealth was thus heavily concentrated in London, with a corresponding concentration of craftsmen and increasing number of shopkeepers. The earliest shopkeepers were mercers, drapers, and grocers, together with a sprinkling of corn chandlers, apothecaries, and others. At first they bought their stock at fairs, but in course of time shopkeepers were supplied directly by middlemen. The sale of other commodities like fish,

Plate VI.22. Print of Wedgwood's showrooms, St James's Square, London, in 1809. (*Jos. Wedgwood & Sons Ltd.*)

meat, and vegetables remained market trades up to the middle of the nineteenth century. Provincial shopkeepers began to appear in the seventeenth century, at first stocking up at fairs, then in London. Country districts were served by hawkers and pedlars who had their regular rounds of the villages.

The Industrial Revolution brought no revolutionary change to retail trade, but it did begin to transform the pattern of wholesale trading. An important characteristic of the period was that the entrepreneur widened his functions, in a few notable instances, to include control and direction of wholesaling and a few retail outlets. We have already referred to the importance and practice of Wedgwood and Boulton in this connection (see pp. 61-2). By the use of trademarks and the publicity given to their special lines they established a direct link with the consumer. For the first time they were able to offer the general public a standard of design and craftsmanship which they could recognise for themselves, rather than relying on the shopkeeper's valuation. Boulton and Wedgwood's sales techniques were widely copied. Before the end of the eighteenth century Peter Stubs of Warrington, a file-maker, was using his own trade marks; the

spread of this practice, and the increase in the scale of production, gradually reduced the number of middlemen.

This period also saw the direct linking of manufacturer and consumer through a group of itinerant wholesalers known variously as "Manchester men", "Shrewsbury men", "Sheffield men", and perhaps other titles. They bought at the mills and factories and delivered goods to the shops by packhorse, often providing credit. They gradually took over the trade of the London merchants, though not without spirited opposition and some acrimonious exchanges. The "Scotch Drapers" or "Scotchmen" provided a direct channel between the mill and the consumer, sometimes working as agents for firms in Lancashire, the West Riding, or Glasgow. Like the pedlars they travelled on foot along a familiar route, but differed from their predecessors in that they specialised in the new cheap textiles, and offered credit to the housewives on whom they regularly called.

The Industrial Revolution in textiles and the metallurgical industries established or confirmed new centres not only of manufacturing, but, in due course, of merchanting as well. London lost ground, relatively speaking, to the new industrial towns of the north of England, though it retained and extended its leadership in finance and credit. In its place Manchester became the national and international centre of cotton textiles, Leeds of woollen textiles, Bradford of worsted, Nottingham of lace and hosiery, Birmingham of hardware, and Stoke-on-Trent of ceramics. Alongside the austere functional factory buildings, or perhaps in a separate quarter of the town, there appeared the elaborate and often pretentious warehouses of the merchants. The commercial attractiveness of the north is illustrated by the fact that Manchester, Birmingham, Bradford, Nottingham, and other industrial towns acquired a "German" colony of merchants, just as London and a few leading ports (like Exeter and Bristol) had done in previous centuries. This transfer of trade to the provincial cities is still commemorated by many proud Victorian warehouses at their hearts and by shining brass nameplates with surnames of Dutch, German, French, and Jewish origin.

WATTS'S WAREHOUSE, MANCHESTER.

Plate VI.23.   A mid-nineteenth-century Manchester cotton warehouse.

Plate VII.1.   Collapsed flue from lead works on the North Pennine moors.

134

VII

Social Consequences of Industrialism

So far we have considered the Industrial Revolution primarily in terms of economic progress, and have neglected its social and political consequences. The effect of rapid economic change on society and the response of wage earners, manufacturers, and the government to the changing needs of an increasingly urban and industrial society are important indeed. Before embarking on this study one point should be made; there is no doubt that sections of the working class suffered unemployment, hunger, and demoralisation at various times over the period covered by this book, and considerable emphasis has been laid on this evil aspect of the period by many writers. It is important, however, not to confuse the social consequences of industrialism with the general results of war and of rapid population growth. It is easy to blame all the suffering of the period on rapid industrialisation, but other factors played their part (as unindustrialised Ireland shows). In these first two sections we shall try to isolate some of the characteristic social consequences of war and of the eighteenth-century population explosion from the results of industrialism.

Economic and Social Consequences of Eighteenth-Century Wars

Political historians often remind us that Britain was at war for more than half the years of the eighteenth century. None of these wars, except perhaps the last (the war with Revolutionary and Napoleonic France) engaged the nation emotionally, physically, or economically in anything like the way twentieth-century wars have done. Eighteenth-century wars were managed by an officer élite drawn from the upper classes and fought by harshly disciplined soldiers and sailors largely drawn from the fitter men to be found among the unemployed and those in irregular employment. The loss of manpower to the economy was relatively trivial; and battles were fought on the high seas or on foreign (or colonial) territory so that the only economic assets that were destroyed were merchant ships and their men and cargoes.

The immediate consequence of the outbreak of war was the curtailment of trade between Britain and the enemy powers concerned. Some British industries depended heavily on overseas markets and the effect of the sudden cutting-off of such an outlet could be catastrophic. When the American colonists began to place an embargo on British exports in 1765, the whole Birmingham and Black Country district immediately felt alarm. "We are all in the greatest consternation about the event of it", Dr John Ash of Birmingham wrote, "and have also this additional reflection, that distress is already at *our* door. Many of our merchants . . . . or rather factors, have nearly their whole capital locked up in North America . . . . More than half the iron goods made in this populous country and three parts in four of the nails were taken off by the American trade; and in all probability from three to fifteen thousand manufacturers [workers] in these branches of trade will be entirely out of work in ten or fourteen days . . . The toy trade may perhaps keep us from immediate ruin . . . . " Ash recognised growing unemployment as a threat to public order, and proposed that the local newspapers be censored of American news, "lest they might in any shape tend to excite insurrections of the common people". Reports from other manufacturing districts of the country suggest that the Birmingham situation was by no means unusual, and Dr Ash's response was characteristic of business and professional men. While it is true that British success in war was followed by territorial acquisitions and hence new markets, and that government loans and subsidies to foreign powers helped to sustain the overseas demand for products of British industry, there can be little doubt that these indirect benefits of war hardly counterbalanced the losses due to dislocation of trade.

War distorted, too, the normal peace-time pattern of economic development. Certainly some industries were stimulated, particularly metal. Speaking of the progress of the iron industry, Professor Ashton notes that "most of the great new works based on the use of coke for smelting and refining were brought into being in 1756-63, 1775-83, and 1793-1802"—the major periods of war in the second half of the century. In the Napoleonic Wars sections of the clothing industry, particularly the West of England industry, prospered on government contracts for uniforms, while some branches of the hosiery industry did well supplying worsted stockings (Leicester) and sailors' jackets (Nottingham). Animal breeders benefited from the inflated demand for horses (for the cavalry and transport), leather (boots and saddlery), and meat (victualling the forces), while farmers generally profited from the cutting-off of supplies of grain from the Continent. But the artificial level of demand collapsed at the first sign of peace, and the whole country suffered in a depression for four years after the peace of 1815. There was also a fall of agricultural prices as a result of good harvests and the flooding of the labour market by rapid demobilisation and Irish immigration. Moreover the West of England suffered permanent economic injury, for its concentration as a result of inflated war-time demand on the old-fashioned broadcloth during the crucial period of transition to the factory system of production must be counted an important factor in the early decline of the region. A sharp rise in the price of wool due to war-time shortages checked the growth of the worsted industry and, according to one leading manufacturer, "large mills and factories originally destined to the working of woollens have been compelled to devote their works to cotton". Working people turned to cotton as a cheap substitute for wool, a fortunate circumstance for Lancashire, which was thereby enabled to maintain the momentum of its growth despite the instability of trade and the frequency of bankruptcy.

The shortages of the war years created an inflation of prices, particularly of foodstuffs. Price inflation encourages entrepreneurs because it reduces the burden of debt and encourages people to buy sooner rather than later. But wage earners, whose incomes tended to be fixed by the custom of the trade and were difficult to adjust upwards, inevitably suffered a deterioration in the value of their earnings. Supplies of coal to London, and of softwood timber from the Baltic (for housing), declined as they depended on transport by sea. The shipping lanes were dangerous, merchant seamen were drafted into the Navy, and ships lost could not be quickly replaced. The statistics of excise duty collected on bricks shows that building declined during the French Wars. It is possible that the notorious jerry-building and urban congestion of the early years of the nineteenth century were at least partly the consequence of war-time shortages and the low priority that government and local authorities gave to measures of social welfare.

Population Growth and Local Government

The congestion of housing that became serious in London in the seventeenth century and in Edinburgh, Dublin, and many provincial towns in the eighteenth century, was the immediate consequence of population growth and migration from the countryside to the towns. The consequent deterioration in the quality of town life has often been blamed on industrialism, but urban squalor was just as characteristic of commercial towns (like Liverpool and Bristol) and centres of government (like Westminster and Edinburgh) as it was of the new centres of industry. The smoke from steam-powered mills certainly polluted the atmosphere of the manufacturing towns, but it should not be overlooked that the breweries of the capital towns were amongst the earliest users of Watt engines, while the largest concentrations of Newcomen engines were found in the "rural" coalfields up to about 1800.

The failure to take adequate steps to deal with the rapid growth of towns is largely to be explained by lack of experience of urban problems. At the beginning of the eighteenth century provincial towns were only villages by the standards of to-day, and problems of water supply, sanitation, lighting, paving and cleaning of streets, and of town planning had hardly presented themselves. The rapid growth of towns was quite unprecedented, and it was a long time before the educated classes realised what was happening let alone tried to do something about it. Until the enthusiasm for statistical investigation of the 1830s there was a general failure to appreciate the extent of the problems brought by urbanisation, such as the threat to health which pollution of water supplies, overcrowding, and lack of sanitation presented. In any case, the techniques of inspection, planning, and municipal engineering hardly existed; they represent some of the less well-known achievements of the later nineteenth century and of the present century.

There was also a lack of adequate machinery of government to take responsibility for new social needs. Over the centuries about 200 towns had received charters from the monarchy and thus acquired independence of the county magistrates. A handful of these towns had a democratically elected corporation, London, Norwich, and Ipswich being the important examples. But by the eighteenth century most of the governing bodies were self-perpetuating oligarchies; among those were the corporations of Leeds, Coventry, Bristol, Liverpool, Nottingham, and Leicester. A few of these privileged élites, notably that of Liverpool, were conscious of the growing economic and social needs of the town they governed, but most of them had a very limited conception of their functions. Their role varied in detail from one chartered town to the next, but generally they regulated streets and markets and made themselves responsible for maintaining civil order. All too often the corporation took on the appearance of an exclusive wining and dining club, supported by its hereditary estates, and only shaken out of its lethargy when some serious disorder broke out in the market place or amongst the craftsmen of the town.

But by no means all industrial towns had a charter until after the passing of the first general measure of reform, the Municipal Corporations Act of 1835. Birmingham and Sheffield had no independent magistracy, and Manchester was governed by a "Court Leet" until 1846. Both chartered and unincorporated towns invariably had improvement commissions, which were appointed by private Act of Parliament to undertake specific functions such as paving, cleaning, lighting and policing the town (or some of its principal streets) and erecting markets. Like the turnpike trusts they represented a private but limited response to public (*i.e.* government) neglect.

The inexperience of county J.P.s, and perhaps also their reluctance to frustrate the profitable enterprise of a neighbouring landowner, led to considerable loss of amenity in rural as well as urban districts. Barren spoil heaps, land poisoned by the refuse of chemical works, marshes and ponds left by mining subsidence, and abandoned pit-head gear were allowed to disfigure the countryside of the mining districts. Vegetation has gradually overlaid many of the tips, but in a few instances, as our photograph shows, the blighting of the landscape seems permanent. It is only within the last few years that local authorities, impelled by the desperate shortage of building land, have begun the expensive process of restoration of what are now known, in the jargon of planners, as "areas of dereliction".

Factory Discipline and the Factory Community

The pioneers of the factory system faced considerable opposition, particularly from the workpeople

Plate VII.2. Moorland poisoned by fumes from lead flues (see Plate IV.22) in Allendale, Northumberland.

137

who (quite correctly) foresaw the displacement of their skills. There was some problem in recruiting workers, particularly those with regular and sober habits. The early cotton mills, which were often situated in remote parts of the Pennines, solved their shortage of labour by importing hundreds of pauper children from populous districts (particularly London) and boarding and training them to the work. Their condition could be akin to slavery. In the towns it was not so difficult to engage workers as to train them to the punctuality, regularity, and high standards demanded by factory owners of the type of Arkwright, Boulton, and Wedgwood. The other difficult problem was the opposition of workers to change, sometimes expressed in mob fury or as a by-product of political demonstrations, sometimes by organised groups (trade unions and political clubs), occasionally as petitions to the local government authority (borough councils or county J.P.s), or to Parliament. From whichever quarter opposition came, the ultimate victory of the factory-owning class could not be assured.

The attempt to train and indoctrinate workers to make them willing factory operatives constitutes one of the most unpleasant chapters of the history of the Industrial Revolution. The pioneers of change were very often high-minded men whose radical economic ideas were paralleled by progressive political and religious ideas, but as their ideas filtered through to lesser men they suffered considerable dilution of quality. Discipline was often, if not invariably, enforced by deterrents, particularly corporal punishment (for juveniles), heavy fines, and dismissal without notice. Incentives, such as bonus payments and promotion by merit, were much less common. Harsh discipline was a universal feature of life during the whole period covered by this book, as the rules of schools and workhouses reveal, but the factory extended this stern paternalism to the ordinary adult worker.

It was soon realised in fact that coercive measures only had a limited effect and what was needed was a fundamental change in the habits and outlook of a working class who had for generations worked and played as necessity, or fancy, or the village revelries took them. What the factory masters called irregular and dissolute habits were part of the established pattern of living in pre-industrial England. Nonconformity and Methodism stood out for a more disciplined life but, in the eighteenth century, they were only minority movements. The factory masters decided

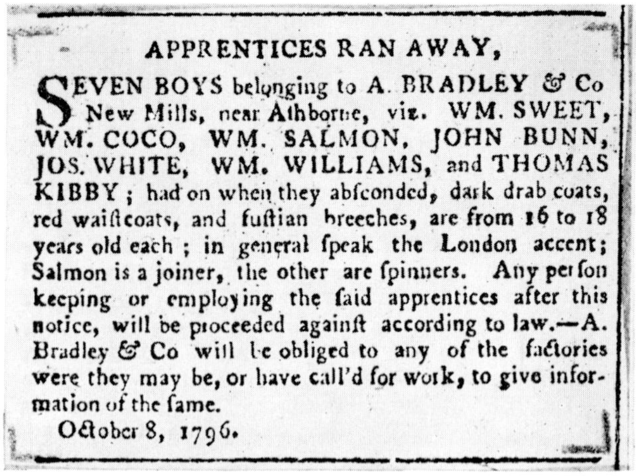
APPRENTICES RAN AWAY,

SEVEN BOYS belonging to A. BRADLEY & Co New Mills, near Athborne, viz. WM. SWEET, WM. COCO, WM. SALMON, JOHN BUNN, JOS. WHITE, WM. WILLIAMS, and THOMAS KIBBY; had on when they abſconded, dark drab coats, red waiſtcoats, and fuſtian breeches, are from 16 to 18 years old each; in general ſpeak the London accent; Salmon is a joiner, the other are ſpinners. Any perſon keeping or employing the ſaid apprentices after this notice, will be proceeded againſt according to law.—A. Bradley & Co will be obliged to any of the factories were they may be, or have call'd for work, to give information of the ſame.

October 8, 1796.

Plate VII.3. Advertisement in the *Derby Mercury*. (*Derby Public Library*.)

what was required was a moral reformation of the worker, and with characteristic energy they set out to implement their conclusion. Various means were used to bring about this reformation of character. Many industrialists founded or supported churches and chapels—Ambrose Crowley opened a chapel for his workers as early as 1705—and towards the end of the century Sunday Schools found similar favour as the idea popularised by Robert Raikes spread. Numbers of firms established or patronised friendly societies among their workers so as to encourage the idea of self-help and thrift. The rules of Boulton and Watt's club at Soho were well known and copied by numbers of contemporaries. Even Major Cartwright, well known as "the father of English radicalism", wrote to Boulton and Watt for a copy of these rules to adapt them for his worsted mill at Retford (Notts).

The historical significance of this process of indoctrination must not be underestimated. The adjustment of labour to the regularity and discipline of factory work involved much more than a change of habits. It demanded a revolution of ideology. As we have seen, the eighteenth-century worker was content to work for a subsistence, had no sense of economy of time, and was generally indifferent to the development of his abilities. The eighteenth-century entrepreneur was anxious to make the best possible use of his time and capabilities to increase his income and improve his standards of living. If he was religious he believed that every man was a steward of God for his time, talents, and money; so that his hard work was both pleasing to God and useful to his

Plate VII.4. School at Cromford.

Plate VII.5. Cromford Church.

fellow men. The new virtues that the workers were persuaded to adopt were those requisite for a material civilisation: regularity, punctuality, obedience, thrift, providence, sobriety, and industry. The factory environment established in many cases by high-minded spiritual men, thus fostered the values of the acquisitive society of our own day.

Factory masters claimed that they achieved the greatest success in reforming their workers in the factory communities that sprang up in the country-side. In order to attract skilled labour from the established manufacturing districts they had to offer both good wages, housing, and sometimes other benefits. The great majority of these industrial settlements in the countryside were quite small affairs, a water mill and six or eight cottages and perhaps (in the cotton mill era) an apprentice house for imported juvenile labour. The mill owner or manager lived in a mansion nearby, and often took it upon himself to direct the morals of the workers, just as the squire or laird were still wont to do in rural Britain.

A handful of highly successful entrepreneurs who were able to purchase large country estates in the districts about their mills, and who employed consider-ably more workers than the average, offered more amenities like schools and churches, shops and markets, and a variety of other incentives to their workers, such as the opportunity of an allotment, or subsidised provisions and coal, or membership of sick clubs which gave benefits during illness. In the

139

Plate VII.6. New Lanark; The "House of Character-Training".

eighteenth century the best known factory community was probably Arkwright's Cromford, which was built on the foundations of a declining lead mining village between 1771 and 1792. Cromford was in fact the darling of a brilliantly successful entrepreneur, trying to create a showplace; there was no such display at his other mills, except where his former partners copied his methods.

The Strutts at Belper, David Dale at New Lanark, Samuel Oldknow at Mellor, and the Evans' at Darley Abbey (Derby) all had early connections with Arkwright and built on his ideas. Other wealthy entrepreneurs preferred to buy up an established community, as Sir Robert Peel bought Tamworth, Joseph Wilkes bought Measham, and John Heathcoat bought part of Tiverton. After Cromford, the best-known eighteenth-century community was Josiah Wedgwood's Etruria, but Wedgwood's initiative in leaving the polluted atmosphere of the Burslem bottle kilns for new pastures found no imitators. Boulton's Soho was nearly a financial failure and, like Etruria, was a unique feature of its district.

In the early decades of the nineteenth century, the advent of steam power rendered many country mills redundant, and several communities disappeared. A few surviving second generation factory patriarchs made their isolated factory communities an end in themselves. David Dale's mills were taken over by his son-in-law, Robert Owen, who tried to develop the community to demonstrate the feasibility of his socialist ideology. Owen's reputation as the founder of the Co-operative movement rests on his campaign for "villages of co-operation", based on an idealisation of New Lanark. Working people opened co-operative stores to raise money to buy land to establish co-operative communities; the little stores prospered while the utopian communities broke up, as many before had done, and not a few since. Thomas Ashton of Hyde (Manchester) built up a community of workers whose providence and sobriety were a by-word in the improving literature of the day. The community was given the maximum publicity in Dr James Kay's *Moral and Physical Condition of the Working Classes employed in the Cotton Manufacture in Manchester* (1832), where it was treated as a model of what working-class life might be. The Gregs at Styall (Cheshire) and the Ashworths at Turton (Lancashire) also exercised their minds in problems of producing subordinate, sober, and industrious workers. Their views of social issues were not hidden from the world of their day.

Jedediah Strutt's sons were more genuinely radical than most of their contemporaries among the middle class. William Strutt is said to have distributed copies of Tom Paine's *Rights of Man* among his workers, and his brother Joseph worked for the acquittal of the leaders of the Pentrich insurrection of 1817. The brothers' philanthropy in Derby included the first hospital, park, and Lancasterian school in the town. But they cherished rather inflated ideas about the civilising influence of Belper. "It is well known in this neighbourhood that before the establishment of these works", they said, "the inhabitants were notorious for vice and immorality, and many of the children were maintained by begging; now their industry, decorous behaviour, attendance on public worship, and general good conduct, compared with the neighbouring villages, where no manufactures are established, is very conspicuous." It is not in doubt that the Strutts brought more regular employment and other benefits to a declining nailing village. But the recent publication of a Belper working man's diary, with accounts of women fighting in the streets and a mob pulling a house down, warn us to be cautious about the eulogies that have sometimes been written of this and other communities.

What *is* clear is that in the second half of the eighteenth century a number of industrial towns and villages benefited from the idealism of some wealthy industrialists. Towns, like Liverpool, Manchester, and Birmingham benefited from the tireless leadership of wealthy Unitarian families, like the Strutts, Ashtons, Gregs, and Wedgwoods, while other industrial centres, like Nottingham, saw rapid municipal progress under Evangelical leadership. Religious idealism was to play an important part in social and municipal progress in the nineteenth century.

The Standard of Living of the Working Classes

In the second half of the nineteenth century it became apparent to most observers that the working classes were benefiting from industrialism in terms of higher real wages, shorter hours, more varied diet, and more regular food supplies, and an improvement in domestic comforts. The point on which contemporaries, and economic historians ever since, have differed, is whether this improvement in the standard of living was cumulative from the beginnings of industrialism in the eighteenth century, or whether the onset of the Industrial Revolution had brought a deterioration in the quality of working-class life that was only made good in the second half of the nineteenth century. The debate is still continuing, but a certain amount of common ground has been established and the outstanding issues have been defined. It is therefore possible to make an interim appraisal of the position.

Before looking at particular regions and classes of people, it is useful to make a number of general points about labour and economic growth. Any country that industrialises must divert an important proportion of its national income into investment in order to build the sinews of modern industry—roads, canals, railways, docks, factories, mines, furnaces, foundries, and the rest. Part of the national income must be diverted from spending on consumer goods to investment in producer goods, in the reasonable expectation of greater gain in the future. During the period of investment entrepreneurs characteristically restricted their own drawings from their firms, in order to increase the flow of investment funds back into the business. Subject to the limitations imposed by the need to attract skilled labour, they tried to subject the workers to the financial stringency they imposed on themselves. The period between 1790 and 1850 is one in which few groups of workers made substantial gains in incomes.

The growth of industry was paralleled by an increase of population and, as we have already noted (Chapter II), it is not clear to what extent the two movements were interdependent. The important point here is that the larger population demanded more food, more clothing, more houses, more schools, hospitals, transport services, and every other kind of amenity. The growing national product had to be shared among a larger number of people and part of the return from investment was necessarily channelled into providing more goods and services for the extra numbers. The experience of several Oriental and Latin-American states to-day shows that rapid population growth can easily swallow up the annual increment of national income provided by industrial investment. In eighteenth-century Britain this was

CROMFORD

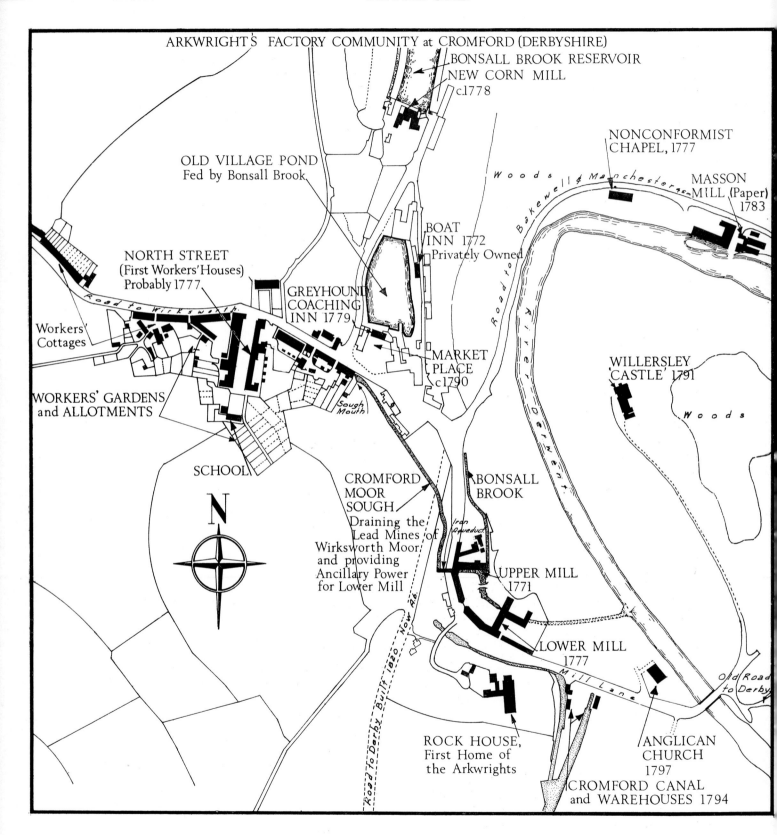

ARKWRIGHT'S FACTORY COMMUNITY at CROMFORD (DERBYSHIRE)

BONSALL BROOK RESERVOIR

NEW CORN MILL c.1778

NONCONFORMIST CHAPEL, 1777

MASSON MILL (Paper) 1783

OLD VILLAGE POND Fed by Bonsall Brook

Woods

Road to Bakewell & Manchester 1820

BOAT INN 1772 Privately Owned

NORTH STREET (First Workers' Houses) Probably 1777

River Derwent

Road to Wirksworth

GREYHOUND COACHING INN 1779

Workers' Cottages

MARKET PLACE c1790

WILLERSLEY 'CASTLE' 1791

Woods

WORKERS' GARDENS and ALLOTMENTS

Sough Mouth

SCHOOL

N

CROMFORD MOOR SOUGH

Draining the Lead Mines of Wirksworth Moor and providing Ancillary Power for Lower Mill

BONSALL BROOK

Iron Aqueduct

UPPER MILL 1771

Road to Derby Built 1820. Now A6.

LOWER MILL 1777

Mill Lane

Old Road to Derby

ROCK HOUSE, First Home of the Arkwrights

ANGLICAN CHURCH 1797

CROMFORD CANAL and WAREHOUSES 1794

Plate VII.7.   Cottages for workpeople at Belper.

Plate VII.8.   A view of a small rural complex.   Note the houses opposite the mill.   Cold Edge, Wanistalls.

Plate VII.9.   A general view of New Lanark.

Plate VII.10.   The mill-manager's house at Cromford.

Plate VII.11.   The second home of the Arkwrights at
Cromford.

fortunately not the case, but the per capita dividend of industrial progress was inevitably smaller when it had to be divided among a larger population.

Another drain on the national resources in the early nineteenth century was the adverse movement of the terms of trade. The price of British exports—mostly manufactured goods—fell relative to the price of the foodstuffs and raw materials that the country imported. This movement of prices was particularly pronounced in the years 1800-15 and 1830-40. In these years foreign countries benefited from the British Industrial Revolution during years when many entrepreneurs were struggling to keep solvent and many workers found all their energies absorbed in a fight to keep above the bread-line.

A period of fundamental technical change is a time of insecurity for trained workers, for invention often devalues or displaces traditional skills. But it is equally a time of opportunity, for invention unlocks doors to new industries which place a premium on workers that can serve them. The experience of other periods and countries suggests that large differentials in wage rates are characteristic of periods of fundamental technical change. For this reason the Industrial Revolution was a period of contrasting prosperity that defeats attempts at generalisation. The expansion of the various industries we have looked at created unprecedented opportunities for workers to earn high wages and set themselves up as independent manufacturers. In Manchester and Stockport, not only established weavers, but shopkeepers, hatters, carters, joiners, clock-makers, and many other artisans became masters in the industry in the period after about 1788. When a survey of the lace industry was made in 1829 it was said that only eight out of more than 1,200 masters in the industry had not been drawn from the ranks of the workmen; most of them had been framework knitters or framesmiths. In Birmingham the "little mesters" were everywhere; in the jewellery trade, for instance, it was said that nine out of ten of the workshops were owned by men who had worked their way up from an apprenticeship in the business. Even the coal industry knew instances of upward social mobility, for an able man might become a "butty" (charter master) and some local newspapers (like the *Wolverhampton Chronicle*) carried advertisements for these men. In every district machine and engine builders were at a premium.

The prosperous condition of these workers must be contrasted with many of those whose skills were displaced. Where the declining trade was a small one, and there was alternative employment, the workers may have suffered little more than the problem of adjustment to new habits of work. An interesting illustration of this point is provided by the decline of the old tenter-field bleaching industry around Manchester in the last two decades of the eighteenth century. No loud complaints were heard, and many of the whitsters, as the bleachers were called, were probably absorbed into the ranks of the country manufacturers. The numbers listed in the Manchester directories are as follows:

	1772	1781	1788	1794	1797	1804	1815
Whitsters	82	88	50	18	1	-	-
Country manufacturers	112	219	202	266	265	311	411

But where large numbers of particular craftsmen were heavily concentrated in one district offering little alternative employment the result of the devaluation of their skills could be disastrous. The introduction of wide frames into the hosiery industry about 1810, at a time when the collapse of the United States market and the Napoleonic blockade compelled an attempt to find new markets by cutting prices, caused a further decline in the living standard of the framework knitters, whose occupation was already overcrowded. The woolcombers, whose unions had done everything they could to prevent the adoption of Cartwright's combing machine in the 1790s, suffered a steady deterioration in income and status from the time improved combing machines began to be widely used, after about 1825. A similar fate befell the handloom weavers as steam looms were widely adopted in the 1830s, and the nailmakers after the first nail-making machine was patented in 1830. The numbers of hand workers who were superseded within a generation were very considerable in some regions. In 1833 there were reckoned to be 200,000-250,000 handloom weavers in the cotton trade. A popular estimate puts the number of Black Country nailers and dependants at 50,000 about 1830, but this may well be an overstatement. The influx of Irish (particularly into north-west England) and the passing of the Poor Law Amendment Act of 1834 (see p. 153), aggravated the social problem of these concentrations of poverty and misery.

The most important characteristic of working-class expenditure during the period covered by this book,

Plate VII.12. A reconstructed working-class interior at Shibden Hall Folk Museum, Halifax.

Plate VII.13. A reconstructed bar at Shibden Hall Folk Museum, Halifax.

and indeed for most of the nineteenth century, was the high proportion of income devoted to food. Four or five basic food-stuffs—bread, potatoes, cheese, and beer, and perhaps meat, sugar, and tea—absorbed most of the weekly wages of the family. The remainder was taken up by rent and fuel.

In the countryside the diet of the poor class of labourers was even less varied than this. "In the South of England", according to Sir Frederick Morton Eden in his inquiry into *The State of the Poor* (1797), "the poorest labourers are habituated to the unvarying meal of dry bread and cheese from week's end to week's end." In the North of England, Scotland, and Wales the poorest labourers showed more ingenuity in varying their diet by baking various kinds of oatmeal cakes and barley bread, and by using more potatoes and making barley soups. The availability of cheaper fuel supplies (coal, and in less accessible districts, timber), enabled the northerners, Scots, and Welsh, to be more independent and comfortable.

Eden published over forty different working-class family budgets from different parts of the country. One example is reprinted here to illustrate a typical working-class expenditure account:-

WEEKLY EXPENDITURE OF FARM LABOURER AND HIS FAMILY (SEVEN CHILDREN) AT STREATLEY, BERKSHIRE, 1797

	s.	d.
8 half-peck loaves at 1s. 9d.	14	0
2 lb. cheese	1	2
2 lb. butter	1	6
2 lb. sugar	1	6
2 oz. tea		4½
½ lb. oatmeal		1½
½ lb. bacon		3
Milk		2
Total expenditure on food	19	1
House rent		10½
Candles, soap, salt, etc. (average)		11
Clothes and shoes (average)	2	4
Fuel is chiefly beech wood collected in the woods; what is bought averages		4½
Total weekly expenditure	23	7

Prices were particularly high in 1797 and this family budget, despite a working wife and two boys employed on the land, was only balanced by subsidies from the parish.

Scattered information available for the next thirty or forty years does not show any very striking changes in patterns of consumption. Carefully compiled statistics of national consumption of

several commodities—beer, cotton, coal, soap, and candles, for instance—suggest an upward trend. There was also a steady move from the coarse grains (rye, barley, oats) to wheat. This is not to suggest, however, that the improvement in popular diet was universal; clearly the gains were very uneven, and some groups did not benefit at all.

"SUBSISTENCE LEVEL" FOR A MARRIED MAN, HIS WIFE, AND FOUR CHILDREN IN 1825
(*according to a correspondent of the "Nottingham Review,"* 30 *September* 1825)

	s.	d.
6 quartern loaves	5	0
1½ lb. sugar	1	3
¾ lb. tea	2	6
1 lb. cheese		10
5 lb. meat	4	2
Flour	1	4
Potatoes		8
Malt liquor	1	6
Milk (for children)		6
Total spent on food	17	9
Rent	2	0
Rates	1	0
Coal	1	0
Clothing	3	9
Shoes	1	2
Candles (lighting)		9
Soap		10
Total expenditure	28	3

The budget lacks variety by modern standards, but the relatively heavy consumption of meat does not suggest a pattern of expenditure directed by a

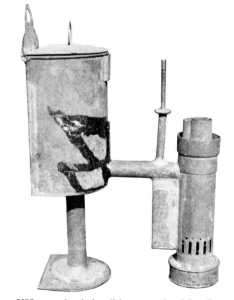

Plate VII.14. A whale-oil lamp used at New Lanark.

struggle for survival. Tea and sugar had been items of popular consumption since the middle of the eighteenth century, and the family consumption of cheese, butter, and milk reaches that of a modern family. However, this diet would be based on that of the prosperous lace hands, whose families (according to the novelist Mary Howitt) "were always well-fed". It would have little meaning to the depressed framework knitters, whose family earnings would rarely exceed fifteen shillings.

A study of working-class housing in the late eighteenth and early nineteenth centuries emphasises the considerable contrasts between income groups that have already been observed. The most usual kind of urban dwelling was a back-to-back house consisting of two or three rooms placed on top of each other. This pattern of building was popular because it was so cheap, it saved bricks and labour—only one outer wall had to be built for each house—and it saved land. A further saving could be made by building the back-to-back terraces around narrow courts, for the builder did not have to make the road up, except for the "front" houses. The upper room of the house was very often used as a workshop by weavers, framework knitters, or other domestic workers. Water was obtained from a pump at the centre of the court, or from water carriers, and there was often a line of "privies" across the end of the court opposite its entrance to the road.

The fact that these courts and terraces have become slums in this century should not blind us to the fact that they were superior to the accommodation available to most people before they were built, and that there were plenty of worse houses inhabited at the time. In her study of *London Life in the Eighteenth Century*, Dr M. D. George comes to the conclusion that overcrowding was general, despite the regulated re-building after the Great Fire of 1666. Workers had to live near their workplace owing to the absence of any cheap means of transport and the unpleasantness and danger of walking through the streets after dark. The standard dwelling of the London artisan, even in a "genteel trade", seems to have been a single room, which in many cases served as a workshop and bedroom as well as living space. The poorest workers shared lodging rooms with fifteen or twenty others for 1d. or 2d. a night, while in many cases sheds and stalls served as homes for most of the eighteenth century. Cellars and garrets were the typical homes and workplaces of small dealers and artisans; the second and

third floor of a house would form the home of a more substantial family. The ground floor would form the home of the owner of the house, a shopkeeper or craftsman of independent status. Information for the provinces is more fragmentary, but implies that standards were not significantly better than those in London for most of the eighteenth century. In Manchester, for instance, the Court Leet records contain references to "houses without back-sides" in the sixteenth century, while in the early part of the next century there are details of gross overcrowding "wherebye it appeareth there are full twenty persons at the least dwelling all within one house". In Nottingham, Mansfield, Buxton, and some other towns, cave dwellings were still in use at the beginning of the nineteenth century.

In the Tudor period, timber, thatch, and wattle and daub were the invariable building materials except in those parts of the country where stone was cheap. Brick and slate replaced the traditional materials only very gradually during the course of the next two centuries, beginning with wealthy merchants and farmers, and spreading slowly down the social hierarchy to reach the better-off artisans towards the end of the eighteenth century. The new materials were partly the consequence of diminishing timber and increasing coal supplies (used to bake bricks), but partly also a recognition of the fact that brick and slate provided dryer and warmer homes. Dr Aikin explains that in Manchester in the 1690s the merchants began to extend their scale of operations and improve their incomes; one early consequence was that they "began to build modern brick houses in place of those of wood and plaster". The solid, symmetrical early Georgian houses of many provincial towns suggests that Manchester's experience was fairly typical. The long brick terraces were the response of the workers to the style set by their immediate superiors, and in one form or another they were the accepted form of building for most of the nineteenth century.

Country labourers and the poorly-paid urban workers did not reach the standard of the back-to-back terrace houses much before 1830. Eden reported that on the coast of Yorkshire "many of the cottages are miserable hovels, built of mud and straw" (1797), while in Cornwall labourers lived between two mud banks at the beginning of the nineteenth century. In the nailing districts of the Black Country "mud" cottages survived to within living memory. In the mining and framework

Plates VII.15 and 16. Education for the workers. *Top*, an eighteenth-century school at Halesowen, Worcs., whose pupils would largely be drawn from the lower middle classes and tradespeople (like Dr Johnson's at Lichfield). *Below*, a National School at Bingley of 1814, erected probably to cater for a certain proportion of working-class pupils.

knitting districts of Derbyshire, a village (Ilkeston) was recalled in the following terms: "its streets were dirty and unpaved, save by a single narrow stepping stone, or 'Derbyshire Causeway'; many of the houses were little better than huts inside or outside, and were noisome and destitute of most of the conveniences of life". In Wigan (Lancashire) many miners' families had houses with only one room in 1842, and "in by far the greatest number furniture is almost unheard of; as to chairs, they do not feel the want of them, as the habit is to sit down upon the heels of their clogs". The handloom weavers of Manchester and some adjacent cotton towns were said to be "largely cellar dwellers" in 1826. The most harrowing descriptions of all are of the homes of the immigrant Irish, written by Friedrich Engels.

149

Plate VII.17.   Cottages at Fazeley, Tamworth, built by Sir Robert Peel for the workers at his cotton mill about the time of the
first Factory Act (1802).   (*Chapman.*)

"Passing along a rough bank, among stakes and washing lines, one penetrates into this chaos of small one-storied, one-room huts, in most of which there is no artificial floor; kitchen, living and sleeping room are in one. In such a hole, scarcely five feet long by six feet broad, I found two beds . . . ."

This picture of working-class life must be balanced by recognising that the better-paid artisans were building houses superior to the back-to-back terraces occupied by most urban workers and their families. The earliest building societies, which were societies of men of small means who clubbed together to buy a plot of land and build a terrace of cottages, appeared in the 1770s. They seem to have originated in Birmingham and its neighbourhood, where skilled workers commonly earned two or three times the 10s. a week that labourers received. In provincial towns like Birmingham, Coventry, Bradford, and Nottingham the artisan élite built their own houses in the adjacent countryside, with enclosed yards and gardens reaching a standard that would satisfy any public health inspector to-day.

The Origins of Government Social Policy

In Chapter II we saw that in our period the government had no economic policy beyond the generally-felt need to leave merchants and manufacturers as free from restraint as possible. Whig and Tory governments alike allowed the Tudor and Stuart statutes that regulated industry to become atrophied by disuse, while the Justices of the Counties and County Boroughs showed increasing reluctance to "interfere" with the free development of commerce and industry. In effect government economic policy was merely acquiescence in commercial and manufacturing norms and practice, a simple faith in the value of unshackled individual enterprise (which would be harmonised by the necessary equation of supply and demand), and a passion for economy in public expenditure.

This is not to suggest, however, that there was no response to changing economic and social needs. While the principle of *laisser-faire* received almost universal assent among the middle classes, in practice particular needs were felt to justify exceptions to the general rule requiring the government to maintain a minimum role in the economic life of the nation. It would be misleading to suggest that governments were wilfully neglectful of those who needed protection, like the displaced spinners and weavers, and those exploited by the truck system, or jerry-built housing. The truth was that Parliament, an upper-class assembly before 1832, was ignorant

Plate VII.18. Late eighteenth-century houses in Woodcock Street, Birmingham, built by one of the early Building Clubs. In the early nineteenth century back-to-back terraces were built on the gardens. (*Chapman.*)

Plate VII.19. *Right*, shows the front door of one of the houses; imitation of upper middle-class tastes is evident. (*Chapman.*)

Manchester Literary and Philosophic Society, whose foundation in 1781 has already been referred to. In the 1790s, the Society began to make statistical enquiries into the causes of and incidence of early mortality in various quarters of the town. The outcome was to identify the correlation between overcrowded living and working conditions and early death. Dr Percival's conviction that the conditions under which women and children laboured in the cotton factories were a prime cause of high mortality rates led directly to the first factory Act, Sir Robert Peel's Health and Morals of Apprentices Act of 1802. The Act laid down that no apprentice was to be employed for more than 12 hours a day, that night work was forbidden, and that some religious and other instruction had to be given. The Justices who were responsible for administering the Act were

of these needs, blinkered by the conventional idea of *laisser-faire*, and harassed by the fear of revolution that was so prevalent during and after the French Wars. It was only very slowly that Parliament began to recognise the necessity for social reforms, and then only on the basis of being exceptions to the commonly accepted policy.

The origin of social welfare legislation is to be found in the scientific study of society, *i.e.* in social investigations producing statistics identifying critical needs. The starting point was the work of the

Plate VII.20. Foundry workers' houses in the country at Penny Bridge (Salop). These are substantially built and are an example of what some factory masters could and did provide.

not so vigilant as they might have been, but the Act was not a dead letter. Robert Owen became a member of the "Lit. and Phil." in 1793 and conceived a passion for reform that made him the next important name in the factory reform movement. Dr Percival also established the pioneer Manchester Board of Health (1796), though it had no true successor for more than a generation. Unfortunately for social progress, many of the members of the learned societies of the 1780s and 1790s were Radicals who had identified themselves with the ideals of the French Revolution, and during the ensuing reaction of the War years they thought it prudent to remove themselves from the public eye.

It was not until the early 1830s that the study of social pathology again became popular. By this time public opinion had become more sensitive to social injustice; the spread of Evangelical religion was persuading men that political issues were necessarily moral issues. The success of the anti-slavery agitation (1787-1807) inspired a succession of other protests with the Christian conscience at their centre; an epidemic, mine disaster, or other exposure of human suffering was likely to produce an in-

dignant group to campaign for support or protection of those who could not help themselves. From the 1820s Parliament became more and more responsive to this kind of pressure from the growing electorate.

In the late 1820s interest in statistical inquiries into welfare revived; the most important landmark was the foundation of the Manchester Statistical Society (1833). The period between 1832 and 1854 saw a chain of Royal Commissions and Select Committees investigating child labour conditions of work in factories and mines, education, the poor law, depressed handloom weavers and knitters, prisons, asylums, and the health of towns. The inquiry was often precipitated by some wave of moral indignation, but the factual information which alone could form the basis of legislation was provided by doctors, engineers, clergymen, merchants, and manufacturers, who were driven by "the stench of urban poverty" into investigating its origins and characteristics. During this period no less than sixteen separate government inspectorates were set up. The legislation and the work of the inspectors (whose inquiries disclosed new and urgent social needs)

152

provided one of the foundations for modern welfare legislation.

It was at one time supposed that the principal inspiration of welfare legislation in the nineteenth century was the work of a number of London intellectuals known as the Utilitarians. Jeremy Bentham and a group of disciples wrote volumes on the application of the principle of "the greatest happiness of the greatest number" to English law, and the most practical *social* reformer among the group was Edwin Chadwick, a civil servant who worked steadfastly to persuade Parliament and public opinion to recognise the connection between poverty and insanitary living conditions. Chadwick managed to draw together, in a series of official reports, the expertise of doctors like James Kay of Manchester, Southwood Smith of London, and Thomas Hawksley, the engineer who pioneered high pressure water supply. In other respects recent scholarship has tended to play down the importance of the Utilitarians. Two pieces of legislation which were Utilitarian measures, the Poor Law Amendment Act of 1834 and the repeal of the Combination Acts in 1825, are now thought to have been based on the narrow assumptions of the group, rather than on a realistic appraisal of the real needs of poor law and trade union reform. The Poor Law of 1834 was based on the assumption derived from the Classical Economists that long-term unemployment was a myth and that men could find jobs if only they went to look for them. Hence they were not to be offered relief except in the workhouse. The Commissioners ignored the effect of the trade cycle and of redundancy caused by mechanisation that displaced traditional skills. The 1834 inquiry produced ample evidence of unemployment arising from these causes, but blind adherence to abstract political theory resulted in Parliament and the administration disregarding the pressing human needs of an industrialising country. The repeal of the Combination Acts was the only survivor of a comprehensive measure of reform prepared by Gravenor Henson, an experienced and moderate trade union leader, and Peter Moore, Radical M.P. for Coventry. Moore and Henson had proposed to repeal almost 400 clauses or complete Acts that they thought were unfair to the employee, and to protect the worker against common forms of exploitation like the truck system (payment in goods instead of cash) and an employer's evasion of a contract of employment. But, except for the achievement of Chadwick in respect of public health and factory legislation, Utilitarianism can hardly be regarded as an enlightened movement.

The Response of the Working Classes

The gradual decay of regulation of industry and commerce by the central and local government authorities forced working people back on to their own resources. The characteristic response of the workers to this was the friendly society, a group of people who joined together to insure one another against the contingencies of sickness, unemployment, and perhaps old age. The members of the friendly society were very often the craftsmen of a particular trade who, when their incomes or conditions of work were threatened, might take on the functions of a trade union. Not all friendly societies were trade unions (even in a contingency sense), and not all trade unions were permanent enough to offer friendly society benefits, but in practice there was so much common ground between them that they might almost be considered one movement. This growth of friendly societies was helped by the general approval that the governing classes gave to them (because they were thought to encourage the working classes in habits of regularity and providence) while workmen's "combinations" were anathema to the upper and middle classes. The funds of friendly societies who registered themselves with the local Justices were protected under an Act of 1793, while trade unions were illegal under the Common Law until 1825, and for long after that time had no legal status.

The origins of the trade union movement are obscure for obvious reasons: illegal bodies keep few records. The earliest unions (like the West of England woolcombers and weavers) were in existence in the first part of the eighteenth century, but trade unions were probably not common until the last decade or two of the century. The growth of the class of permanent wage earners (men with no prospect of ever becoming an independent manufacturer), the decline of state regulation, and the success of the French Revolution, which encouraged ideas of freedom and equality, all contrived to establish pockets of trade union activity throughout the manufacturing districts. At the end of the eighteenth century, periods of good trade (like 1791-2, 1809-10, and 1824-5) were accompanied by a rush of wage demands, and sometimes strikes and lock-outs, news of which found their way into the increasing numbers of local newspapers.

The characteristic features of trade unions before 1825 can be discerned in the reports of the Home Office agents and in Justices' dispatches, and in intercepted and confiscated correspondence. The membership, officials, and organisation were kept secret because of fear of prosecution. Strikers, when arrested, maintained that they had been intimidated by others, and knew nothing of the union. Freemasonry, with its signs, passwords, and oaths of fidelity suggested many ideas. The unions usually had a methodical, democratic organisation. The Wesleyan (Methodist) movement and the new radical political societies provided trade unionists with ideas on representation, delegation, and federation. Tom Paine's popular *Rights of Man* introduced unionists to fraternal ideas and friendly society benefits fitted in with this ideal. Social mobility was growing in the eighteenth century, but the opportunity for a working man to climb the social ladder depended on unusually favourable circumstances; the consequence was that even at this early period, the trade union movement threw up numbers of fearless and talented leaders.

The surviving records suggest that the early trade unions were concentrated among two over-lapping groups of workers. They were common among skilled workers, particularly those whose craft had once been regulated, such as tailors, compositors, weavers, framework knitters, shoe-makers, cutlers, hatters, bakers, and so on. They were also very common among men whose trade was highly concentrated in particular localities, like the coal miners of Bristol, Wigan, Sheffield, and Dudley, the fishermen of Yarmouth, Tyneside, and Aberdeen, and the silk workers of Spitalfields and Coventry.

A few of the more successful societies illustrate some of the achievements of trade unions before 1825. The London Journeymen Tailors' Society is said to have had a membership of 15,000 men in 1800. There were branches all over London based on the public houses. The union came into prominence at this time when it organised a strike for an increase in wages from 25s. to 30s. a week. In January 1801 the London Justices felt compelled to intervene to make a settlement granting the men 27s. The Lancashire Cotton Weavers' Society was a successful union of handloom weavers. It had its headquarters at Bolton and branches at Manchester, Salford, Stockport, Oldham, Wigan, Blackburn, Chorley, Newton,

Warrington, and a number of other centres of the industry. The central committee consisted of a President, Secretary, and twenty-eight delegates, and met monthly. The Society petitioned Parliament to fix wages and, when this failed, promoted the Weavers' Minimum Wage Bill (1808) which was not, however, successful.

The Union Society of Framework Knitters had its headquarters at the Newton's Head Inn, Nottingham, and in 1812 was already well established through the hosiery districts of Nottinghamshire and Derbyshire. In 1814 it was reported as "making very rapid progress throughout Leicestershire, London, Godalming, Tewkesbury, and Northamptonshire . . .". The Society laid down its own minimum wage rates, and struck against any firm which did not pay the rate. The full-time secretary, Gravenor Henson, an able organiser and writer, was paid three guineas a week at a time when knitters in the common branches rarely exceeded 15s. The Society promoted a measure of protection for the industry, the Framework Knitters Bill of 1812, of which more will be said in a moment.

In many instances it is difficult to be sure whether a workers' demonstration or strike was directed by a union or just a spontaneous reaction against something that was commonly felt to be unjust. Before 1825 the history of labour is crowded with innumerable instances of riots, demonstrations, and other eruptions of popular fury, and it is too easy to dismiss these events as the blind reactions of ignorant people. A close study of the events urges that workers were informed by a sense of justice and "fair" prices and wages, as for instance in the frequent market riots and anti-truck demonstrations. There was certainly organisation behind some of these while others, at least, showed unanimity of popular feeling.

From the point of view of this book, the most interesting expressions of working-class belief were the riots and sabotage that often accompanied the introduction of labour-saving machinery. Where the new forms of industry offered workers opportunities of sharing in the enterprise and profits they were ready to contribute to change, but in situations where they could only see themselves as losers they were not slow to raise their objections. From the first they detected the real meaning of the transition to factory production for them, as the following quotation from a petition of Leicester spinners to Parliament (1788) amply demonstrates:

Sometimes we are told we shall have employment in the (factory) woollen manufacture, though the nature of our employment may be changed. Were such changes gradual, the evil would be less; old persons would go off and new ones be brought up to the new-fashioned employment. But the evil is sudden; is at at hand; spinning mills are now setting up all around us . . . and our masters show what their expectations are by undervaluing our work and beating down our wages.

Failing assurance from Parliament, the spinners' menfolk, the woolcombers, took the law into their own hands, and in a fortnight's fury of rioting so intimidated Leicester Corporation that they agreed to ban mechanised spinning from the town and all places within a thirty-mile radius.

The Leicester case is a particularly interesting but by no means unique instance of successful opposition. In 1790 Edmund Cartwright, the inventor of the power loom, entered into an agreement to put 400 of his looms into operation in a factory in Manchester. The opposition of the handloom weavers

was instantly aroused and in a letter to the proprietors, they declared that they had sworn together to destroy the factory, even "if we die for it and we have your lives for ruining our trade". The factory was burned to the ground under mysterious circumstances, and the adoption of the power loom was delayed by more than a decade.

In the West Country practically every innovation was greeted with a united opposition from the workers in the craft affected. The most striking instance of the effect of this opposition is connected with the spinning jenny. The introduction of a few of those machines in Shepton Mallet (Somerset) in 1776—a dozen years after Hargreaves's invention— was followed by their immediate destruction. A meeting of fifty principal clothiers of Gloucestershire, Wiltshire, and Somerset resolved to adopt the machine. Even twenty years later (1796), when Thomas Fox ordered some jennies for his factory

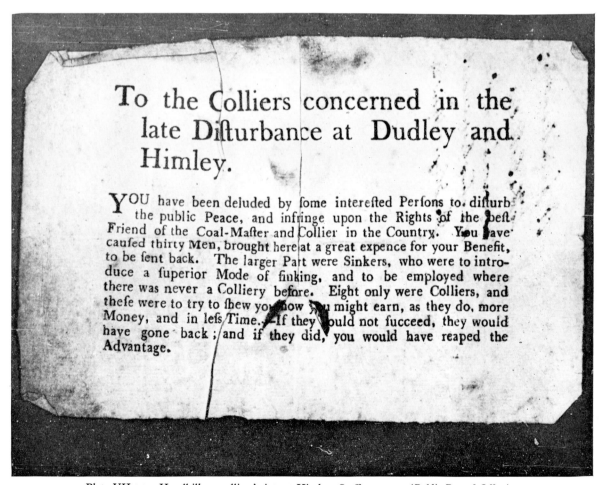

Plate VII.21. Handbill on colliers' riots at Himley, Staffs., 1797. (*Public Record Office.*)

at Wellington (Somerset) his partners left in fear of the buildings being burned down.

Opposition to new machinery was also active in East Anglia. A local historian of Norwich recalled that the town had suffered from "the existence of a violent and odiously virulent party spirit . . . No man of either political party . . . . could introduce machinery into this city . . . . but he would in all probability, at some paltry election contest (particularly if he took an active part in it) be held up as an obnoxious individual . . . . and his property and perhaps his life endangered thereby . . .". The position is overstated in the sense that innovations *were* successfully introduced, but the quotation reflects the very real frustration of many manufacturers.

Though the textile trades offer the largest number of instances of opposition to labour-saving machinery, resistance to innovation was not of course limited to this sector of the economy. When Charles Beaumont tried to introduce Newcastle methods into Viscount Dudley's coal-mines, the result was riots at Himley Hall, and thirty men (twenty-two sinkers and eight miners) brought from the north-east had to be sent back home without work. A West Bromwich colliery proprietor advised Beaumont that the owners "will not be able to reduce the wages of the colliers; indeed I think it would be bad policy so to do considering the scarcity of them and the dangers attending the profession". There was also opposition to the introduction of farm machinery; in 1830 there were reports from Kent, Sussex, and elsewhere of breaking of threshing machines at a time when wages were depressed.

A great deal had been written about the nocturnal machine-breakers and terrorists known as the Luddites. The original Luddites were armed gangs of framework knitters from the industrial villages of Nottinghamshire, but gangs of Lancashire handloom weavers and West Riding shearmen with similar aims in view were soon given the same name. The only thing that the desperate craftsmen of the three regions had in common was that they were skilled men whose wages had been depressed by the interruption of trade during the French wars. The introduction of the wide stocking frame, the power loom, and the shearing frame led to redundancies and spelt the end of the golden years for the operatives of the older machines. Rising food prices in 1811-12 encouraged working-class support and solidarity, and the activities of Home Office *agents provocateurs* made insecure workers even more restless. Nevertheless, remarkably little damage was done in Lancashire and Yorkshire. Two factories near Manchester containing power looms were attacked, a few workshops in the vicinity of Huddersfield containing shearing frames were destroyed, but the vigorous action of a few magistrates ended the sabotage within a few months.

In Nottinghamshire the Luddites had a more complicated origin and were successful for a longer period. The conflict is best understood in terms of the substantial difference in earnings between knitters at the centre of the industry, who were engaged on the most skilled and remunerative work, and the knitters in the rural manufacturing villages, who were engaged on the "common branches" of the trade. The artisan élite responded to the wide frames by promoting a Bill in Parliament, "for preventing frauds and abuses in the framework knitting manufacture and in the payment of persons employed therein", while the country workers, who were the first to feel any contraction in trade, such as that which followed the closing of the United States market in 1811, were impatient of constitutional action. Their anger and frustration exploded into a chain of nocturnal attacks which the Nottingham leadership, in London lobbying for the Bill, were powerless to prevent, despite the embarrassment to their cause. The destruction of wide frames continued through 1811 and 1812, and revived in 1816 when the machines at Heathcoat's first lace factory at Loughborough (Leicestershire) were smashed to pieces. The Pentrich Revolution of 1817, though provoked by an infamous Home Office spy known as Oliver, has the same economic background, for Pentrich, a Derbyshire hamlet about 15 miles from Nottingham, stood on the margin of the hosiery manufacturing district. The leader, Jeremiah Brandreth, was "a half-starved, illiterate, and unemployed framework knitter". Labour unrest in the Nottingham area between 1811 and 1817 is perhaps the most striking commentary on the varying fortunes of workers in the Industrial Revolution.

VIII

Conclusion: The Course of Economic Change

The phrase "Industrial Revolution" still attaches strongly to any discussion of the origins of industrialism in Britain, and in order to avoid pedantry we have used it freely in this book. But at the close of our study we find it just as difficult as other recent writers on the subject to define the chronological limits of change and, particularly, to confine the "Revolution" to the late eighteenth and early nineteenth centuries. It is certainly true that most of the important technical changes in cotton and iron were crowded into the last thirty years of the eighteenth century, but careful investigation of the contribution of these two industries to the national income at the period leaves some doubt about whether they were really responsible for transforming the British economy. "At the beginning of the nineteenth century it is doubtful whether they accounted together for much more than 10 per cent. of the British national income: at the beginning of the 1780s their share may have been as high as 3 per cent. Even assuming a high degree of interdependence with other industries .... their direct effect on the rate of growth of an economy whose population was already increasing at the rate of nearly $1\frac{1}{2}$ per cent. per annum could not have been decisive."[1] Moreover, as we have seen, the process of industrialisation began at the end of the sixteenth century with the growth of coal and its associated industries. In the course of two-and-a-half centuries of growth there were a number of more intense periods of activity—the beginning and end of the seventeenth century, and a period of increasing activity from the 1740s onwards. The proper significance of the period from c.1780 to 1830, invariably referred to as the Industrial Revolution, is that it was the greatest and

most spectacular of a series of developments up to that time, though in terms of the rate of growth of the national economy, its proud place was soon to be usurped in the era of railway development.

If statistics of production for the eighteenth and early nineteenth centuries are scarce and for the most part unreliable those for earlier periods are practically non-existent. This absence of quantitative evidence makes the evaluation of the changes of the reign of Elizabeth and the period up to the Civil Wars most problematical. These were clearly the great pioneering days for the coal trade, glass, paper, and some of the metal industries, but their impact on the national economy was probably small. The great centre of growth was London, where mercantile energy attracted the successful from every port and market town of the country. The rapid growth of its population was the real foundation of the early prosperity of Tyneside, which until the eighteenth century was the most important of the coalfields. The population of London included the discriminating market of noblemen and gentlemen from the provinces, whose refined tastes fostered the growth of many of what we would call luxury industries. The mass market of London was the forcing house of consumption industries producing on a large scale for a popular market, like beer, paper, coal, and pewter, and it shortly began to call forth centres of regional specialisation both for industrial and manufacturing products. The busy commerce of London also laid the foundations of a banking and credit system at this early period.

The "Defoe period" is convenient shorthand for a whole range of commercial and manufacturing activities that were resumed or taken up after the Restoration. The variety defeats any attempt to discover a single key to their interpretation, except

---

[1] Phyllis Deane and W. A. Cole, *British Economic Growth, 1688-1959* (1962).

157

that, apart from new skills brought by the Huguenot refugees, many of the important developments were commercial rather then industrial. In transport, the period saw the beginning of river navigations, the first phase of dock and harbour construction, and a handful of early turnpikes. The London banking system was established, crowned by the foundation of the Bank of England in 1694, and the first provincial banks appeared. In manufacturing, there is evidence of vigour from the registration of patents, whose numbers reached their first peak in the 1690s. Huguenots brought new techniques and refined old ones: fine textiles, watches, paper, and precision instruments were all specialities of these highly skilled Frenchmen. Huguenot paper makers settled in Kent, Hampshire, and Somerset, but most of the refugee artisans found a home in London, reinforcing the concentration of talent in the metropolis that we have already noticed.

However, from this period some London trades began to migrate into the provinces in search of cheaper labour and rents, and more freedom from corporate restriction. It was towards the end of the seventeenth century that the hosiery industry began to leave London for Nottingham, and the Dutch engine loom for Manchester, both assisted by metropolitan capital. The stocking frame and the engine loom played a crucial role in the transition to the factory system at a later stage of economic development. The Derby silk mill, the first modern factory, also owed its origin to a London merchant-entrepreneur; and the first two silk mills at Stockport were supported by capital from London. The great Crowley ironworks at Newcastle, another concern far in advance of its time, was also planned and financed from London.

Talent and enterprise was not, of course, limited to London, as the great provincial families of ironmasters readily show. One regional study of industry points out that all the pre-conditions for major industrial change—for an Industrial Revolution—were present in this period. At any rate, Britain entered the eighteenth century possessed of many active and thrusting entrepreneurs who, though concentrated in London and for the most part possessed of a mercantile (rather than manufacturing) background, were beginning to disperse their interests. The entrepreneurs commanded capital and growing colonial and domestic markets, and they were ready to patronise mechanical talent. Government and parliament were increasingly prepared to

share their commercial outlook. When the right time arrived they were ready to spread their wings and initiate the so-called "take-off into self-sustained growth" of the later eighteenth century. A study of the activities of the entrepreneurs provides the key to understanding the course of change.

In all societies, some individuals have a talent for accumulating and directing the use of capital; such individuals were particularly numerous in England, and English society, by its social, political, and legal institutions, was particularly adapted to produce and encourage them. In a country where a population of rich landlords and merchants, substantial farmers, tradesmen, and artisans, provided a market for consumption goods of all kinds, and where even the wage earners, except in times of unemployment, usually had a surplus to spend above basic subsistence, there was great scope for successful enterprise. At the same time, profit-making was regarded as a highly meritorious pursuit in all ranks of society from the highest to the lowest. The internal market was buoyant; the external market, especially in the colonies, was expanding; old-fashioned restrictions such as guild regulations and apprenticeship laws no longer set up barriers as they did in France and other continental countries to the spread of industry, and the countryside as well as the towns were humming with the noise of spindle and loom, of hammer and anvil, of mill-wheels and sails, with the rumble of carts and the tramp of pack horses, with the noise and bustle of sheep and cattle fairs, of cloth market and corn exchanges. If anyone doubts this he should turn to the pages of Arthur Young's *Travels in France* where he comments again and again on the almost empty roads compared with those of England, with the difficulty he met with of hiring a post-chaise for a journey, and on the miserable inns compared to those of England and the abundance of fleas and the scantiness of the fare publicans provided. It is not surprising that on this background of ceaseless economic activity and universal search for profits, a number of outstanding figures should emerge as inventors and leaders of enterprise who are as familiar to us as the great generals and politicians of the period, and not less important.

But besides the leaders whom we hear about in the textbooks, there was a whole host of other men, often quite poor men, who were busy inventing new or improving existing industrial processes. In 1752, Dean Tucker wrote of "infinite numbers daily inventing machines for shortening business", and a Frenchman wrote that every manufacturer in Birmingham "was ceaselessly occupied in inventing new means of cutting costs and thereby increasing his profits". We know, also, that many of these "manufacturers"—often ordinary mechanics in their own workshops—were so determined to press on with their ideas that they applied to the Commissioners of Patents to obtain the sole right to put them on the market. This was especially noticeable in the second half of the century. Up to 1760, the number of patents only occasionally reached double figures in any one year, but in 1766 the number rose to thirty-one and in 1769 to thirty-six; and in the three last decades the numbers were 297, 512, and 655 respectively.

Since the great majority of these inventions were concerned with different forms of economic activity the acceleration in the rate of invention is itself an important part of the economic history of the period. Why the sudden increase? No single, or certain, answer can be given; but this can be said, that they all had one characteristic in common: they were all concerned with the problem of meeting the growing demand for consumption goods of a population that was growing at an unprecedented rate and at the same time was possessed of purchasing power to provide surplus over basic needs. The inventors were responding to the stimulus of the market and at the same time, by lowering prices, widening its range.

The inventors did not, however, confine their attention to the methods of production. They were also greatly concerned with the methods of distribution, above all with the problem of how to reduce the time that elapsed between the despatch of goods and their arrival in the market. Time was money—money spent on men's wages, the upkeep of pack horses, on the goods that had not yet been paid for—and manufacturers looked anxiously for ways and means of saving time and making their money circulate faster. The roads in the early eighteenth century were uniformly bad—according to some travellers, the worst in Europe; but England was blest with an excellent river system, perhaps the best in Europe, for the purpose of inland trade. There were six main rivers penetrating into the heart of this country: the Thames, Severn, Trent, Great Ouse, Yorkshire Ouse, and the Tees, and no important centre of population was more than fifteen miles from one of them. It was therefore possible to send bulky goods by a land carrier over a relatively short distance to a river by which they could be carried to urban markets and to the greatest highway of all, the sea that encircles the coast; and, it should be remembered, there were no barriers in the form of feudal tolls to check the flow as was the case, for instance, on the rivers of France and Germany. It was now possible to improve river navigation by straightening out the curves and avoiding the shallows by means of cuts controlled by locks at each end, and by 1750 there were a thousand miles of navigable waterways for the use of internal commerce. It was only a step from this to the artificial waterway system, but, although it had been talked about in the seventeenth century, it did not make its appearance until the second half of the eighteenth century. In the meantime, there were bitter complaints that coal was piling up at the pit-heads (usually in isolated country sites) while the coal-consuming industries—pig iron, pottery, brick-making—and also the rising centres of urban population were crying out for coal for industrial and domestic purposes.

The first result of this increased pressure on the transport system was a flood of turnpike Acts connecting the coal-producing areas with the towns or with river ports. In the first half of the century, about eight turnpike Acts a year had been passed; in the period 1750 to 1754 there were no less than ninety-three, mainly for roads in the coal-producing areas north of the Trent; and regional enquiries suggest that this much neglected phase of economic expansion was connected with the acceleration in the growth of the population, especially in the towns, and with the rebuilding of the countryside which was now in full swing as a result of the rising prosperity of agriculture. An urban and rural building boom was in progress which made itself felt throughout the entire structure of the economy.

The turnpikes, however, were quite incapable of meeting the needs of the time and it was inevitable that water would be utilised to take the burden from the roads. James Brindley showed how this could be done in the Bridgwater Canal in 1761; and by puddling the sides and bottom with clay he demonstrated the possibility of extending the use of the existing waterways to provide a network of eventually 10,000 miles of artificial waterways. This transformed the internal commerce of the country.

As a result of improved transport the same amount of capital could be made to do more work, and could either circulate more quickly or be put into fixed capital like machines and buildings. The canal itself, while being the greatest single consumer of capital before the coming of the railways, was also a great saver of capital; at the same time it brought fresh forms of capital into existence by stimulating investment in mines, quarries, factories, dairies, and other specialised forms of industry and agriculture along its banks; and a contemporary scale map will often reveal narrow-gauge railway lines sprouting from the course of a canal like ribs from a backbone showing that a new structure of the local economy had come about as a result of it.

Besides these forms of economy in the use of labour and natural resources and capital, entirely new resources were discovered by the work of scientists to serve the same economic purpose. Perhaps the most notable example was the utilisation of chemical means to speed up the processess of bleaching. Experiments had been going forward with success in the large-scale manufacture of chemicals in the first half of the century, as may be seen by the fact that whereas sulphuric acid was 1s. 6d. to 2s. 6d. *per ounce* in 1700, by 1780 it was $7\frac{1}{2}$d. *per pound*. When chlorine and bleaching powder were introduced in the 1780s and '90s a real revolution was effected in the later stages of textile manufacture. Instead of successive immersions in sour milk and ashes and stretchings on tenter poles in the sunlight, a process that might occupy the whole of the summer months, the cloth could now be bleached in a few days. Without this saving of time, it would have been impossible for the cotton industry to meet the growing demand for calicoes and muslins at home and overseas. Everyone wanted cotton goods, and as prices went down output went up. From 38s. per pound in 1786 cotton yarn fell to 2s. 11d. in 1832, and exports of cotton goods represented 40 per cent. of the total value of British exports in the first half of the nineteenth century.

It is for this reason—the almost infinite cost-elasticity of cotton manufacture—that the cotton industry has been regarded as the main "growth centre" of the Industrial Revolution. It radiated its effects into wider and wider segments of the whole economy, and by absorbing immense quantities of raw cotton from the Southern states of the U.S.A. it provided an ever-widening market on the American continent, not only for British goods, but for the goods of any nation which could sell at a competitive price. Trade was multi-lateral, and a "multiplying effect" was set off in the entire range of

exchange as a result of the phenomenal growth of cotton manufacture.

It is possible, however, to exaggerate the importance of the cotton industry as a stimulating factor in the growth of the economy; we should remember it depended on imported raw material for which exchange value had to be found, and this, once paid to America, was more likely to be spent on products manufactured there than in Britain. The capital outlay for the establishment of the cotton factories was relatively small, and the feed-back to the purchasing power of the internal market far less than, for instance, in the case of railways and iron and steel shipping. If we are to think in terms of what it has become fashionable to describe as "the take-off into sustained growth", perhaps we should have to advance the date beyond the period of this book to the age of railways and steam shipping. At the same time we should remember that sea-going commerce had been helped, while that of our European competitors had been hindered, by the long wars with Napoleon. Between 1790-4 and 1800-4 British exports to Europe, which had long been stagnant, almost doubled and those to North America went up by more than half, and Britain's trading position after the end of the war was immensely strong, especially in regard to the entrepôt and carrying trade. The steady dismantling of the Navigation System and the growth of Free Trade strengthened it still further; and when the breakthrough in shipping occurred with the screw-driven iron steamship in the 1850s, Britain's position was supreme.

The question may well be asked: What is meant by sustained growth? The simplest and shortest answer is that the growth of the economy in terms of investment for total production (input and output as the economists say) kept pace with population growth; and since population was now rising by nearly 200,000 per year, the total production had also to maintain a similar rate of growth if there was not to be a set-back owing to population pressure. Some observers feared that this would happen, but as we know, the economy more than succeeded in keeping pace with population: while population growth was about 1·3 per cent. per annum between 1790 and 1850, the rate of total production has been estimated at about 2·8 per cent. per annum.

It might be assumed from this that, in terms of the standard of living, conditions should have improved substantially for the mass of people during these years; and for an increasing proportion, especially those in the new industries, using the latest machinery, this was true; but for very large numbers like handloom weavers, framework knitters, agricultural labourers, *i.e.* those who were still using traditional methods of production, conditions were no better, and in many cases worse. The factory workers were relatively well paid but they suffered from the misery of unaccustomed discipline involved in machine production, and all classes of workers shared in the deplorable results of the growth of urban population without the corresponding growth of urban services and amenities.

A still more important cause of distress was the fluctuating nature of the economy. The fairly regular succession of booms and slumps—the trade cycle— brought successive crises alternating with periods of prosperity for both masters and men; and although each successive boom reached a higher level than the preceding one, each intervening slump brought frustration and despair to hundreds and thousands of helpless victims of a system over which they could exert little influence. The friendly societies were dependent on the tiny subscriptions of their members; and the theories of the time, especially the population theories of Malthus, and the wage fund theory of the classical economists, forbade any large-scale diversion of capital by the organs of the State from productive investment to what we now call social overheads. It was a disastrous decision and probably did more than anything to make the Industrial Revolution the searing experience it was for many. It alienated the working classes from the new system of production and provided am-

munition for the Marxist doctrines of the class war and exploitation of the proletariat; and since population growth went forward in a relentless upward trend while the economy advanced in periodic leaps, followed by intervals of preparation for the next forward leap, there were periods when the economic structure based on machine industry appeared dangerously unstable.

The gradual elimination of obsolete methods of production, the increase of international trade, and the growing power of the British economy to supplement the home production of food by imports from abroad, removed these fears and gave rise instead to a mood of confidence and complacency in the achievements of the new system of production. At the same time, the development of a sense of responsibility by the community as a whole, working through the organs of the State, for the maintenance of public health, improved factory conditions, the limitation of the working day, and the widening recognition of the role of collective bargaining, laid the foundations of the society we have to-day. The coming of machine industry had made it possible to satisfy, on a progressively rising scale, the material wants of all, even of the poorest, and it gradually became realised that this possibility extended also to include the enjoyment of the fruits of the mind and spirit in an environment of freedom. Other countries industrialising later were able to some degree to provide for the adverse social effects Britain experienced through her mistakes and ignorance. Looked at in these terms, the Industrial Revolution wherever it has occurred may be one of the most hopeful events in the history of mankind.

Plate VIII.   Machinery in a wool mill at Tal-y-Bent, North Wales.

Graphs and Figures

Fig. 1

AN INDEX OF REAL WAGES OF LABOURERS IN LANCASHIRE, 1700–1796

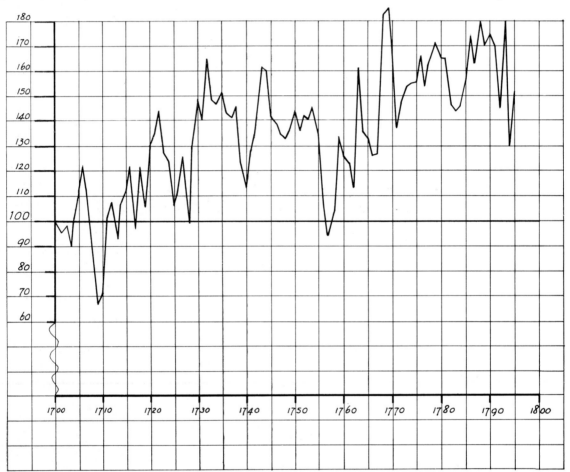

Source: E. W. Gilboy, "The Cost of Living and Wages in Eighteenth-Century England", *Review of Economic Statistics* (1936) [1700 = 100].

Fig. 2

THREE ESTIMATES OF ENGLAND'S POPULATION IN THE EIGHTEENTH CENTURY

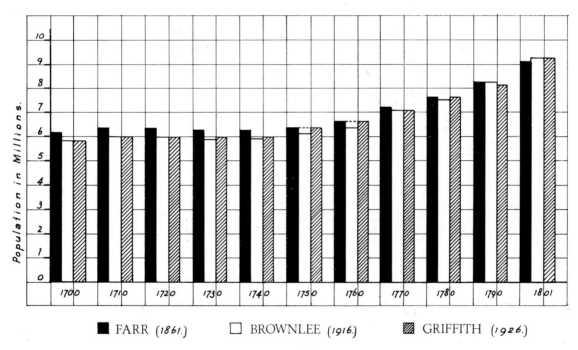

■ FARR *(1861.)*   □ BROWNLEE *(1916.)*   ▨ GRIFFITH *(1926.)*

The dotted columns indicate Brownlee's alternative estimates.

Source: J. D. Chambers, *Vale of Trent* (1960), p. 23.

Fig. 3

ILLUSTRATION OF GLASS CRYSTALS

Philos Trans Vol. LXVI Tab. VI p542.

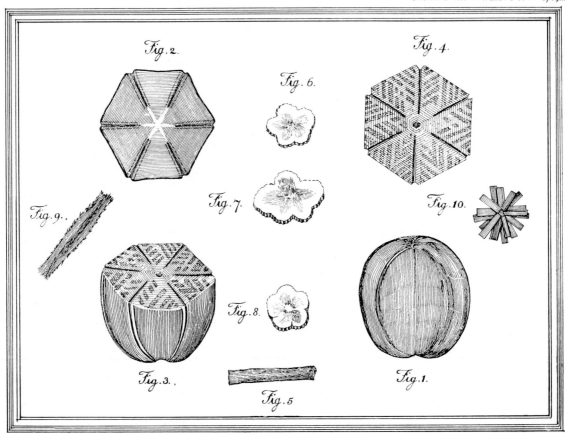

Source: James Keir, "On the Crystallisations observed in glass", *Trans. Royal Soc.*, 1776. Keir (1735-1820) became a glass manufacturer at Stourbridge in 1775 (see Chapter II, p. 35).

Fig. 4

ANNUAL INCOME OF ENGLISH MIDDLE–CLASS HOUSEHOLDS, 1688

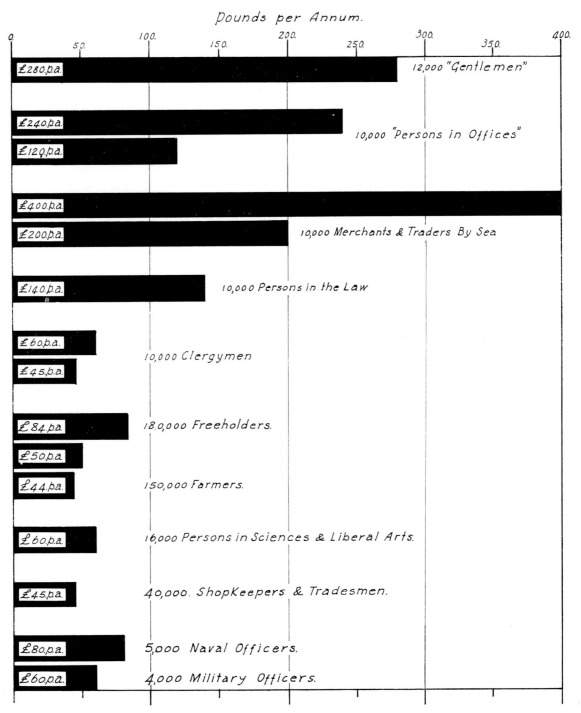

Source: Gregory King's survey.

Fig. 5

THE GROWTH OF THE COTTON INDUSTRY: IMPORTS OF RAW COTTON, 1750–1800

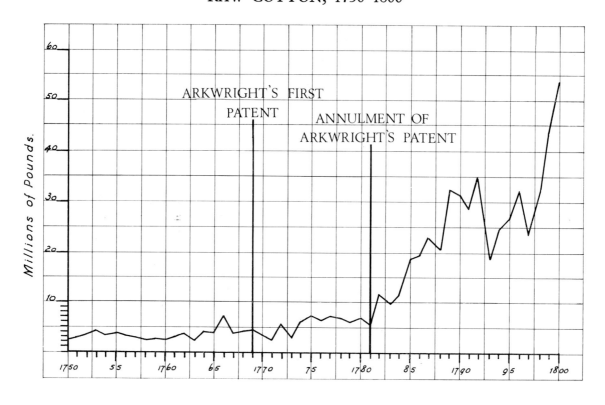

Fig. 6

ARKWRIGHT'S BUSINESS INTERESTS

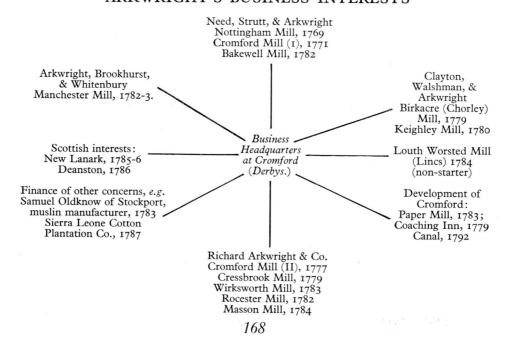

Fig. 7

DISTRIBUTION OF COTTON MILLS IN WEST RIDING, *c.* 1802

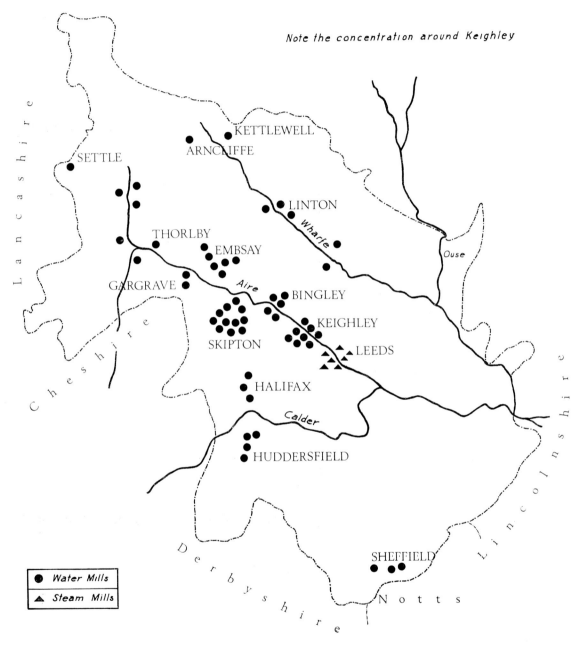

Sources: (1) Water Mills: Returns of County J.P.s under Peel's Health and Morals of Apprentices Act, 1802. Only factories with more than twenty people were registered. (2) Steam Mills: Boulton and Watt MSS. Other firms may have supplied steam engines.

Fig. 8

ESTIMATED GROWTH OF WOOLLEN MANUFACTURE IN ENGLAND AND WALES IN THE EIGHTEENTH CENTURY

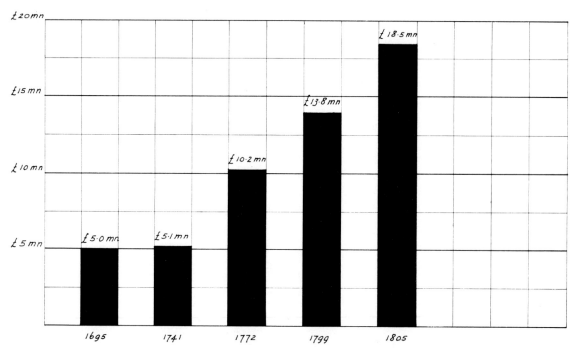

Source: P. Deane, "The Output of the British Woollen Industry in the Eighteenth Century", *Journal of Economic History*, XVII (1957).

Fig. 9

THE PRICE OF BOBBIN-NET LACE (per sq. yd.) IN
NOTTINGHAM MARKET, 1809–1850

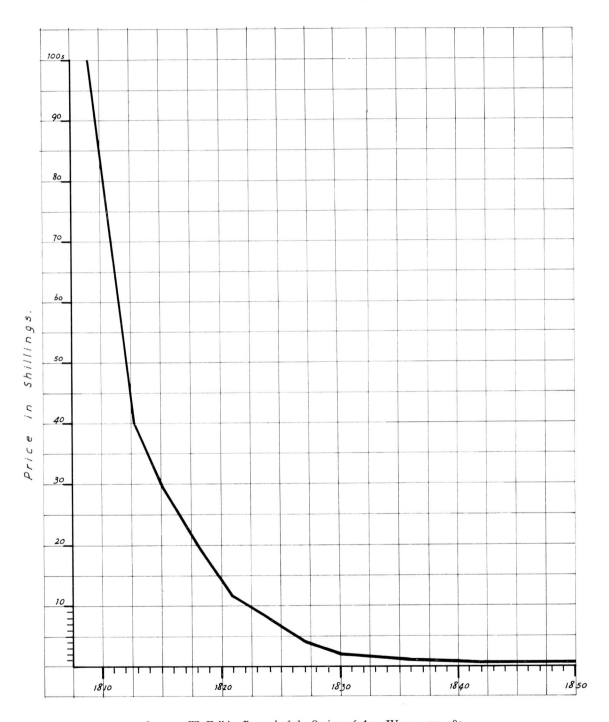

Source: W. Felkin, *Journal of the Society of Arts*, IV, pp. 479, 483.

Fig. 10

THE STRUCTURE OF THE COTTON INDUSTRY ABOUT 1815

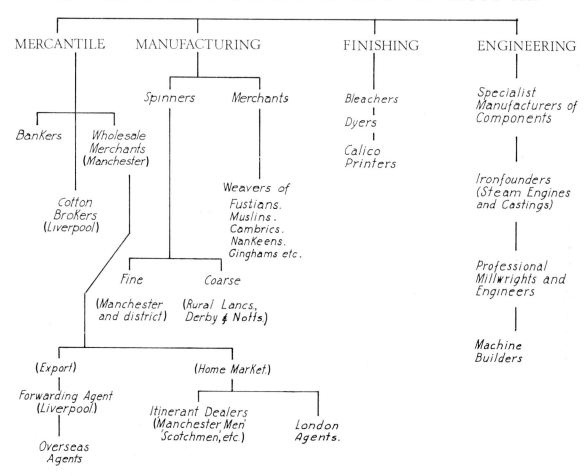

Figures

Fig. 11

COAL OUTPUT IN THE UNITED KINGDOM, 1800–1850

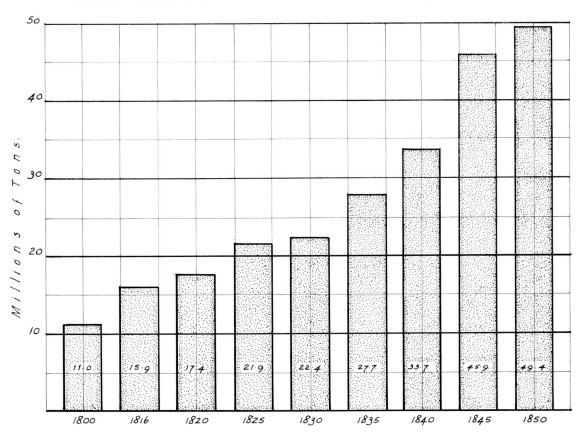

Source: P. Deane and W. A. Cole, *British Economic Growth*, 1688-1959 (1962), p. 216.

Fig. 12

THE QUANTITIES OF PIG IRON MADE IN 1830

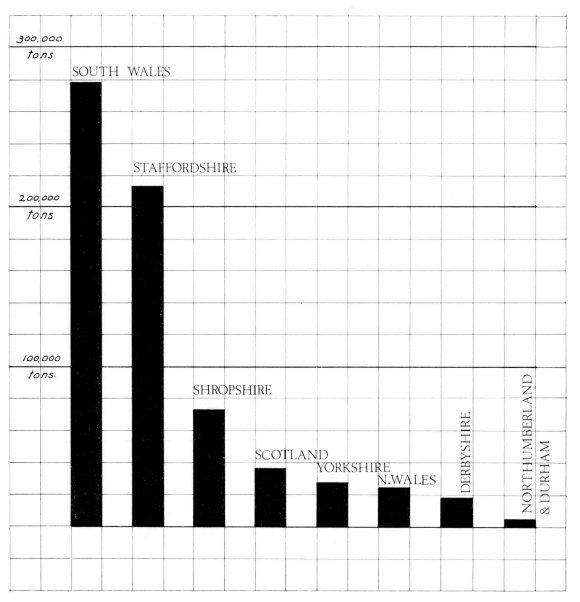

Source: H. Scrivener, *History of the Iron Trade* (1841), pp. 134-5.

Fig. 13

THE INDUSTRIAL EMPIRE OF JOHN AND WILLIAM WILKINSON

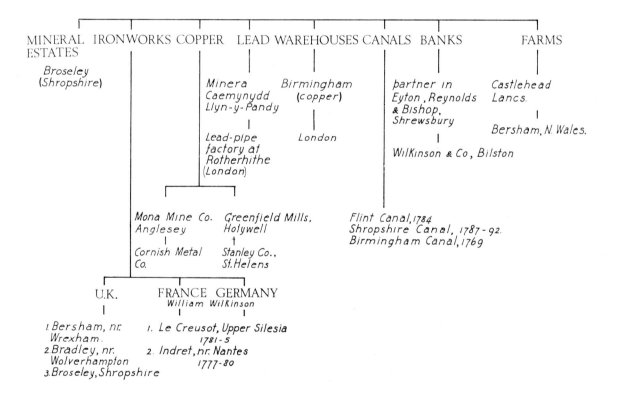

Fig. 14

INCREASE OF WET DOCK AND BASIN ACCOMMODATION IN ENGLAND, 1700–1830

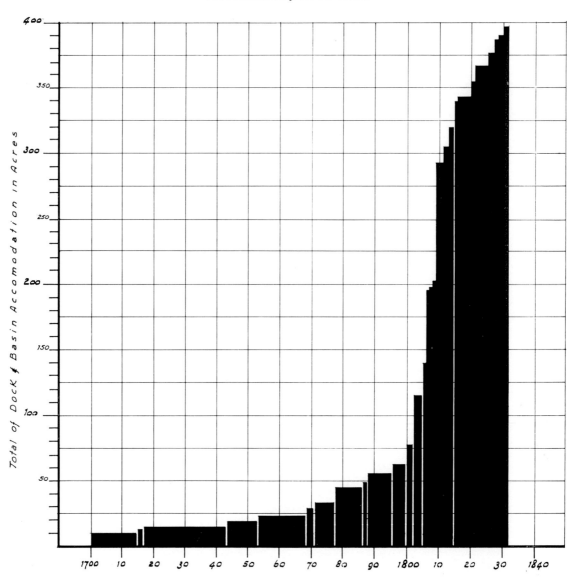

Source: D. Swann, "The Pace and Progress of Port Investment in England, 1660-1830". *Yorkshire Bulletin of Economic and Social Research*, Vol. XII (1960), p. 38.

Reading List

T. S. Ashton, *The Industrial Revolution* (Oxford University Press, 1948).

P. Mantoux, *The Industrial Revolution in the Eighteenth Century* (1928; University Paperback, 1964).

W. H. B. Court, *A Concise Economic History of Britain* (Cambridge University Press, 1954).

P. Mathias, *The First Industrial Nation. An Economic History of Britain*, 1700-1914 (Methuen, 1969).

D. S. Landes, *The Unbound Prometheus: Technological Change and Industrial Development in Western Europe from 1750 to the Present* (Cambridge University Press, 1969).

M. W. Flinn, *The Origins of the Industrial Revolution* (Longmans, 1966).

S. Pollard, *The Genesis of Modern Management. A Study of the Industrial Revolution in Great Britain* (Edward Arnold, 1965).

David and Charles Industrial Archaeology series is a growing list of titles by regional specialists, directing the student to some of the best physical survivals of early industrialisation in Britain.

Index

179

Index

PRINTED IN GREAT BRITAIN BY UNIVERSITY TUTORIAL PRESS LTD, FOXTON, NR CAMBRIDGE